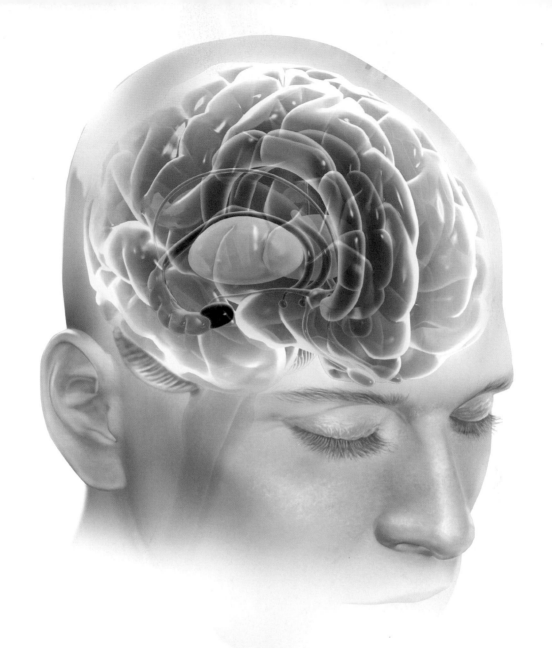

CONCISE ENCYCLOPEDIA OF THE
HUMAN BODY

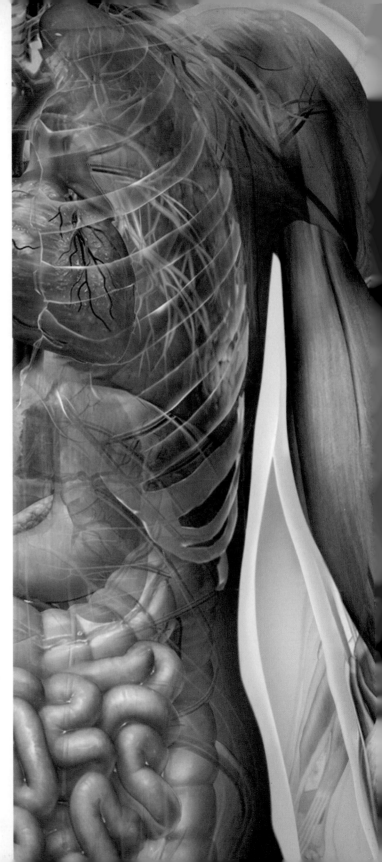

RED LEMON PRESS

First published in Great Britain by
Weldon Owen
Kings Road Publishing
2.07 The Plaza
535 Kings Road
Chelsea, London, SW10 0SZ
Weldon Owen Pty Ltd

Much of the text in this book is taken from *The Illustrated Atlas of the Human Body*, written by Beverly McMillan and originally published by Weldon Owen Pty Ltd in 2008. All the information in this edition has been completely revised and updated.

Additional text by: Simon Holland

Designed by: Peter Clayman

Editorial consultant: Dr. Patricia Macnair

Design assistance: Krina Patel, Katie Knutton

Editorial assistance: Lydia Halliday

Original illustrations by: Argosy Publishing

Please see page 288 for full details of the illustrations and photographic images reproduced in this book.

Produced for Red Lemon Press by DUTCH&DANE

ISBN 978-1-78342-080-3

A CIP catalogue for this book is available from the British Library.

Printed and bound in China.

10 9 8 7 6 5 4 3 2

Red Lemon Press is part of the Bonnier Publishing Group.

www.bonnierpublishing.com

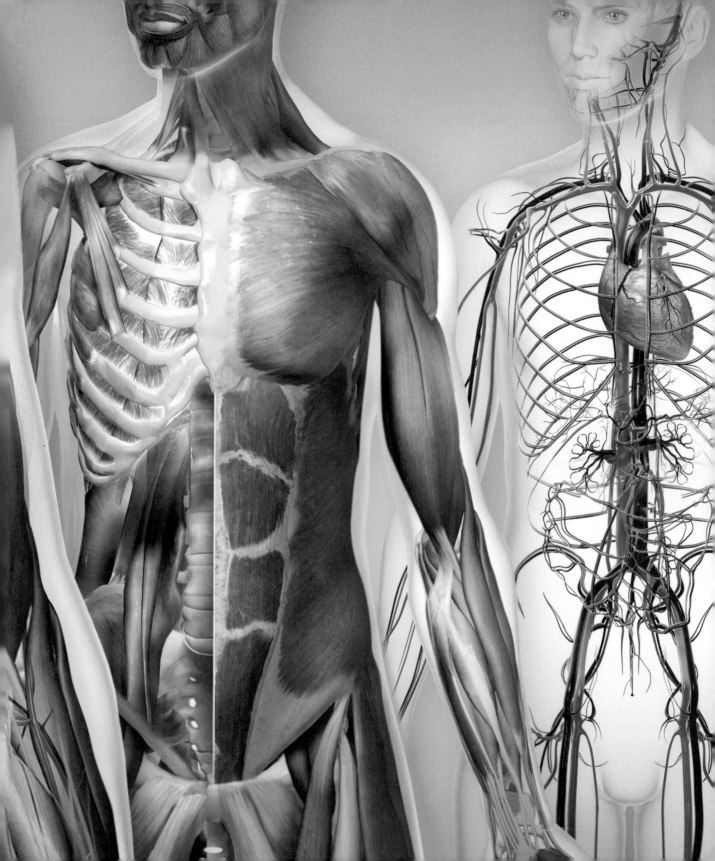

CONTENTS

YOU WILL FIND ICONS AT THE BOTTOM OF THE PAGES IN THIS BOOK,
WHICH ARE GUIDES TO FURTHER INFORMATION:

 Key facts

 Dictionary definitions

 Cross-references to other, relevant pages

 Books and programs

BODY IMAGING

Imaging technologies, used to see inside the human body, are major tools in the diagnosis and treatment of diseases and disorders. They have also enabled scientists to deepen their understanding of the body's intricate systems and their functions. These pages show, and briefly explain, the range of imaging techniques reproduced in this encyclopedia.

X-rays and related imaging

X-rays provide a general view of hard, dense structures. Many modern techniques combine images from X-rays, radioisotopes, or magnetic fields with computer and color enhancements. Such technologies include computed tomography (CT), positron emission tomography (PET), and magnetic resonance imaging (MRI). Each achieves a particular type of image, such as the high-contrast views of soft tissues provided by MRI (right).

Composite MRI scan of a whole human female (front view)

Magnetic resonance imaging (MRI)

MRI uses a combination of magnetism and radiowaves to map the presence of chemical elements in soft tissues. It produces detailed, high-contrast images of organs and their parts. Functional MRI (or fMRI) provides real-time images of oxygen use in tissues, an indicator of cell activity.

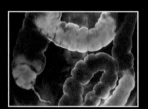

Colored X-ray images
X-rays are shortwave electromagnetic waves that are absorbed well by dense masses. Structures such as bones or tumors show up as clearly outlined, light areas. Fat and hollow organs appear dark and fuzzy.

Colored X-ray of the colon

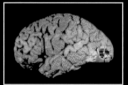
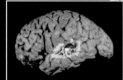

Seeing   **Hearing**

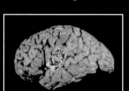
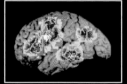

Thinking   **Speaking**

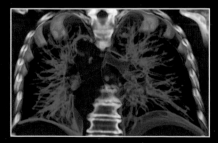

Colored CT scan of healthy lungs

3D computed tomography (CT) scanning

In 3D CT scanning, X-rays are beamed into the body from a device that rotates, moving all around the patient. The resulting computer-combined images build up an extremely clear, three-dimensional view of the area of interest.

PET scans of brain activity during different human functions

Positron emission tomography (PET)

PET tracks the uptake by cells of radioactively labeled substances. Colors show up the areas of a tissue or organ that are either more or less metabolically active. PET is often used to pinpoint areas of the brain that are active when subjects are reading, speaking, or performing a cognitive or problem-solving task.

 SEE PAGE 20 FOR AN SEM IMAGE OF MITOSIS—THE PROCESS BY WHICH CELLS REPRODUCE AND NEW LIFE IS CREATED.

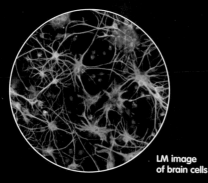

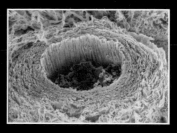

Scanning electron microscopy (SEM)

A scanning electron microscope sweeps a focused beam of electrons across the surface of a specimen, which has in some cases been thinly coated with gold or some other metallic material. The electrons are then converted, by computer, into a 3D image.

LM image of brain cells

Colored SEM of the surface of a slice through a blood vessel

Light micrograph (LM) images

A micrograph, or photomicrograph, is any image taken through a microscope (or other magnifying device) to create an enlarged picture. Specimens or tissues are sometimes stained with a dye to highlight tiny details or particles of interest.

Transmission electron microscopy (TEM)

With TEM, electrons are beamed through a specimen—often something extremely small—to produce a detailed image of its internal parts. The specimen in this case is a healthy human cell.

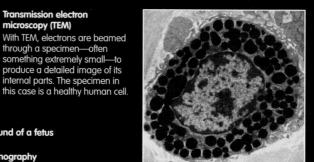

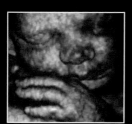

3D ultrasound of a fetus

3D ultrasonography

In ultrasound, the echoes of pulsed sound waves generate images. It is often used as a non-invasive way to monitor the growth, health, and position of a fetus, before birth. In 3D ultrasound, a computer manipulates the data to build up a more detailed image.

TEM of a human mast cell in body tissue

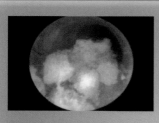

Endoscopic views of kidney stones in the ureter

ENDOSCOPY

An endoscope is a narrow, hollow (and usually flexible) tube that contains a light source and a fiber-optic viewing device, which may be connected to a video monitor. Once an endoscope has been passed into the body—through either a natural opening or an incision in the abdomen, for example—surgical instruments can be threaded through the tube and controlled remotely. This greatly aids the treatment or diagnosis of a problem.

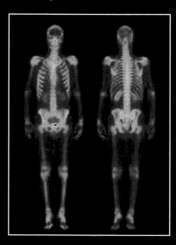

"Gamma" scans of the human skeleton

Nuclear scanning

In nuclear medicine, a mildly radioactive substance is used to create images. A "radioisotope" is introduced to the body, and then a detection device tracks the path or destination of the isotope. This can be used to show up cancer deposits or infection in the bones, for example.

ORGAN SYSTEMS

The complex form and functioning of the human body and its intricate systems have preoccupied a broad range of scientists for many hundreds of years. In this technological age, we are virtually at the cutting edge of medical science—and yet many discoveries are still to be made. Using this encyclopedia, you can develop your own knowledge by examining each of the body's 12 main organ systems.

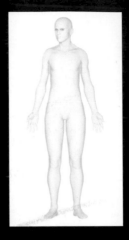

Integumentary system
This system consists of the skin and structures such as hair and nails. Skin is a barrier against water loss and microbes. It also protects deeper tissues from physical damage, helps to control body temperature, and contains sensory receptors. Glands embedded in the skin excrete certain body wastes.

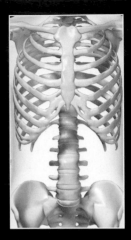

Skeletal system
The skeleton supports the body's soft tissues and protects our vital organs. Bones provide rigid attachment sites for skeletal muscles, serving as levers in body movements. Bones also store the minerals calcium and phosphorus, while bone marrow generates red blood cells.

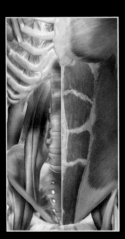

Muscular system
Hundreds of skeletal muscles work with bones to move the body and its parts, under our voluntary (conscious) control. Skeletal muscles also produce body heat and some maintain the upright human posture. The body's smooth and cardiac muscles are not consciously controllable, so they are classed as "involuntary."

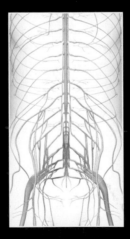

Nervous system
This system brings together and integrates the activities of all other organ systems. In tandem with our sensory organs and receptors, it detects stimuli from outside and inside the body and organizes and controls our bodily and behavioral responses.

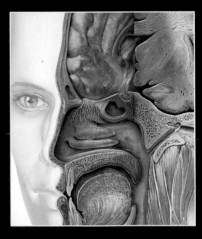

Sensory system
This system of organs and receptors brings information to the body, allowing it to receive, manage, and respond to changes that are both internal and external. There are two groups of human senses—the general senses, such as touch, pressure, and pain, and the special senses of vision, hearing, smell, taste, and balance.

 FIND OUT MORE ABOUT HOW THE SKIN SUPPORTS THE OTHER BODY SYSTEMS ON *PAGES 36–37*.

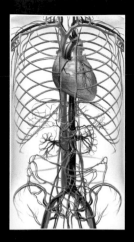

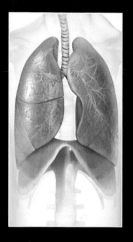

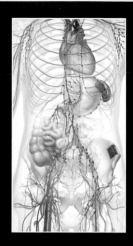

Endocrine system

Endocrine organs produce hormones, chemicals that play major roles in influencing or controlling both the short- and long-term functions of the body. The system's operations are closely coordinated with the activities of the nervous system.

Cardiovascular system

The blood-pumping heart and blood-transporting vessels rapidly move oxygen, nutrients, and many other materials to and from the body's cells. The system also helps to stabilize body temperature and our internal chemical conditions.

Respiratory system

This system extracts oxygen from the air and delivers it to the bloodstream for circulation throughout the body. It also removes excess carbon dioxide, a waste product of respiration, and helps to manage the body's acid-base balance.

Lymphatic system

This network of filtering organs and vessels collects and returns tissue fluid to the bloodstream. It also produces cells and substances that are specially adapted to protect the body from tissue damage and infection.

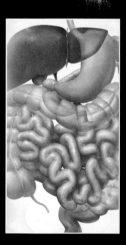

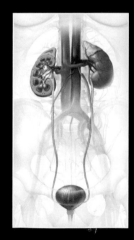

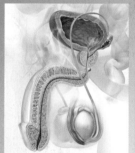

Digestive system

This system takes in bulk loads of food and breaks it down, mechanically and chemically, to extract nutrients for body cells. Parts of the system are specialized to realize digestive enzymes, absorb nutrients, and eliminate undigested food residues.

Urinary system

This is the body's filtering system, which has primary responsibility for maintaining the proper chemical balance of the blood and tissue fluid. It removes blood-borne wastes and excess water, excreting them from the body in our urine.

THE REPRODUCTIVE SYSTEMS

The female reproductive system produces eggs, the female sex cells, and nurtures developing young. The male system forms sperm, the male sex cells, and transfers sperm to the female via sexual intercourse. Both systems produce hormones that have widespread effects in the male and female body.

BODY BASICS

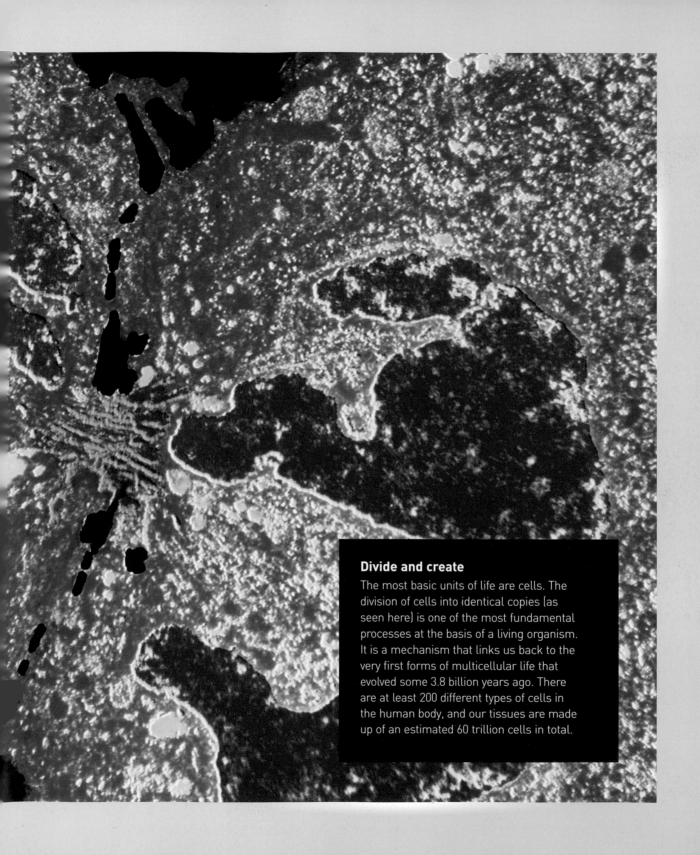

Divide and create

The most basic units of life are cells. The division of cells into identical copies (as seen here) is one of the most fundamental processes at the basis of a living organism. It is a mechanism that links us back to the very first forms of multicellular life that evolved some 3.8 billion years ago. There are at least 200 different types of cells in the human body, and our tissues are made up of an estimated 60 trillion cells in total.

BODY UNITS

In the human body, a remarkable assortment of structures form a complex living unit—a whole being that is far more than the sum of its parts. This feat of biological engineering depends on the organization of its body parts into integrated, functional units. The multitude of tasks required for normal operations are cleverly divided among 11 main organ systems. Moment to moment, all of these parts interact to keep the whole body alive and thriving.

Organ systems

Within each of these systems, one or two—or more—individual organs cooperate to perform a given role, such as circulating blood around the body or extracting nutrients from food. The lungs (right) are the primary respiratory organs through which oxygen enters the body and carbon dioxide—as a waste product—is removed.

The lungs

Cartilage
The strong but flexible connective tissue that supports and shapes the soft tissues in lots of different parts of the body—such as the trachea, the nose, and the outer ear.

THE LATIN WORD *HUMANUS* MEANS "OF MAN, HUMAN." *HUMANUS* PROBABLY DERIVED FROM THE WORD *HOMO*, MEANING "MAN."

Nerve
Contains nervous tissue, connective tissue, and blood vessels that carry messages.

Blood vessel
A tubular organ that transports blood as part of the circulatory system.

Skeletal muscle
Contains the most common type of muscle tissue in the body—specialized for moving the bones of the skeleton.

Ligament
The connective tissue that holds the bones together to stabilize joints.

Basic cell structure
A typical cell contains a variety of structures inside a membrane.

The skin
This organ contains nerve tissues, connective tissues, and an epithelial layer on top—the dermis.

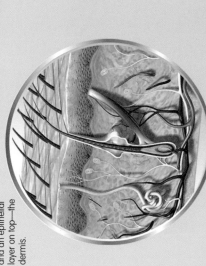

Tissues

Each organ is a blend of a number of tissues: The nervous tissue that conveys and processes information; connective tissues such as bone, cartilage, collagen, and elastin; and epithelial tissue, which forms the outer layer and internal linings of the organ. Epithelial tissue holds the body and its organs together, giving them form, strength, and shape.

Cells

The building blocks of tissues, an estimated 60 trillion cells, are the body's smallest living units. There are at least 200 different types of cells in the human body. (See pages 18–19 for more on cells.)

CELLS

Cells are the smallest units of life, and most of them are so tiny that they are only visible under a microscope. Most cells are specialized, and have a structure which enables them to perform a particular function. These jobs include connecting body parts, fighting disease, storing nutrients, controlling bodily functions, as well as manufacturing the chemicals and substances needed by the body.

Specialized cells

All body cells have a similar basic structure (see pages 18–19), but they vary greatly in size, shape, and the functions they perform. The shape of the cell usually reflects the role it plays in the day-to-day working of the body.

Dendrite

Neurons

Nerve cells have hundreds of "dendrites" that branch off to collect incoming signals, and one long "axon," to take the outgoing signals on.

Axon

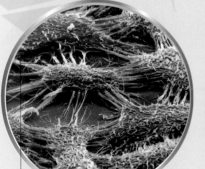

Epithelial cells

Epithelial cells help to form the skin and the linings of body cavities and organs. Many of these cells have a flattened or boxlike shape.

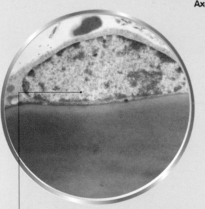

Adipose cells

These cells are like tiny balloons that can fill up to store fat.

Smooth muscle cells

Smooth muscle cells have an elastic, stretchy quality. They allow movement to occur in tissues and organs that humans do not consciously control, such as the intestines.

Tail

Midpiece

Head

Plasma membrane

White blood cells
These cells form part of the body's defense against invading germs. Their outer layer is designed to attract, trap, and destroy the alien microbes.

Sperm cells
The long tail of a man's sperm cell enables it to swim through fluid to locate and fertilize the ovum (egg) of a female. Sperm cells are highly complex and specialized.

STEM CELLS

Unlike most cell types, which are locked into a specialized role, "stem" cells—especially those from embryos—retain their potential to generate a variety of different specialized cell types. The body uses them for vital functions such as repairing worn out cells in the gut or producing new blood cells in bone marrow. In medicine, stem cells can be used to regrow damaged body parts and treat those suffering from cell-destroying disorders.

Stem cells from a human embryo

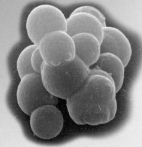

Red blood cells
These cells resemble thin disks. Their biconcave disk shape makes it easier for them to pick up and deliver oxygen to the various tissues of the body.

CELL ANALYSIS

The cell's plasma membrane encloses its internal parts and allows the ceaseless movement of substances into and out of the cell. The nucleus is one of many organelles (or "little organs") within the cell, and it houses the genetic material DNA. Guided by instructions in DNA, these tiny components perform specialized operations that help to keep cells alive and allow each one to play its particular biological role in the body.

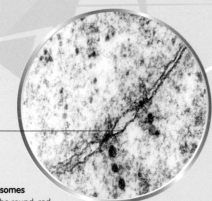

Ribosomes
are the round, red specks in this image. They connect amino acids together to assemble proteins. They are located on the rough endoplasmic reticulum.

Golgi apparatus
processes and releases proteins and lipids that are used in the cell or packaged for sending elsewhere.

 GOLGI, CAMILLO (1844–1926) WAS AN ITALIAN ANATOMIST WHO DESCRIBED THE STRUCTURE IN THE CYTOPLASM OF MOST CELLS.

Nucleus
contains a cell's DNA,
keeping it separate
from the organelles.

Nucleolus
is the dense, central
area where all cell
activity is controlled.

Lysosomes
are fluid filled
membranes
(shown here as
blue) which contain
enzymes that break
down unwanted
materials (shown in
pink and green).

Rough endoplasmic reticulum
plays an important part in the
formation of proteins, along with
the ribosomes.

Mitochondria
convert molecules in
sugars into a usable
fuel called ATP,
providing enery
for the cell.

**Smooth
endoplasmic
reticulum**
plays a part in the
creation and storage
of steroids and lipids.
It also regulates and
releases calcium ions.

Plasma membrane
Different proteins in the
double-layered membrane
identify chemicals, bind
substances (such as
hormones), and help to
move other substances
into and out of the cell.

The plasma membrane
The plasma membrane actively
controls which chemicals are able
to enter or exit the cell. A range
of "lock and key" type receptors
recognize and bind different
chemicals, opening channels to
transport these substances through
the membrane. This process is
crucial in controlling factors such
as the cell's internal pH balance
and its salt content.

CHROMOSOMES

The countless processes and events that build and operate the body are guided by a chemical called DNA, or deoxyribonucleic acid. The nucleus of every cell contains lengthy strands of DNA, which are organized into separate threads called chromosomes. These chromosomes carry genetic information. They are passed from parents to their offspring, which is why children have similar characteristics to their parents.

AN X CHROMOSOME

MITOSIS

Body cells reproduce themselves by dividing into two identical copies. This process, known as mitosis, allows tissues to grow and repair themselves. This SEM image of mitosis shows the cell's genetic material (colored red) separating into two identical populations. Nuclear membranes are reforming around the material. Soon, the creation of two new "daughter" cells will be complete. This is how genetic information is copied and passed on.

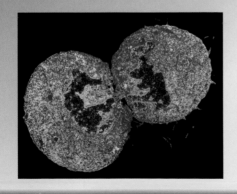

DNA "backbone"

Solenoids
When not active, DNA is packaged up into units.

 ON AVERAGE, ONLY ABOUT *0.1 PERCENT* OF OUR GENES DISTINGUISH ONE HUMAN INDIVIDUAL FROM ANOTHER.

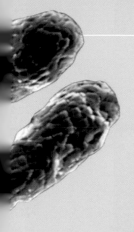

The full set

The nucleus of every cell contains 46 chromosomes, arranged in 23 pairs (shown here, right). Each chromosome pair carries hundreds of specific sets of genes. The final pair determines the sex of the human. The "XY" pair, seen at the very end, shows that this is a standard set of male chromosomes. A standard female set would have two "X" chromosomes at the end.

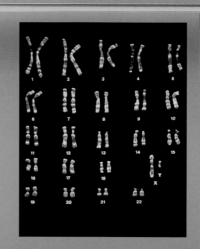

Genes

A gene is a distinct unit of chemical instructions for how the body is formed and run. Genes are encoded into our DNA and stored along the chromosomes in each cell nucleus. A human has around 21,500 genes in total. They are the combination of two genetic sets—one from a mother, the other from a father.

Genetic transmission

When the genes stored on the chromosomes are eventually inherited, from one generation of humans to the next, they are passed on in whole "chunks". They are not blended or mixed together, like liquids in a cocktail.

Nucleosomes

DNA is wound around proteins called histones (shown in purple) to form these basic units.

DNA molecules

in each human cell are twisted and folded into what we call their "double helix" formation (for further analysis, see pages 22–23).

Chromosome duplication

Each DNA molecule is a double strand wound up into a "helix." When a cell is preparing to divide, its chromosomes "unravel" and are duplicated—so that each daughter cell receives the full set of 46 chromosomes.

THE DNA STRAND

DNA consists of pairs of chemical units called nucleotides or base pairs, which are lined up in parallel strands like the rails of a ladder. Most of the time, the strands are twisted into a spiraling double helix. Some sections are genes—these specific lengths of the DNA carry the code for particular characteristics. Other sections have support roles, such as helping to turn a specific gene "on" or "off." Genes are constantly being switched on and off as our cells adapt and respond to different stimuli and challenges.

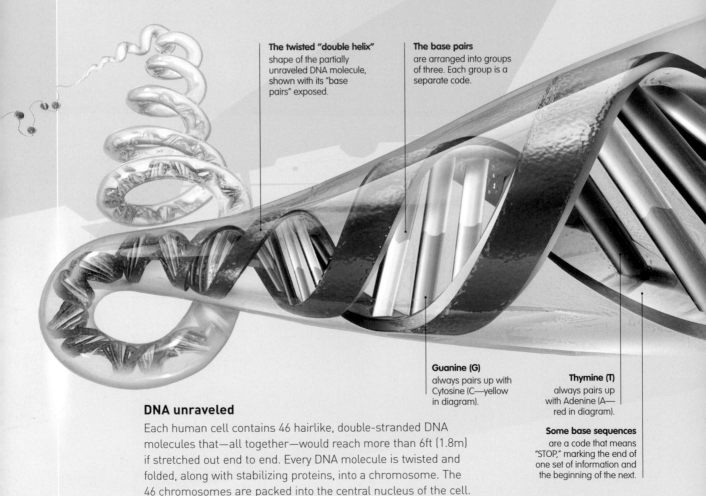

The twisted "double helix"
shape of the partially unraveled DNA molecule, shown with its "base pairs" exposed.

The base pairs
are arranged into groups of three. Each group is a separate code.

Guanine (G)
always pairs up with Cytosine (C—yellow in diagram).

Thymine (T)
always pairs up with Adenine (A— red in diagram).

Some base sequences
are a code that means "STOP," marking the end of one set of information and the beginning of the next.

DNA unraveled

Each human cell contains 46 hairlike, double-stranded DNA molecules that—all together—would reach more than 6ft (1.8m) if stretched out end to end. Every DNA molecule is twisted and folded, along with stabilizing proteins, into a chromosome. The 46 chromosomes are packed into the central nucleus of the cell.

SANGER, FREDERICK (1918–2013) WAS A BRITISH BIOLOGIST WHO ESTABLISHED THE COMPLETE NUCLEOTIDE SEQUENCE OF A VIRAL DNA IN 1977.

DNA IDENTITIES

No two people have the same DNA. Even identical twins have a few dozen differences. In each person, fragments are repeated multiple times in the two parallel DNA strands. These "random repeats" normally differ from person to person, and so they provide a "fingerprint" for matching blood or tissue to the individual it came from. DNA fingerprinting is used to link suspects to crime scenes, and to identify the parents of a child.

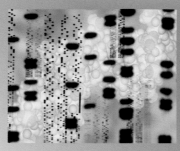

Cytosine (C)
always pairs up with base Guanine (G—green in diagram).

Adenine (A)
always pairs up with base Thymine (T—purple in diagram).

Base pairs

The genetic information in the DNA molecule is encoded into a sequence of chemicals, known as bases. The four nucleotide bases are adenine (A), cytosine (C), guanine (G), and thymine (T). They form "base pairs," with each pair making up a specific rung in the ladderlike structure of DNA.

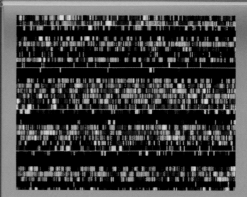

De-coding DNA

Using gene-sequencing technology, today's researchers can work out the number and order of nucleotides in DNA—and closely pinpoint where one gene stops and another begins. This has revealed that the human genetic heritage—also known as the "genome"—consists of about 21,500 genes. Studying the human genome is an important part of discovering the role that genes play in health and disease.

TISSUE TYPES

The body contains four basic types of tissues: epithelial tissue, muscle tissue, nervous tissue, and connective tissue. Each type is a group of similar cells that perform a particular function.

Hairlike cilia
(light green) on the surface of the cells beat rhythmically to brush the mucus up the bronchial passages, removing bits of trapped debris.

Epithelial tissue

Epithelial tissue is a major component of body coverings, most notably the skin and the linings of body cavities and tubes. The epithelium that lines the upper bronchial passages (above) includes gland cells that secrete a mucus, for trapping debris. This helps to protect the upper passages from infection.

Skeletal muscle cells
are long cylinders. They are fused together, giving them the appearance of continuous tissue.

Connective tissues
(shown in white) separate the skeletal muscle fibers.

Muscle tissue

There are three types of muscular tissue in the body: skeletal muscle, smooth muscle, and cardiac muscle. They are all specialized for generating different types of movement. In skeletal muscle (above), special junctions fuse the cells together and enable them to contract (squeeze together) as a unit.

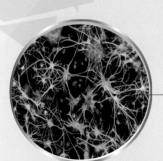

Astrocytes
are star-shaped and belong to a class of cells known as neuroglia (meaning "nerve glue").

Nervous tissue

Nervous tissue consists of neurons (nerve cells) involved in the body's communications and other cells that support the neurons' operations. For example, astrocytes (above) provide structural and nutritional support to the neurons. The astrocytes are the most common type of "neuroglial" cell.

Tendons
are an example of connective tissues that physically bind or anchor a body part, as this cross-section shows.

Connective tissue

Most of the body's tissues are connective tissues. They are found in bone, cartilage, tendons (shown above), adipose (fat) tissue, and even blood. Most of them are a blend of proteins and a surrounding "matrix," which can be solid (as in bone), liquid (as with blood plasma), or somewhere in between.

TISSUE COMES FROM AN OLD FRENCH WORD, *TISSU* ("WOVEN"), WHICH ITSELF DERIVES FROM A LATIN WORD, *TEXERE* ("TO WEAVE").

Cartilage

Cartilage (shown in green) is a dense, pliable tissue that resists compression (squashing). It is also rigid enough to provide structure and form. Hyaline cartilage at the ends of bones reduces friction in movable joints such as the hips, shoulders, and fingers. It also forms part of the ribs, trachea, and nose. Elastic cartilage is found where flexibility is important, such as in the external ear. Pressure-resistant "fibrocartilage" provides padding in the knees and between the spinal vertebrae.

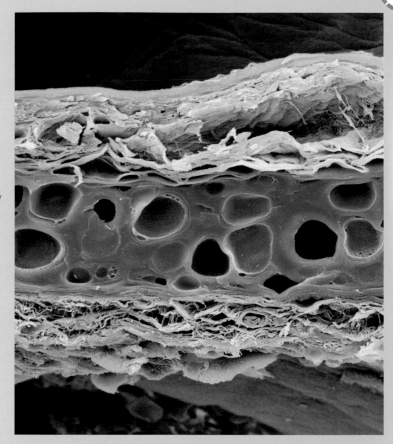

FATTY TISSUE

The body stores fat in adipose tissue. This mainly consists of cells containing fat droplets made from carbohydrates and proteins not used for metabolism. Most adipose tissue occurs just below the skin, where it provides cushioning and insulation. Different people store fat in different places, resulting in a variety of body shapes.

MEMBRANES AND GLANDS

Membranes play major roles in protecting or lining body surfaces and cavities. Most of them consist of epithelium, a tissue that can also form glands. Epithelial membranes combine epithelium with connective tissue to form a thin sheet. They include most of the membranes in the body, and they can be divided into four main groups.

Epithelium
(see page 24) makes up the top layer, containing cells that produce a thick, slippery mucus.

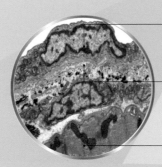

Serous pericardium
is a double-walled sac surrounding the heart.

Serous fluid
in the space between the membranes prevents friction when they move.

Heart

Mucous membranes

Moist, pink mucous membranes line the channels of the digestive, urinary, respiratory, and reproductive systems. Mucus oils surfaces and helps to moisten chewed food. In the nose and bronchial passages it also traps dust, pathogens, and other materials.

Serous membranes

These membranes occur in paired sheets with two layers which can slide along each other. Serous membranes enclose organs that expand and contract, such as the heart and lungs, and also line the chambers in which these organs are located.

Basal layer
of the epidermis (see pages 38–39) is where new cells are formed for the upper epidermis.

Knee joint
is lubricated by synovial fluid, to ease its movement and nourish its cartilage components.

Cutaneous membranes

The skin, a cutaneous membrane, is the most wide-ranging system in the entire body. Cutaneous membranes are thicker with multiple layers of flattened cells, as they protect the body from the outside world.

Synovial membranes

Synovial membranes, consisting only of connective tissue, make up the fourth and final group. They line the movable parts of the body, such as the shoulder and hip joints, and they contain cells that release a lubricating substance—synovial fluid.

WHILE THE *PERICARDIUM* HOUSES THE HEART, THE *PLEURAL MEMBRANE* ENCLOSES THE LUNGS INSIDE THE CHEST—*SEE PAGE 195.*

Gland categories

Glands are structures that secrete substances and they fall into two main categories. Endocrine glands, such as the pituitary (see pages 156–157), release hormones into the bloodstream. Exocrine glands, the second group, secrete substances onto the skin or the internal lining of an organ.

Salivary glands
empty their saliva through small tubes or ducts, into the mouth.

Parotid gland
is located near the ear.

Sudoriferous glands
(sweat glands) release transparent, acidic perspiration onto the skin or into hair follicles.

Sublingual gland
is under the tongue.

Submandibular gland
is at the back of the jaw.

Exocrine glands

Exocrine glands include sweat and sebaceous glands in the skin, salivary glands in the mouth, and other glands that secrete mucus, digestive enzymes, and earwax. Mammary glands in a female's breasts (right) are basically modified sweat glands. Instead of sweating, they "lactate," producing milk for babies to consume.

SWEAT AND SEBACEOUS GLANDS

Perspiration
(sweat) contains a lot of water, which helps to get rid of excess body heat when it evaporates off the surface of the skin.

Sebaceous glands
are common around the base of hair follicles. They secrete an oily substance called sebum (see pages 40–41) onto the hair and skin.

Hair follicle

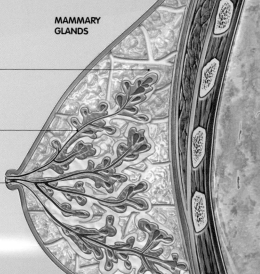

MAMMARY GLANDS

Cuboidal cells
secrete milk.

Lactiferous duct
transmits the milk to the nipple.

Nipple
where babies can feed.

BODY CAVITIES

An organ is a combination of two or more types of tissue that jointly perform one or more body functions. Structures such as the brain, liver, stomach, and lungs are what we normally categorize as organs. However, whole muscles and bones could also be considered to be organs as well, because they include nerves, blood vessels, and various types of connective tissue. Every organ is part of one or more of the body's eleven major organ systems (see pages 10–11). Many of them are housed and protected inside the body's cavities.

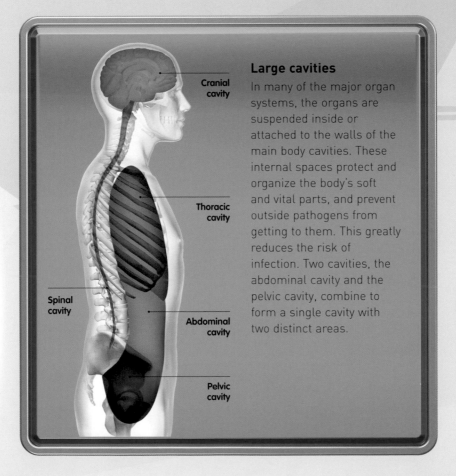

Cranial cavity

Thoracic cavity

Spinal cavity

Abdominal cavity

Pelvic cavity

Large cavities

In many of the major organ systems, the organs are suspended inside or attached to the walls of the main body cavities. These internal spaces protect and organize the body's soft and vital parts, and prevent outside pathogens from getting to them. This greatly reduces the risk of infection. Two cavities, the abdominal cavity and the pelvic cavity, combine to form a single cavity with two distinct areas.

Pleural membrane
lines the pleural cavities and prevents friction (rubbing) as the lungs expand and contract.

 YOU CAN LEARN MORE ABOUT THE FUNCTION OF THE DIAPHRAGM ON *PAGES 195* AND *198*.

SMALL CAVITIES

The body also has lots of smaller cavities, formed by the arrangement of bony parts. In the skull alone there are four pairs of sinus cavities (see page 56), the nasal and ear cavities, the oral cavity (mouth), as well as the orbital cavities that enclose all but the very front of the eyeballs. The brain and spinal cord contain cavities filled with cerebrospinal fluid, and synovial joints—such as the knees, hips, and shoulders—have chambers filled with synovial fluid.

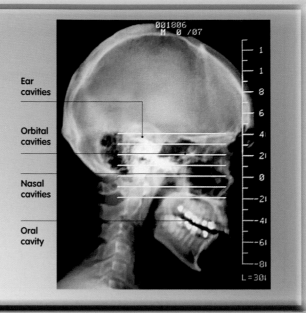

Ear cavities

Orbital cavities

Nasal cavities

Oral cavity

Trachea

Right lung

Left lung

Heart

Pleural cavity is lined with pleural membranes.

Pericardial cavity

The major spaces for organs

The cranial cavity, formed by the bony shell of the skull, encloses the brain, while the spinal cavity, formed by a bony tunnel through the vertebrae, houses the spinal cord. The chest, or thoracic cavity, contains the heart, lungs, and many other structures. A thick sheet of muscle, the diaphragm, separates the thoracic cavity from the abdominal cavity, which holds the stomach, pancreas, liver, and much of the intestine, as well as the kidneys and other organs. The pelvic cavity contains the internal reproductive organs in both males and females, as well as the bladder and the rectum.

Pericardium
(see page 26), peeled back here, is the double-walled sac that encloses the heart and its large vessels.

Ribcage
is made up of 12 pairs of ribs that curve around the chest to protect the heart and the lungs.

TISSUE REPAIR

Tissue damage, especially a cut or tear in the skin where infectious microbes can enter, presents a potentially serious challenge to the body. This is why a series of repair mechanisms begins, almost immediately, when tissues are injured. Sometimes, an organ (or part of an organ) can rebuild all of its tissues entirely—but these cases are rare.

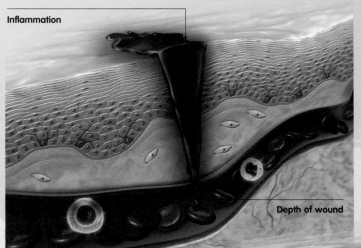

Inflammation

Depth of wound

Blood vessel

Inflammatory response

In a badly grazed knee, for example, an automatic response mobilizes blood cells and proteins to form a blood clot. This stops any bleeding and walls off healthy tissue from microbes. Next, the damaged tissue begins to regenerate as signaling chemicals, called growth factors, spur healthy cells to divide and produce replacements for the dead or dying ones.

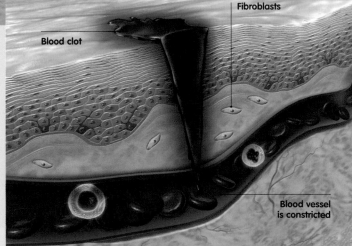

Fibroblasts

Blood clot

Blood vessel is constricted

Phase one: response to a wound

The first response to tissue damage is inflammation, the signs of which are heat, redness, and pain. This is an automatic process that spurs blood cells and proteins into their repair operations. A wound that draws blood, for example, will unleash a flood of chemicals that attract infection-fighting cells, while red blood cells are activated to form a clot that seals the wound.

Phase two: clotting

As blood cells infiltrate the area, fibroblasts (a type of cell involved in repair of tissues) travel to the wound to generate a structural protein called collagen.

 COLLAGEN IS THE MAIN STRUCTURAL PROTEIN FOUND IN THE CONNECTIVE TISSUE OF ANIMALS. IT IS ALSO THE MOST ABUNDANT PROTEIN IN MAMMALS.

Phase three: healing

A scab forms on the external part of the wound, temporarily providing a dry and protective crust. Meanwhile, growth factors stimulate the development of new tissue to fill the wounded area. This leads to the formation of a collagen-rich layer, known as granulation tissue.

Scab

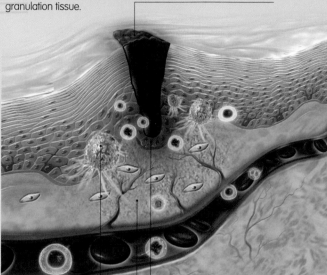

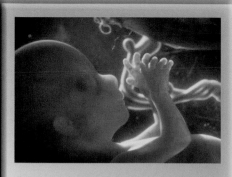

REPAIR IN THE WOMB

With knowledge and skill, surgeons can now operate on fetuses in the womb. If there is evidence of a facial abnormality in the fetus, the surgeon can make precise cuts to repair a cleft lip and palate, for example. The advantage of "in utero" surgery is that it does not result in the scarring that would occur if the body was operated on after the fetus was born, as wounds heal in the womb by a process of regeneration rather than repair.

Infiltration of cells

Granulation tissue

Wound depth is reducing

Scab falls away

Area of scarring

Regenerated tissue

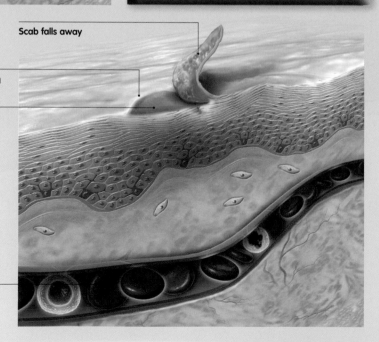

Phase four: scarring

Within a week or two, the scab sloughs off, revealing pale pink, regenerated skin at the wound site. Any collagen remaining from the granulation tissue may gradually form a visible scar.

Normal blood flow resumes in the vessels

CANCEROUS CELLS

The word cancer covers a range of diseases that all share one basic feature: The loss of genetic controls of growth that prevent normal cells from dividing more often than normal. In a cancer cell, a series of gene mutations sets off an abnormally frequent division of cells. This corrupts the highly organized internal structure of the cells. If the immune system does not quickly detect and kill the defective cells, their steadily multiplying offspring may form a cancerous tumor, invade the surrounding tissues, and spread to other locations in the body.

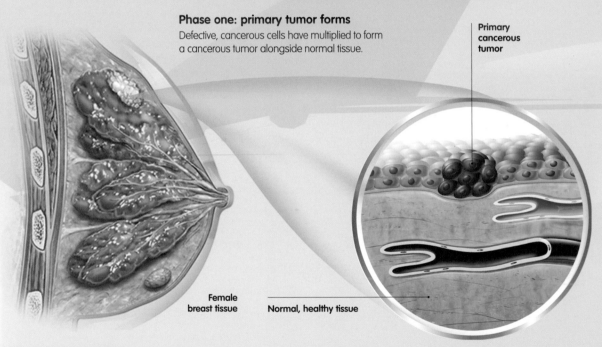

Phase one: primary tumor forms
Defective, cancerous cells have multiplied to form a cancerous tumor alongside normal tissue.

Primary cancerous tumor

Female breast tissue

Normal, healthy tissue

How cancer begins and spreads

The change may begin with a mutation that converts a "proto-oncogene" (a pre-cancer gene) into a cancer-causing oncogene. Usually, other mutations are also required, in which at least one "tumor suppressor" gene is disabled. In about five percent of cancers, one or more of the genetic mutations are inherited. In most cancers, the exact causes of the mutations are not known, but they may include chemical carcinogens (such as asbestos fibers in building materials), viral infections, and radiation from sunlight or medical X-rays.

Phase two: malignant cells break away

Malignant (invasive) cancer cells break away from the primary, or parent, tumor. Next, they release enzymes that allow them to enter blood vessels or lymph vessels.

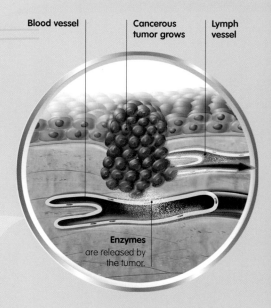

Blood vessel

Cancerous tumor grows

Lymph vessel

Enzymes are released by the tumor.

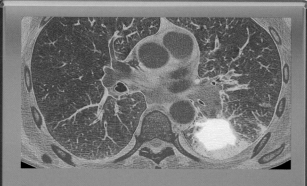

Detecting cancer

A "biopsy" test examines cells, from a sample of tissue or a lymph node, for signs of cancerous changes. For some cancers, a blood test can detect "tumor markers," substances produced either by malignant cells or by normal cells responding to the presence of a cancer. Instead of surgery, doctors can also use MRI, CT (above, the yellow area is a tumor), X-rays, and ultrasound scans to locate tumors.

Phase three: cells invade other tissues

The malignant cells then move through the blood vessels, or lymph vessels, to a new location. Here, they re-enter the tissue.

Phase four: secondary tumor forms

A new, secondary tumor forms in another part of the body, and the process continues to spread the cancer.

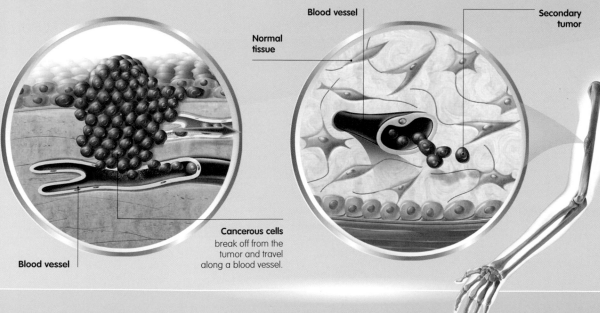

Normal tissue

Blood vessel

Secondary tumor

Blood vessel

Cancerous cells break off from the tumor and travel along a blood vessel.

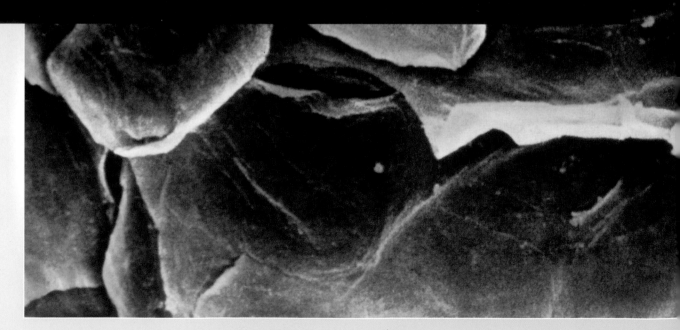

CHAPTER TWO

INTEGUMENTARY SYSTEM

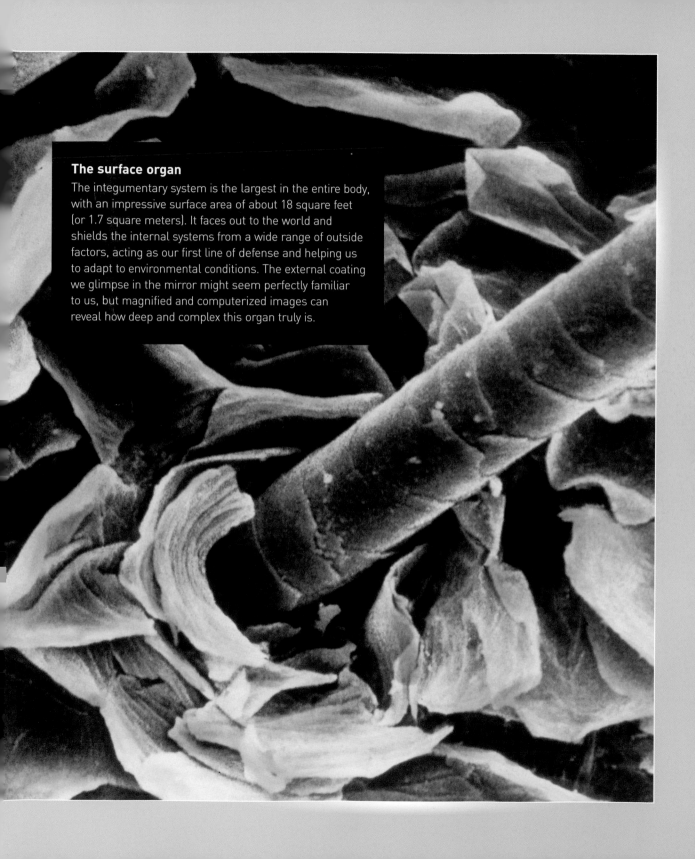

The surface organ

The integumentary system is the largest in the entire body, with an impressive surface area of about 18 square feet (or 1.7 square meters). It faces out to the world and shields the internal systems from a wide range of outside factors, acting as our first line of defense and helping us to adapt to environmental conditions. The external coating we glimpse in the mirror might seem perfectly familiar to us, but magnified and computerized images can reveal how deep and complex this organ truly is.

SKIN COVER

Skin makes up most of the body's outer covering, otherwise known as the integument. It provides an array of essential functions. It forms a barrier to microbes, prevents the excessive loss of body water, absorbs harmful solar radiation, and helps to spread out and get rid of metabolic heat (created by the chemical reactions of the body). Human skin is generally only about as thick as gift wrap. However, it is thicker in some areas—such as the soles of the feet, where it helps to bear the weight of the body.

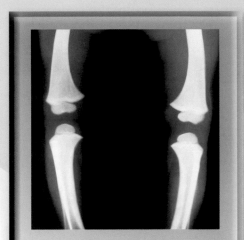

VITAMIN D PRODUCTION

The skin makes cholecalciferol, a key ingredient in vitamin D—essential to the development and maintenance of strong, healthy bones and muscles. In fact, vitamin D is important throughout the body. Research has also shown that vitamin D receptors are present in most, if not all, body cells and that it has potent effects on the growth and differentiation of many types of cells. Deficiency in vitamin D can lead to rickets, a disorder where bones soften, causing skeletal problems (see above).

SUPPORTING ALL THE SYSTEMS

The integumentary system helps to support the operation of the other body systems. In turn, all the other systems contribute in some way to the healthy functioning of the skin and the structures (and substances) obtained from it.

Skeletal system
Skin helps to activate vitamin D, required for the absorption of calcium and phosphate, which are used in the formation of bone tissue. The skeletal system provides structural support for the integument.

Muscular system
By starting the process that leads to the active form of vitamin D in the body, the skin helps to keep muscles strong. In return, the activity of the muscles increases blood flow to the skin.

Lymphatic system
Skin is an external barrier against invading microbes, and the immune system helps to heal wounds in the integument layers.

THE FOLLOWING FOODS ARE KEY *SOURCES OF VITAMIN D*: OILY FISH (SUCH AS SALMON), LIVER, EGGS, AND FORTIFIED CEREALS.

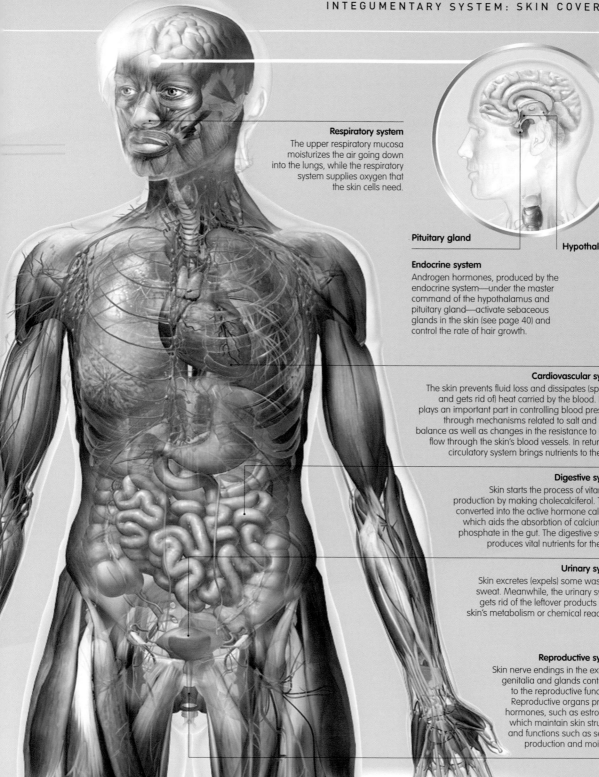

Respiratory system
The upper respiratory mucosa moisturizes the air going down into the lungs, while the respiratory system supplies oxygen that the skin cells need.

Pituitary gland

Hypothalamus

Endocrine system
Androgen hormones, produced by the endocrine system—under the master command of the hypothalamus and pituitary gland—activate sebaceous glands in the skin (see page 40) and control the rate of hair growth.

Cardiovascular system
The skin prevents fluid loss and dissipates (spreads and gets rid of) heat carried by the blood. It also plays an important part in controlling blood pressure, through mechanisms related to salt and water balance as well as changes in the resistance to blood flow through the skin's blood vessels. In return, the circulatory system brings nutrients to the skin.

Digestive system
Skin starts the process of vitamin D production by making cholecalciferol. This is converted into the active hormone calcitriol, which aids the absorbtion of calcium and phosphate in the gut. The digestive system produces vital nutrients for the skin.

Urinary system
Skin excretes (expels) some wastes in sweat. Meanwhile, the urinary system gets rid of the leftover products of the skin's metabolism or chemical reactions.

Reproductive system
Skin nerve endings in the external genitalia and glands contribute to the reproductive functions. Reproductive organs provide hormones, such as estrogens, which maintain skin structure and functions such as sebum production and moisture.

SKIN STRUCTURE

Skin has two layers: the waterproof layer called the epidermis, with cells containing keratin, and the dermis below it. Required to withstand a lifetime of stretches, bumps, and scrapes, the epidermis is constantly regenerating. As dead, outer cells flake or rub off, living cells replace them from below. This is similar to the process that helps cuts to heal (see pages 30–31). The skin also contains sensory receptors (within the dermis) that convey information about touch, temperature, pain, and other stimuli.

The anatomy of skin

Hair follicles, nerves, blood vessels, and oil and sweat glands are all embedded in the dermis layer. The upper epidermis layer consists of dead cells that are rich in a fibrous protein called keratin.

Scaly layer of keratin-rich cells.

Pore

Red blood cells

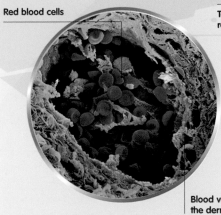

Touch receptor

Blood vessel in the dermis layer

Hair follicle

Body temperature

Blood-monitoring sensors in the hypothalamus (see pages 158–159) can detect changes in core body temperature. When it rises above the optimum level of about 98.2°F (36.8°C), the hypothalamus tells the blood vessels in the skin to dilate (widen). More blood flows to the surface and its excess heat escapes through the skin. This is why skin may appear pink after exercise, for example. When the core temperature drops too low, the vessels contract to reduce heat loss.

Arrector pili muscle attached to a hair follicle. The contraction of this muscle causes the hair to stand on end.

Sebaceous gland

FIND OUT MORE ABOUT THE STRUCTURAL CHANGES THAT THE SKIN UNDERGOES, THROUGH AGING, ON *PAGE 275*.

Pigmentation

Human skin gets some of its color from a yellow-orange pigment called carotene, in the dermis layer—but it gets much more from cells called melanocytes in the epidermis. The melanocytes produce a black-brown pigment called melanin. All humans have the same number of melanocytes, but there are genetic differences in how they are distributed and how much melanin they make.

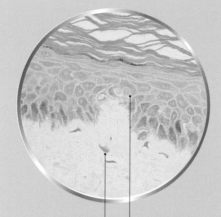

Epidermis layer

Basal epidermal layer

Dermis layer

Nerve

Subcutaneous fat

Blood vessels
These contract and dilate.

Red blood cells
flow through tiny capillaries near the skin's surface. This creates the common pinkish color in fair skin.

Melanocytes
in darker skin produce more melanin than those in fair skin, producing a brown color to the skin.

HOW THE SKIN AGES

A newborn child has delicate, soft skin with a thin epidermis, few functional sweat glands, and a substantial layer of fat to prevent heat loss. In teenage years, hormonal changes increase the size and output of sebaceous (oil) glands, which can contribute to pimples and acne. With increased age, hormonal changes and exposure to sunshine, the epidermis and dermis get thinner. The skin also becomes less elastic, resulting in sagging and wrinkles (see page 275).

SKIN GLANDS

Hair, nails, oil, and sweat glands—all of these structures are buried in the dermis and pass up through the epidermis (see pages 38–39). Sweat mainly consists of water, and its most essential role in the body is to carry away excess body heat as it evaporates from the surface of the skin. Except for the palms and soles of the feet, every part of an adult's skin has sebaceous glands, and the oily sebum they produce lubricates (oils) and softens skin and hair.

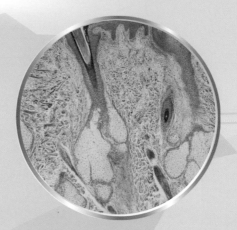

Sebaceous glands

Sebaceous (oil) glands produce an oily substance, sebum, that lubricates hairs and the surface of the skin. This prevents the hair from drying out and reduces water loss from the skin, too. Sebum also plays a part in preventing bacteria and fungi from infecting the skin. In this SEM image (above), the sebaceous glands show up as the pale purple, saclike structures.

Sweat glands

Sweat glands, known as "eccrine" glands, populate much of the human skin. From the scalp—on the top of the head—to the palm of the hands and the soles of the feet, most skin areas contain these glands. They can increase their output of watery sweat, as and when needed, to dissipate (spread and expel) body heat. Large sweat glands, called "apocrine" glands, are concentrated in the armpits and the groin.

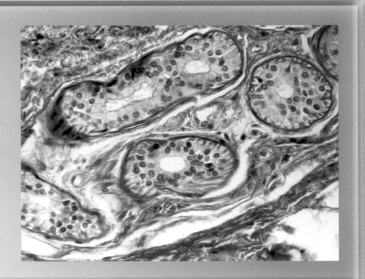

SEBUM IS A LATIN WORD THAT MEANS "GREASE."

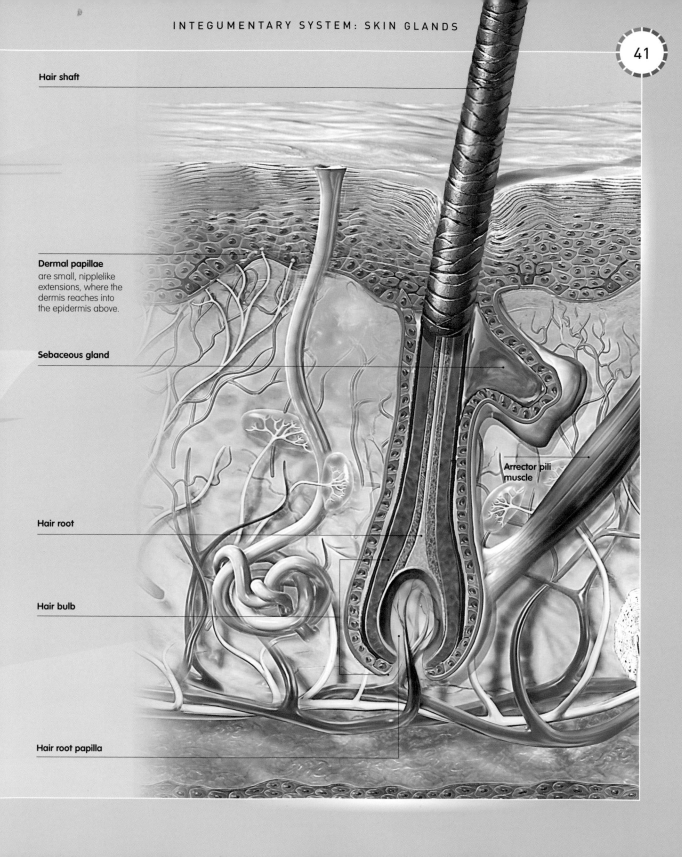

Hair shaft

Dermal papillae
are small, nipplelike
extensions, where the
dermis reaches into
the epidermis above.

Sebaceous gland

Hair root

Hair bulb

Hair root papilla

Arrector pili
muscle

HAIR AND NAILS

Millions of hairs grow on the scalp, on the limbs, in the armpits, and elsewhere. Each flexible shaft of hair consists mainly of fibrous, keratin-rich cells and protrudes from a hair follicle that is rooted in the dermis. As a hair grows, cells in the outer shaft die and may become frayed. Fingernails and toenails contain an especially hard form of keratin. As they grow, the lengthening nails move over the "nail bed" underneath.

Hair follicles

A hair follicle cycles between phases of growth and rest. During the growth phase, the hair lengthens as new cells arise in the root and push dead cells upward. After a resting phase, growth begins anew. A scalp hair, on the head, may grow for up to six years before the follicle rests. Hair on the head grows an average of 6 inches (15cm) each year.

Head hairs

This close-up SEM image (above) shows hairs growing from a human scalp. On average, the human head has about 100,000 hair follicles at different stages of activity. About 75–100 hairs fall out each day—more if a person is on a strict weight-loss diet. We often see the thinning of hair in older men and women. This is because our hormones wane as our bodies age.

Body hair functions

Hairs on the body serve a number of functions. They trap air, which insulates the body to keep it warm. They protect the skin from friction, and from the irritation of external conditions, such as sunshine and wind-blown particles. Hairs also redirect sweat and water, and soak some of it up to prevent further irritation of the skin.

 INDIVIDUAL STRANDS OF HEAD HAIR TYPICALLY GROW UP TO 6 INCHES (OR 15CM) EVERY YEAR, AND HAVE AN AVERAGE LIFESPAN OF SIX YEARS.

Structure of a nail

A nail has three main parts: the nail plate (the visible portion), the embedded root under a fold of skin (the cuticle), and the free edge at the tip. Capillaries (containing blood) in the underlying nail bed give the nail body its pinkish color.

Nail functions

Nails protect the tips of the fingers and toes, as well as the soft tissues around them. They allow us to make precise and delicate movements—and they sometimes serve as tools, in themselves, for picking or pulling at objects.

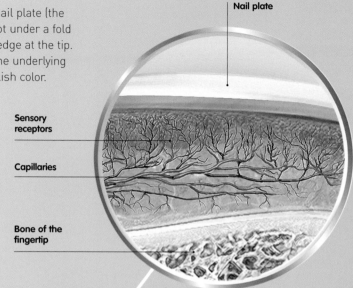

Nail plate

Sensory receptors

Capillaries

Bone of the fingertip

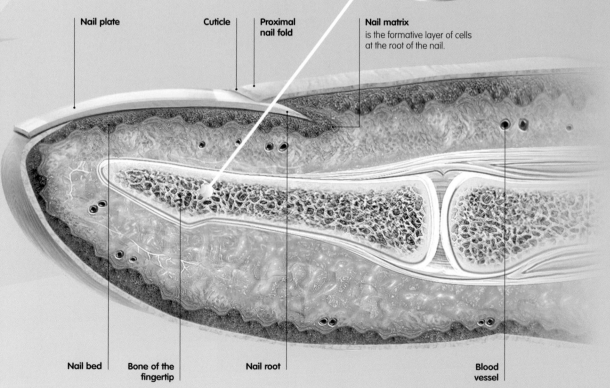

Nail plate

Cuticle

Proximal nail fold

Nail matrix
is the formative layer of cells at the root of the nail.

Nail bed

Bone of the fingertip

Nail root

Blood vessel

SKIN DISORDERS

Skin is exposed to abrasion and contact with irritants, sharp objects, chemicals, hot surfaces, as well as bacteria and other pathogens. Its most widespread disorders fall into a category called dermatitis—which simply means inflammation of the skin. This inflammation may result in a rash, or cause dandruff. Skin cells also turn over, constantly, to produce new cells. This process of division can go out of control, leading to a variety of conditions including skin cancers. There are three main forms of skin cancer: basal cell carcinoma, squamous cell carcinoma, and melanoma. All of them are associated with overexposure to ultraviolet (UV) radiation.

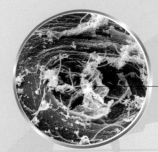

Bacteria on the surface of the skin are revealed by this color-enhanced SEM image.

Micro-organisms
The skin is covered in millions upon millions of micro-organisms at all times. The skin carries many good bacteria which keep the skin healthy. Good hygiene is vital in preventing harmful bacteria from entering the mouth, for example. Occasionally, some micro-organisms manage to invade through damaged or unhealthy parts of the skin.

Psoriasis
Psoriasis occurs when the usual, weeks-long life cycle of skin cells is packed into just a few days, and the skin turnover is rapid. It is marked by thick, whitish, irritated patches that build up on the elbows, knees, and elsewhere. The cause is unknown but triggers include stress, trauma, infections, and hormones.

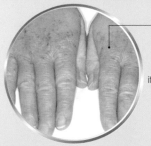

Inflammation of the skin leads to symptoms such as redness, soreness, itching, flaking, rashes, and sometimes small blisters.

Eczema
Nobody knows exactly what causes eczema, but genetics play a major part, and it is a fairly common form of dermatitis. It is often triggered by reactions to drugs, soaps, creams, bacteria, sweat, weather conditions, and metals used in jewelry. Stress and anxiety can also give rise to these itchy, scaly patches of skin.

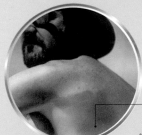

Mild sunburn is classed as a first-degree burn.

Burns
Skin burns are graded according to their coverage, depth, and location. First-degree burns, such as mild sunburn (above), are on the surface and usually heal quickly. Blistering is a sign of a deeper, second-degree burn. Third-degree burns usually cause the skin to die, exposing the underlying tissues to infection.

 CURRENTLY, *2 TO 3 MILLION NON-MELANOMA* SKIN CANCERS AND AROUND *132,000 MELANOMA* SKIN CANCERS OCCUR GLOBALLY EACH YEAR.

Skin cancers

Most skin cancers are slow-growing basal cell carcinomas, treatable through minor surgery. Squamous cell carcinoma develops in the flattened cells at the skin's surface. These cells grow more rapidly and may spread to the nearby lymph nodes. Malignant melanoma is more aggressive. It is often mistaken for a harmless mole on the skin, but may spread before the sufferer realizes that the blemish is abnormal.

SYNTHETIC SKIN

Artificial skin is made of a scaffolding of natural materials such as fibrin or collagen, or from stem cells. Grown in a laboratory, it can repair damage from cancer, burns, and other skin problems. After it has been transplanted into the damaged place, blood vessels can migrate to the area, followed by epithelial cells (see page 16). Over time, the synthetic skin may decay, leaving behind a healthy, new patch of skin.

Basal cell carcinoma
Prolonged exposure to UV rays—from the sun or tanning beds, for example—can damage cells at the base of the epidermis. This leads to the formation of a mound of slow-growing, cancerous cells. Squamous cell carcinomas are more likely to grow and spread.

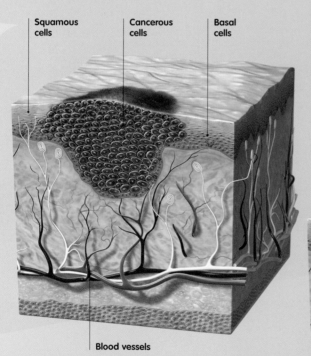

Squamous cells   Cancerous cells   Basal cells

Blood vessels

Melanoma
Melanocytes (see pages 38–39) are pigment-producing cells that give color to the skin. When they are damaged by UV radiation, melanocytes may escape normal growth controls and start to form a dark, irregular lesion in the skin. This type of cancer is highly "metastatic," which means the cells spread and invade other tissues very quickly.

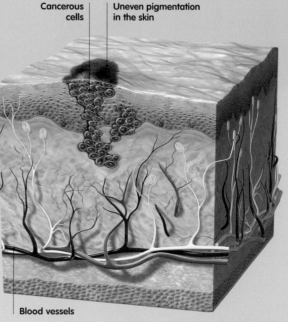

Cancerous cells   Uneven pigmentation in the skin

Blood vessels

SKELETAL SYSTEM

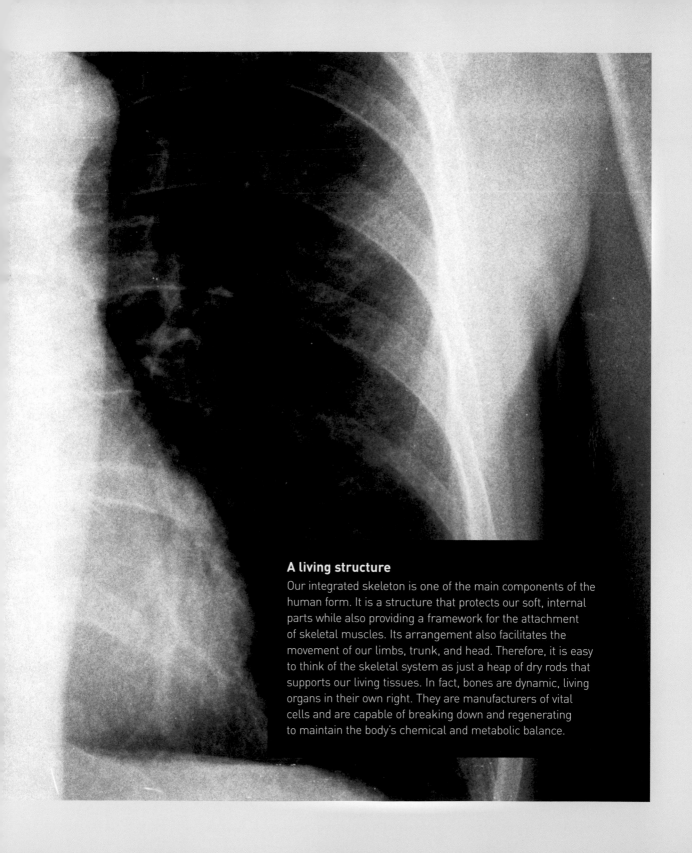

A living structure

Our integrated skeleton is one of the main components of the human form. It is a structure that protects our soft, internal parts while also providing a framework for the attachment of skeletal muscles. Its arrangement also facilitates the movement of our limbs, trunk, and head. Therefore, it is easy to think of the skeletal system as just a heap of dry rods that supports our living tissues. In fact, bones are dynamic, living organs in their own right. They are manufacturers of vital cells and are capable of breaking down and regenerating to maintain the body's chemical and metabolic balance.

THE SKELETON

As humans, we are large, mobile animals. We require a strong bodily framework that allows movement while providing support and protection for our muscles and soft, internal organs. The skeleton is this architectural framework. It is a versatile collection of (usually) 206 bones, each one a living organ—a fine-tuned blend of bone tissue and other components. Anatomically, the skeleton has two main regions: the axial and appendicular skeletons.

The axial skeleton

The parts of the axial skeleton include the skull, the vertebral column (or spine), and the ribcage.

Coccyx
More regularly known as the tailbone, the coccyx is made up of small, fused vertebrae.

Humerus
This long bone supports the upper arm.

Ulna
The upper end of this bone forms the prominent, bony portion of the elbow.

Radius
The radius extends from the elbow down to the thumb side of the lower arm.

Frontal bone
This bone, under the skin of the forehead, forms the front of the skull and the upper eye sockets.

Maxilla
The upper jawbone.

Mandible
A massive bone that forms the lower jaw. It is the only facial bone that moves.

Scapula
This broad bone is also known as the shoulder blade.

Clavicle
The clavicle, or collarbone, provides support in the upper chest.

Rib
Ribs form the protective wall of the chest cavity.

Sternum
The ribs attach to the sternum, or breastbone, which also helps to protect the heart.

Coxal bone (or Ischia)
Also known as the hip bone, this strong bone forms most of the pelvis.

Sacrum
Formed by the fusion of five vertebrae (see pages 54–55).

Femur
The femur, or thighbone, is the longest and strongest bone in the body.

Patella
The patella, or kneecap, is embedded in a major tendon of the knee joint (see pages 64–65).

Tibia
Also known as the shinbone, this sturdy bone helps to bear the weight of the body.

Fibula
The lower end of this smaller leg bone forms the prominent, bony portion of the ankle.

Phalanges
The phalanges are the bones of the fingers and toes.

Carpals
These are the eight bones that form each wrist.

Metacarpals
The metacarpals are the bones of the upper hand.

Phalanges
These are the bones that make up the fingers and toes.

The appendicular skeleton

The bones of the appendicular skeleton, or "hanging" skeleton, include those in the limbs and the pectoral and pelvic girdles.

A variety of bones

A bone's overall form needs to serve its function, and this is why bones come in such a wide array of sizes. There are four basic shapes: long, short, flat, and irregular. Thighbones are required to support the full weight of the upper body, so they are massive in comparison to the tiny bones of the middle ear (see page 56)—or the interlocking finger bones that help to make the hands such accurate and versatile tools.

Tarsals
The tarsals are the main bones of the ankle.

Metatarsals
Related—in their form and function—to the metacarpals of the hand, the metatarsal bones support the form and load-bearing of the upper foot.

BONE STRUCTURE

For the skeleton to support and protect the soft parts of the body, bones must be strong and rigid. The structure of bone tissue helps to meet these demands without making the skeleton too heavy. Like other connective tissues, bone consists of living cells in an "extracellular" matrix of fibers and other substances. These cells include osteoblasts, which form bone, and osteoclasts, which break it down. The bone matrix is the mix of fibers and substances from which the structure of bone develops.

Nerve
Nerves carry neural signals to and from the periosteum.

THE STRUCTURE OF A LONG BONE

Bone marrow
In some bones, marrow fills a cavity or the spaces in the spongy bone. Red marrow, in bones such as the sternum, produces blood cells (see page 207). The long bones of adults contain yellow marrow, which stores fat.

The rock-hard matrix

The bone matrix contains collagen fibers and crystals of hydroxyapatite, a mix of the minerals calcium and phosphate that makes the matrix rock-hard. These are the foundation for the two types of bone tissue. Dense "compact" bone forms the smooth, outer part of bones. "Spongy" bone, in the interior, contains large spaces amid bony struts (see opposite page).

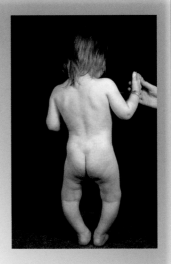

BONE NUTRITION
One of the important roles of vitamin D (see page 36) is to assist the movement of calcium and phosphorus into the bloodstream. These minerals make bones hard and dense. If a young child is deficient in vitamin D, it may develop rickets—a disorder in which bones soften, resulting in bowed legs and other skeletal problems. This photo shows how the lower limbs of the infant have become deformed.

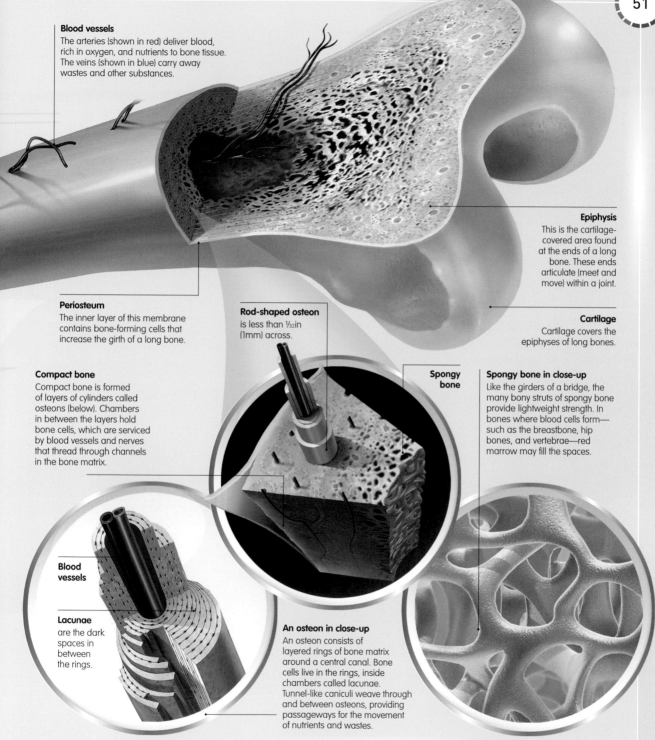

Blood vessels
The arteries (shown in red) deliver blood, rich in oxygen, and nutrients to bone tissue. The veins (shown in blue) carry away wastes and other substances.

Epiphysis
This is the cartilage-covered area found at the ends of a long bone. These ends articulate (meet and move) within a joint.

Periosteum
The inner layer of this membrane contains bone-forming cells that increase the girth of a long bone.

Rod-shaped osteon
is less than 1/32in (1mm) across.

Cartilage
Cartilage covers the epiphyses of long bones.

Compact bone
Compact bone is formed of layers of cylinders called osteons (below). Chambers in between the layers hold bone cells, which are serviced by blood vessels and nerves that thread through channels in the bone matrix.

Spongy bone

Spongy bone in close-up
Like the girders of a bridge, the many bony struts of spongy bone provide lightweight strength. In bones where blood cells form—such as the breastbone, hip bones, and vertebrae—red marrow may fill the spaces.

Blood vessels

Lacunae
are the dark spaces in between the rings.

An osteon in close-up
An osteon consists of layered rings of bone matrix around a central canal. Bone cells live in the rings, inside chambers called lacunae. Tunnel-like caniculi weave through and between osteons, providing passageways for the movement of nutrients and wastes.

GROWTH AND REMODELING

In a give-and-take process known as remodeling, osteoblasts steadily form and lay down bone tissue while osteoclasts steadily destroy it. This is how bones grow longer or wider, take on the correct form and proportions, and—importantly—heal themselves after an injury. The process is continuous, ensuring that old tissue is constantly being replaced with fresh tissue. Over several years, virtually all of the body's bone mass is recycled in this way.

Stress and strength

Healthy bones become stronger through load-bearing activities such as carrying heavy groceries. The "mechanical stress" this creates shifts the balance between osteoblasts and osteoclasts. This means that more bone is laid down than removed during the normal cycle of remodeling.

How a long bone forms

At first, a human fetus has flexible "bones" made of cartilage. As bone cells develop, spongy bone begins to replace the cartilage, and blood vessels invade the developing bone. In time, a marrow cavity opens up, and knobbly epiphyses form at the bone ends.

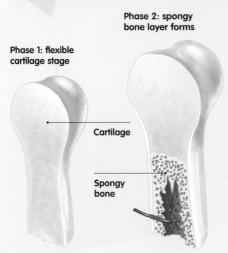

Phase 1: flexible cartilage stage

Cartilage

Spongy bone

Phase 2: spongy bone layer forms

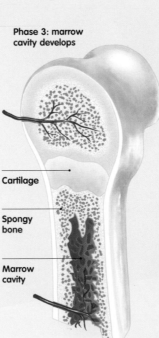

Phase 3: marrow cavity develops

Cartilage

Spongy bone

Marrow cavity

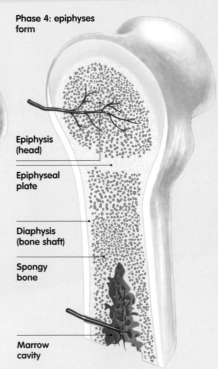

Phase 4: epiphyses form

Epiphysis (head)

Epiphyseal plate

Diaphysis (bone shaft)

Spongy bone

Marrow cavity

CALCIUM (Ca) IS ONE OF THE ALKALINE EARTH METALS. ITS COMPOUNDS OCCUR NATURALLY IN LIMESTONE, FLUORITE, GYMPSUM, AND OTHER MINERALS.

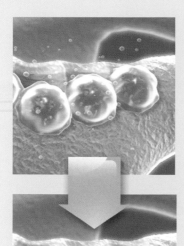

Bone tissue regeneration

Bone tissue remodeling is a continuous process of recycling, comparable to the way in which skin cells turn over, replace, and renew themselves.

Osteoclasts
(shown in pink) are cells that break down bone tissue.

Osteoclasts
at work in the bone lacunae (see page 51).

Bone resorption
is the name of the process by which bone tissue is selectively removed by the osteoclasts.

Calcium supplies

Osteoclasts can also "mine" bone tissue to help ensure an adequate supply of calcium to meet the constant demand from muscles and the nervous system. When too little calcium circulates in the bloodstream, glands in the neck—the parathyroids—release the parathyroid hormone (or PTH). The osteoclasts respond by breaking down bone tissue to release its calcium content, which then quickly enters the blood.

Osteoblasts
(shown in purple) are cells that secrete new bone substance.

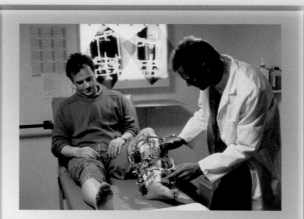

ASSISTED REMODELING
In cases where severe bone damage or fracturing has occurred, or after surgery, an "Ilizarov apparatus" can be used to immobilize the bones in the affected area. A frame of metal rods holds the bones in place and encourages the natural processes of bone growth and remodeling.

Ossification
is the name of the process by which new bone is formed.

UPPER AXIAL SKELETON

The axial skeleton is the body's overall framework. Aligned along a lengthwise axis, its 82 bones support the head, neck, chest, and abdomen. They also protect the vital structures inside these areas, including the brain, the spinal cord, and major organs such as the heart and lungs. Most axial skeleton bones are flat or have an irregular shape.

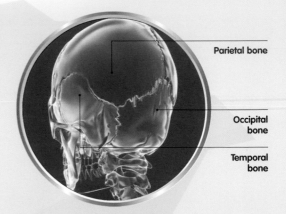

Parietal bone

Occipital bone

Temporal bone

Flat bones of the skull

The body's flat bones include the helmet-like skull bones that enclose and protect the brain. Although relatively thin, these bones are curved like a Roman arch—a design that makes them surprisingly strong. The bones fuse together as the skull develops (see page 56).

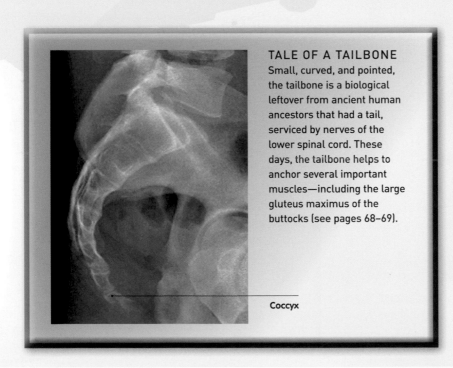

TALE OF A TAILBONE

Small, curved, and pointed, the tailbone is a biological leftover from ancient human ancestors that had a tail, serviced by nerves of the lower spinal cord. These days, the tailbone helps to anchor several important muscles—including the large gluteus maximus of the buttocks (see pages 68–69).

Coccyx

Internal protection

Many of the axial bones are arranged to form protective cavities for soft, delicate body parts, or to allow openings for blood vessels and nerves—including the spinal cord and nerves that link the central nervous system with the rest of the body.

Frontal bone

This bone forms the forehead and the upper eye sockets.

Temporal bone

The ear canal (see pages 136–137) passes through this bone, which forms the lower sides of the cranium (skull).

Hyoid bone

Located in the neck and held in place by muscles and ligaments, this U-shaped bone supports the base of the tongue and muscles associated with the throat. It is the only bone in the body that does not connect to another bone.

Ribs

The 24 ribs, arranged in 12 pairs, are thin bones connected by muscles which work together to lift and expand with breathing.

Ribcage

This bony box is formed by the ribs, the sternum, and the thoracic vertebrae. It protects the organs of the chest and upper abdomen, and helps to support the shoulders and upper limbs.

Parietal bone

The two parietal bones form most of the roof and sides of the cranium.

Occipital bone

A large bone that forms most of the back and lower rear of the cranium.

Temporomandibular joint

The temporal bone and lower jawbone connect at this joint.

Structural support

The long axis of the body runs from the top of the head to the coccyx at the base of the trunk. Its main support is provided by the skull and spinal column, the hyoid bone in the neck, the ribcage, and the sternum (breastbone).

Sternum

Also known as the breastbone, the sternum anchors the inner ends of the upper ten pairs of ribs.

Vertebral column

Commonly known as the spine or backbone, this flexible stack of 33 vertebrae houses the spinal cord and helps to support the pelvic bones.

Intervertebral disk

These disks act as spinal flexing points and shock absorbers. Each one is made up of a ring of cartilage and a softer, elastic center.

Sacrum

Five sacral vertebrae, all fused together, form this triangular bone.

Coccyx

Four tiny vertebrae fuse together to form this structure at the very base of the axial skeleton. It is more commonly known as the tailbone.

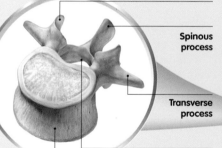

Articular surface

Spinous process

Transverse process

Vertebral foramen
encloses the spinal cord.

Processes
have surfaces designed to form a series of movable joints.

Body

The vertebrae

The flexible part of the spinal column is normally made up of 24 vertebrae. These are prime examples of irregular bones. Stacked on top of each other—with disks of cartilage in between—their rounded, flat bodies combine to bear the weight of the body. Bony projections called processes flare outward around an opening called the vertebral foramen.

THE SKULL

There are 22 cranial and facial bones in the skull. They encase and protect the brain, and provide attachment points for the muscles of the face and neck. They also form protective chambers around the organs that provide our senses of vision, hearing, taste, smell, and balance. The joint between the skull's occipital bone and the first vertebra allows the head to lean forward and backward. There is a pivot joint between the first and second vertebrae, which enables the head to turn left and right. The disks and ligaments that connect and support the first vertebrae of the spine provide a wide range of motion for the head.

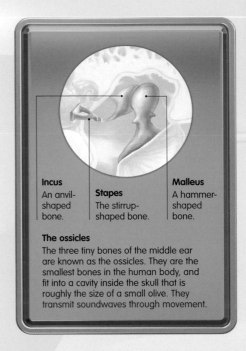

Incus
An anvil-shaped bone.

Stapes
The stirrup-shaped bone.

Malleus
A hammer-shaped bone.

The ossicles
The three tiny bones of the middle ear are known as the ossicles. They are the smallest bones in the human body, and fit into a cavity inside the skull that is roughly the size of a small olive. They transmit soundwaves through movement.

Skull development

At birth, the human skull is made up of 44 separate parts. As the body develops, many of these bony elements gradually fuse together into solid bone. Some skull bones are connected by jagged joints called sutures. In children, the sutures are made up of fibrous connective tissue that flexes as the cranial bones grow and develop. The sutures mineralize and harden over time, a process that can last well into middle age.

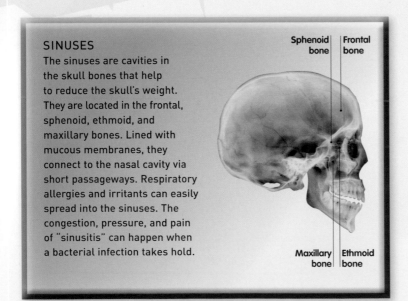

SINUSES
The sinuses are cavities in the skull bones that help to reduce the skull's weight. They are located in the frontal, sphenoid, ethmoid, and maxillary bones. Lined with mucous membranes, they connect to the nasal cavity via short passageways. Respiratory allergies and irritants can easily spread into the sinuses. The congestion, pressure, and pain of "sinusitis" can happen when a bacterial infection takes hold.

Sphenoid bone | Frontal bone
Maxillary bone | Ethmoid bone

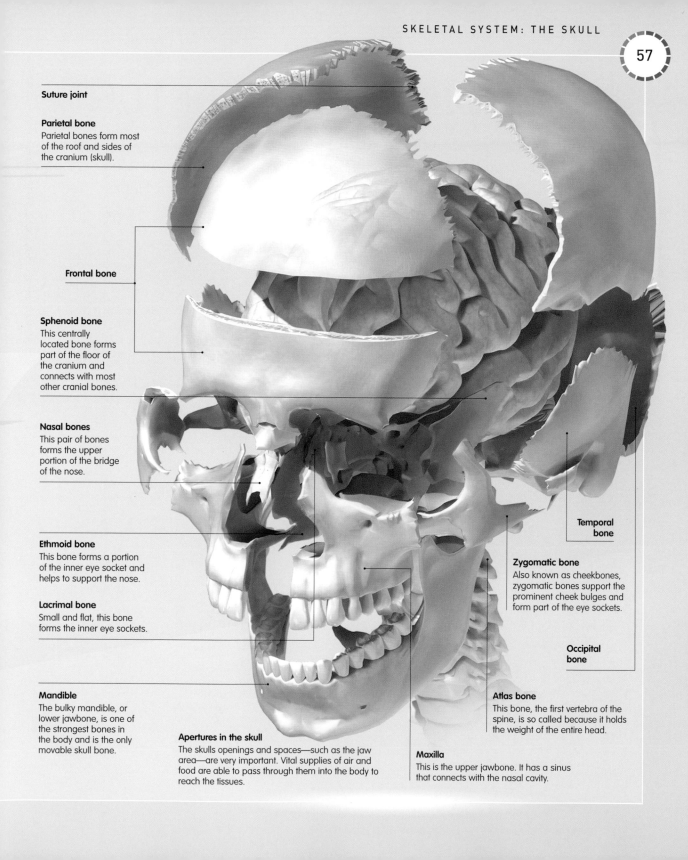

Suture joint

Parietal bone
Parietal bones form most
of the roof and sides of
the cranium (skull).

Frontal bone

Sphenoid bone
This centrally
located bone forms
part of the floor of
the cranium and
connects with most
other cranial bones.

Nasal bones
This pair of bones
forms the upper
portion of the bridge
of the nose.

Ethmoid bone
This bone forms a portion
of the inner eye socket and
helps to support the nose.

Lacrimal bone
Small and flat, this bone
forms the inner eye sockets.

Mandible
The bulky mandible, or
lower jawbone, is one of
the strongest bones in
the body and is the only
movable skull bone.

Apertures in the skull
The skulls openings and spaces—such as the jaw
area—are very important. Vital supplies of air and
food are able to pass through them into the body to
reach the tissues.

**Temporal
bone**

Zygomatic bone
Also known as cheekbones,
zygomatic bones support the
prominent cheek bulges and
form part of the eye sockets.

**Occipital
bone**

Atlas bone
This bone, the first vertebra of the
spine, is so called because it holds
the weight of the entire head.

Maxilla
This is the upper jawbone. It has a sinus
that connects with the nasal cavity.

APPENDICULAR SKELETON

The appendicular skeleton includes the bones of the limbs and the pectoral and pelvic girdles—in other words, all the parts that attach to the axial skeleton and provide a bony infrastructure for most of the body's major movements. Human limbs, especially the wrists and hands, have an intricate structure that allows for precisely controlled movements.

Jointed limbs

Joints such as the shoulder (see page 62), are highly mobile. The shoulder allows the humerus, the long bone of the upper arm, to play its fundamental role in throwing an object, swinging a golf club, or lifting loads overhead.

The pectoral girdles
Males have larger, heavier pectoral girdles in the upper body (shown in blue) compared to those of females (shown in pink). These help to support the wider, more muscular chest and shoulders that males develop after puberty.

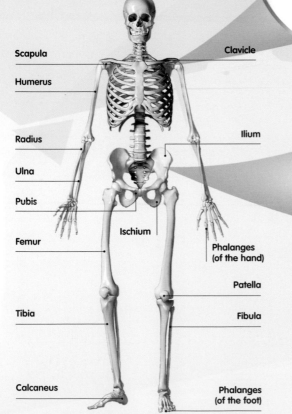

Scapula

Humerus

Radius

Ulna

Pubis

Femur

Ischium

Tibia

Calcaneus

Clavicle

Ilium

Phalanges (of the hand)

Patella

Fibula

Phalanges (of the foot)

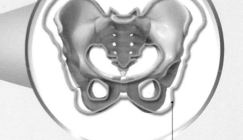

The pelvic girdle
Compared to a male's pelvis, a female's pelvic bones are relatively thin and lightweight—and form a rounder, wider opening (shown in pink) for the purposes of child-bearing. Women's hips have a wider range of motion as well.

STUDY THE MOTOR FUNCTIONS OF THE NERVOUS SYSTEM ON *PAGES 110–111*.

Built to move

The pelvic girdle and lower limbs are bulkier and less flexible than the upper limbs, but they are sturdy enough to support the body's weight against gravity when a person is upright. They also support dynamic bodily movements such as running or jumping.

Dynamic limbs

Using a thought-controlled dynamic—or "bionic"—limb, a person can mentally direct nerve impulses to move the artificial body part. The devices in the limb are "wired" to the functioning motor nerves that remain in the area attached to the replacement limb, for instance in this robotic arm shown above.

Replacement limbs

Artificial limbs—or prosthetics—are widely available for people who were born without limbs, or who have had to have a damaged limb removed. Using "static" prostheses, the wearer can move the artificial limbs by manipulating a system of straps and cables.

HANDS AND FEET

Of the 206 bones in an adult, 126 of them are in the appendicular, or "hanging," skeleton (see page 58)—and most of these are in the hands and feet. Each hand contains 27 bones and each foot has 26 bones. In the hand, there are 19 bones that articulate (join and move) with each other, or with the wrist bones, to provide a wide range of movement. The structure of the feet is designed to be supporting and load-bearing, as well as dexterous.

Manual dexterity

The articulating, interconnecting bones of the hands provide the dexterity to do things such as scratch an itch, play the piano, or deftly communicate using sign language.

The opposable thumb
Many hand movements make use of the "opposable" human thumb, which can move to touch the tips of the other four fingers. This motion is provided by the saddle joint (see pages 64–65) located between the first metacarpal and the wrist bone. It gives humans a unique ability to control fine movements.

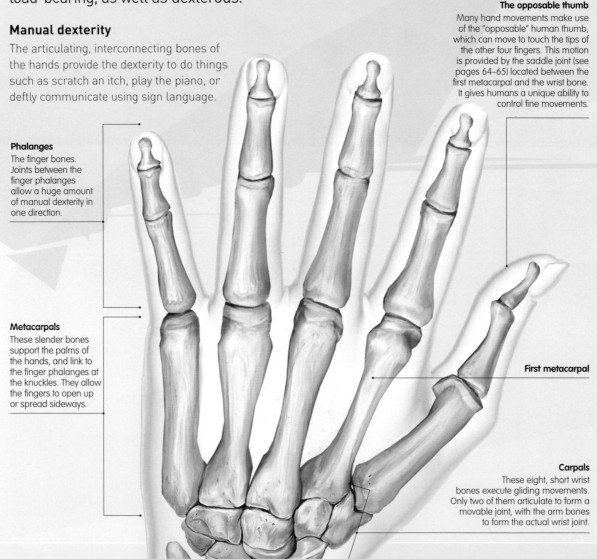

Phalanges
The finger bones. Joints between the finger phalanges allow a huge amount of manual dexterity in one direction.

Metacarpals
These slender bones support the palms of the hands, and link to the finger phalanges at the knuckles. They allow the fingers to open up or spread sideways.

First metacarpal

Carpals
These eight, short wrist bones execute gliding movements. Only two of them articulate to form a movable joint, with the arm bones to form the actual wrist joint.

Foot functions

Human feet are designed to support the entire weight of the body—and yet they are also incredibly flexible. As in the hands, the many bones of the feet combine and articulate to provide a wide range of movements and postures.

Tibia
This large leg bone helps to bear the weight of the body. Its lower end articulates in the ankle joint.

Fibula
The sticklike fibula gives lateral (side-to-side) stability. Its lower end produces the outer, bony "bulge" of the ankle joint.

Calcaneus
Otherwise known as the heel bone, this is one of the longest tarsals. It helps to anchor the longitudinal (lengthwise) arch of the foot (see panel).

Outer longitudinal arch

Inner longitudinal arch

Transverse arch

Arches of support

The bones of the foot combine to form weight-bearing arches—a "transverse," side-to-side arch and two longitudinal (lengthwise) arches. If the tendons and ligaments holding the inner (or medial) longitudinal arch weaken, the arch of the foot will flatten or "fall." This is how people develop the condition commonly known as "flat feet."

Tarsals
These bones collectively support the rear of the foot and help to bear the weight of the body.

Metatarsals
These five long bones help to form the longitudinal (lengthwise) arches of the foot.

Phalanges
The toe bones. As with the finger bones, the toe phalanges connect via joints that make the toes relatively flexible.

Medial process of tuberosity | Talus bone

Tuber calcanei
The area of the calcaneus that forms the bottom of the heel.

Sustentaculum tali
A curved area where the talus bone articulates the upper calcaneus.

Sulcus (or groove)
for the attachment of the flexor hallicus longus muscle (see page 69).

Load-bearing bone
The calcaneus is the largest and strongest of seven tarsal bones that form the rear of each foot. Together with the talus bone, which rests on top of it, the bulky calcaneus supports much of the body's weight when a person is upright. The thick Achilles tendon (see page 69) attaches three calf muscles to the back surface of the calcaneus. Stabilizing ligaments attach the calcaneus to the fibula, one of the two long bones in the lower leg.

CATARRHINES INCLUDE OLD WORLD MONKEYS, GIBBONS, GREAT APES, AND HUMANS. THEY ALL SHARE AN IMPORTANT FEATURE—THE *OPPOSABLE THUMB*.

BONE CONNECTIONS

For the human skeleton's parts to move, the bones need to link at joints. These connections come in three main types. In freely movable—or synovial—joints, such as the knee and shoulder, a cavity separates the adjoining bones and the bone ends are covered with cartilage and ligaments to add stability. The other two categories are cartilaginous joints and fibrous joints, which are much less mobile.

Synovial joints

Of all the synovial joints, the shoulder has the greatest range of motion. Because of the need for maximum rotation, the joint is reinforced by only a few ligaments. However, additional stability is provided by tendons extending from the bicep muscle and from the muscles that form the "rotator cuff" around the joint.

Fibrous capsule

Clavicle bone

Bursa

Articular cartilage

Humerus bone

Sternum (breastbone)

Biceps tendon

Articular capsule

Synovial cavity

Posterior sacroiliac ligament

The pelvic bones

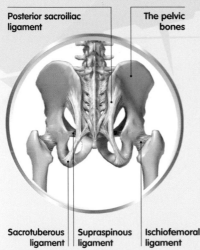

Sacrotuberous ligament | Supraspinous ligament | Ischiofemoral ligament

Cartilaginous joints

The joints between the ribs and the sternum are good examples of cartilaginous joints. Flexible cartilage fills the spaces between the bones, allowing enough movement for the chest cavity to expand and contract during the constant action of breathing.

Rib

Cartilage

Supportive ligaments

The fibrous ligaments that connect the hip bones to the thigh bones, to the sacrum (at the lower end of the spine), and to each other (at the pubic symphysis) are exceedingly strong. The pelvis supports internal organs, as well as the spine.

 LEARN ABOUT OSTEOARTHRITIS AND THE EFFECTS OF AGING ON JOINTS ON *PAGE 275*.

Stability plus mobility

The knee joint is stabilized and strengthened by numerous ligaments, the cartilage menisci of the tibia, and tendons from the strong muscles of the thigh and leg. Because of all this support, the knee joint is limited to a hingelike motion. Twisting or sideways movements can easily tear a ligament or cause some other knee injury.

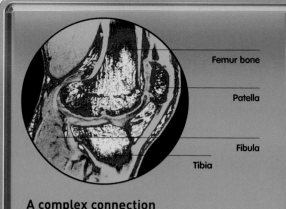

Femur bone

Patella

Fibula

Tibia

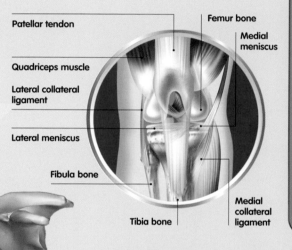

Patellar tendon

Femur bone

Medial meniscus

Quadriceps muscle

Lateral collateral ligament

Lateral meniscus

Fibula bone

Tibia bone

Medial collateral ligament

A complex connection

The knee is the body's bulkiest and most complicated joint. Its fluid-filled cavity encloses the rear and sides of the articulating femur and tibia. The kneecap, or patella, rests on top, curving over the bulging knobs at the end of the femur. The tendon of the thigh's quadriceps muscle encloses the patella, which glides across the end of the femur when the knee bends. The knee joint also contains "bursae"—pouches of synovial fluid that form a part of the joint capsule and reduce friction.

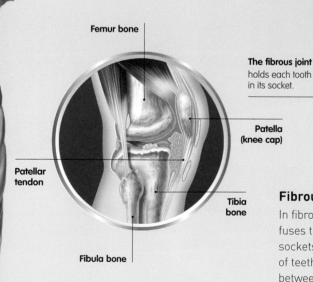

Femur bone

The fibrous joint holds each tooth in its socket.

Patella (knee cap)

Patellar tendon

Tibia bone

Fibula bone

Periodontal or "around the tooth" ligament

Periodontal membrane

Blood vessels in the jaw.

Fibrous joints

In fibrous joints, a seam of tough connective tissue fuses the bones where they join, such as in the tooth sockets and where flat skull bones meet. In the case of teeth, a ligament provides an additional connection between the tooth root and the underlying jaw bone.

SYNOVIAL JOINTS

In a synovial joint, a strong connective tissue "capsule" encloses the ends of the bones that form the joint. Within this capsule there is a membrane-lined cavity filled with synovial fluid, which lubricates the joint. Both bone ends are cushioned with a layer of smooth cartilage, which helps to prevent damage. Built to flex, extend, and rotate, synovial joints are the mechanical foundation for the vast majority of body movements.

Plane joints

Plane, or gliding, joints connect the flat bones of the body—such as the articulating processes of the vertebrae (see page 55) and the hand bones below the wrist. The joints allow the bones to glide past one another, but they are unable to rotate.

Saddle joints

In these joints, the end of one articulating bone is roughly U-shaped, and the end of the other bone fits into it—just as a horse rider fits into a saddle. The thumb articulates with the neighboring carpal bone in this type of joint, which allows humans to move their thumbs in a variety of ways.

Ellipsoidal joints

The radius bone of the forearm and the bones of the wrist articulate (join and move) in this type of joint—as do the finger bones that join at the knuckles of the hand. As the oval tip of one bone moves within a matching, shallow cup in the other, the wrists and fingers can flex, extend, and "circle" through an imaginary cone-shaped area.

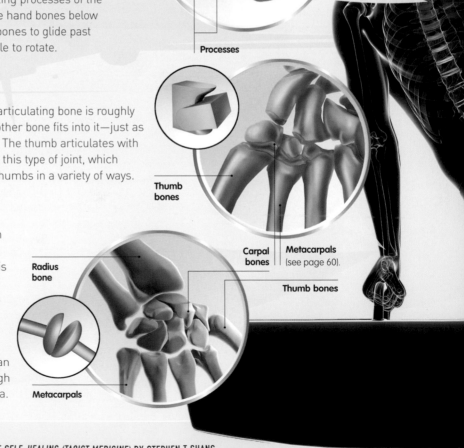

Processes

Thumb bones

Radius bone

Carpal bones

Metacarpals (see page 60).

Thumb bones

Metacarpals

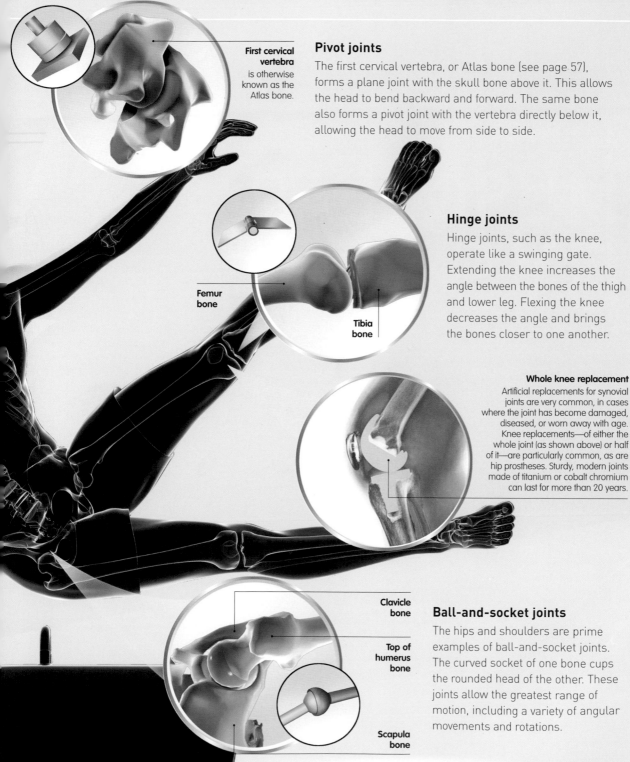

First cervical vertebra is otherwise known as the Atlas bone.

Pivot joints

The first cervical vertebra, or Atlas bone (see page 57), forms a plane joint with the skull bone above it. This allows the head to bend backward and forward. The same bone also forms a pivot joint with the vertebra directly below it, allowing the head to move from side to side.

Femur bone

Tibia bone

Hinge joints

Hinge joints, such as the knee, operate like a swinging gate. Extending the knee increases the angle between the bones of the thigh and lower leg. Flexing the knee decreases the angle and brings the bones closer to one another.

Whole knee replacement
Artificial replacements for synovial joints are very common, in cases where the joint has become damaged, diseased, or worn away with age. Knee replacements—of either the whole joint (as shown above) or half of it—are particularly common, as are hip prostheses. Sturdy, modern joints made of titanium or cobalt chromium can last for more than 20 years.

Clavicle bone

Top of humerus bone

Scapula bone

Ball-and-socket joints

The hips and shoulders are prime examples of ball-and-socket joints. The curved socket of one bone cups the rounded head of the other. These joints allow the greatest range of motion, including a variety of angular movements and rotations.

CHAPTER FOUR

MUSCULAR
SYSTEM

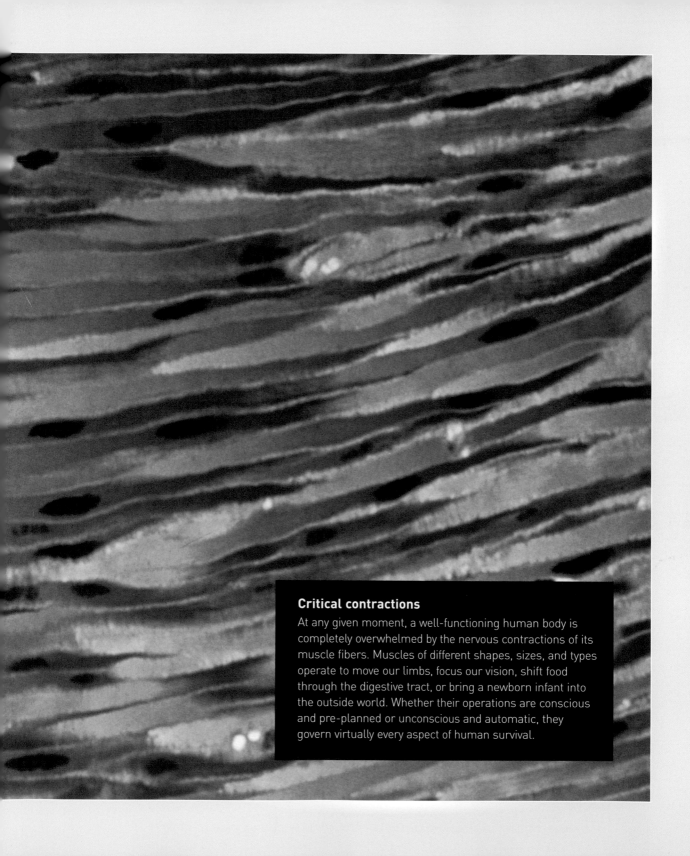

Critical contractions

At any given moment, a well-functioning human body is completely overwhelmed by the nervous contractions of its muscle fibers. Muscles of different shapes, sizes, and types operate to move our limbs, focus our vision, shift food through the digestive tract, or bring a newborn infant into the outside world. Whether their operations are conscious and pre-planned or unconscious and automatic, they govern virtually every aspect of human survival.

Muscle gallery

The body has more than 600 skeletal muscles, some long and slender, others triangular, circular, or another shape entirely. The most familiar skeletal muscles are the superficial ones, such as the biceps of the upper arm and the large muscles of the chest, thigh, and back. Deeper muscles also play vital roles in moving the limbs, spine, and other body parts.

Frontalis
is a muscle that covers the frontal skull and forehead.

Orbicularis oris
is a circular muscle.

Sternocleidomastoid
is one of a pair of deep muscles running from the sternum (breastbone) and clavicle to the side of the skull.

Platysma
is a broad, flat muscle attached to the jawbone and to the skin of the lower face.

Brachialis

Rectus abdominus

Sartorius
is a strap-like muscle. It is the longest muscle in the body.

Orbicularis oculi
is a circular muscle that surrounds the eye.

Zygomaticus major
runs diagonally from the cheekbone to the mouth.

Deltoid
is a triangular muscle, shaped like the splaying formation of a river delta (hence its name).

Biceps brachii

Pectoralis major
is a very large, superficial muscle of the upper chest.

External oblique

Opponens pollicis

Opponens digiti minimi

Flexor digitorum group
consists of two long muscles.

Interossia group
includes numerous small muscles.

Quadriceps femoris
is a large and fleshy muscle group made up of four parts.

Adductor longus
is one of the large muscles of the thigh.

Tibialis anterior

Fibularis group
is made up of two muscles running alongside the lower leg.

MUSCLE GROUPS

There are three types of muscle tissue: skeletal muscle, smooth muscle, and cardiac muscle. By weight, the human body is about 40 percent skeletal muscle. A few skeletal muscles attach to the skin, but most of them are firmly connected to bones by tendons. Unlike cardiac muscle (see pages 178–179) or the smooth muscle of the internal organs, skeletal muscles are under our conscious control.

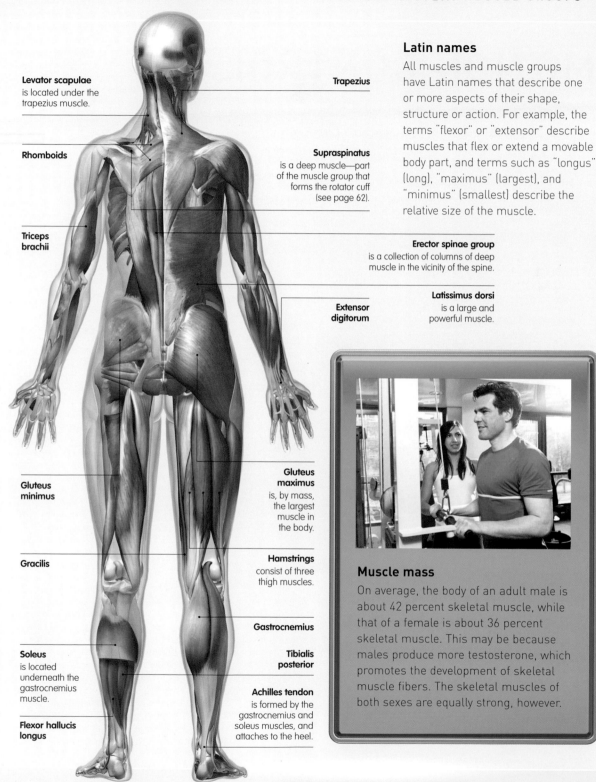

Levator scapulae is located under the trapezius muscle.

Rhomboids

Triceps brachii

Gluteus minimus

Gracilis

Soleus is located underneath the gastrocnemius muscle.

Flexor hallucis longus

Trapezius

Supraspinatus is a deep muscle—part of the muscle group that forms the rotator cuff (see page 62).

Erector spinae group is a collection of columns of deep muscle in the vicinity of the spine.

Extensor digitorum

Latissimus dorsi is a large and powerful muscle.

Gluteus maximus is, by mass, the largest muscle in the body.

Hamstrings consist of three thigh muscles.

Gastrocnemius

Tibialis posterior

Achilles tendon is formed by the gastrocnemius and soleus muscles, and attaches to the heel.

Latin names

All muscles and muscle groups have Latin names that describe one or more aspects of their shape, structure or action. For example, the terms "flexor" or "extensor" describe muscles that flex or extend a movable body part, and terms such as "longus" (long), "maximus" (largest), and "minimus" (smallest) describe the relative size of the muscle.

Muscle mass

On average, the body of an adult male is about 42 percent skeletal muscle, while that of a female is about 36 percent skeletal muscle. This may be because males produce more testosterone, which promotes the development of skeletal muscle fibers. The skeletal muscles of both sexes are equally strong, however.

MOTION CONTROL

As the human body has evolved, individual muscles and groups of muscles have adapted to suit the performance of the major body movements, such as walking, running, lifting, and turning the head. Some of the smaller muscles have also adapted to facilitate the very fine, delicate movements of the hands and feet, for example.

Pairs and groups

Skeletal muscles often work in pairs or larger groups. One muscle serves as a "prime mover," providing most of the required force. One or more assisting, or "synergist," muscles may add either force or stability. When a prime mover contracts, one or more "antagonist" muscles—on the opposite side of the joint—can reverse or adjust the action.

Triceps brachii
The triceps extends or straightens the arm and forearm.

Sternocleidomastoids
The contractions of these two muscles help to bend the head forward or turn it from side to side.

Upper body: front view

Brachialis
This muscle assists the flexing of the forearm.

The gluteus muscles
The gluteus maximus is a massive muscle that operates during walking, running, and climbing, as it extends and rotates the thigh outward. The gluteus minimus, beneath it, assists the gluteus maximus in lifting and rotating the thigh.

Deltoids
The deltoids are responsible for the rotating, flexing, and extending movements of the arms.

Pectoralis major
Movements involved in pushing, throwing, and climbing utilize this large upper chest muscle.

Biceps brachii
This muscle flexes the elbow joint, drawing the forearm upward.

External oblique
This large muscle assists the movements that bend or rotate the spine laterally (sideways), and those that compress the upper abdomen.

Rectus abdominus
A muscle that compresses the abdomen, depresses the chest cavity, and helps to bend the spine forward.

Adductor longus
Movements that flex, extend, or rotate the thigh bring this muscle into action.

Quadriceps femoris
This muscle group flexes the thigh at the hips and extends the leg at the knee in walking, running, and climbing.

Sartorius
This long muscle bends the thigh at the hip, rotates the thigh outward, and helps to flex the knee.

 SARTORIUS COMES FROM THE LATIN. SARTOR ("TAILOR"). THE MUSCLE IS USED WHEN CROSSING THE LEGS IN THE SEWING POSTURE OF A TAILOR.

Gastrocnemius and soleus

This muscle bends the calf at the knee during walking. It extends the foot during jumping. Underneath the gastrocnemius, the soleus muscle flexes and helps to support the foot during walking and other upright forms of locomotion.

Achilles tendon

Lower leg: side view

Lower leg: front view

Tibialis anterior

A muscle that flexes the foot downward, draws its inner side upward, and stabilizes the arch of the foot.

Extensor digitorum

This connects, via these tendons, to the four fingers. It contracts to extend or flare them.

Fibularis group

Two muscles help to flex the foot downward or bend it upward at the outer ankle.

Upper body: rear view

Trapezius

The trapezius is a large muscle that draws back the head, lifts the shoulder blade, and helps to support the shoulder joint. The levator scapulae muscle, beneath the trapezius, assists in raising the shoulder blades.

Opponens digiti minimi

Several muscles power the fine hand movements. This small interior muscle helps to draw the little finger forward to touch the thumb.

Ventral surface of hand

Hand: palm

Rhomboids

Below the trapezius, these muscles draw the shoulder blades back, or downward, and also help to stabilize them.

Erector spinae group

These are columns of muscles that act in spinal movements and help us to maintain an upright posture.

Flexor digitorum group

These muscles contract to flex the wrist and fingers.

Interossia group

This group includes lots of small muscles that act to raise, lower, flex, and extend the fingers.

Opponens pollicis

This muscle moves the thumb to touch the tip of the finger, enabling us to work with tools, use writing and painting implements, and so on.

Latissimus dorsi

This powerful muscle plays a part in arm motions such as reaching overhead, pushing a heavy object, rowing, or striking a blow.

Hamstrings

Acting together, the three muscles in this group bend the knee and draw the thigh backward.

Powerful posterior muscles (left)

The muscles of the upper and lower back have major roles in moving the head, neck, spine, and arms, while those of the buttocks and backs of the thighs and legs generate much of the power humans need to move their hips and bend the knees. Not surprisingly, these muscles and muscle groups include some of the largest and strongest skeletal muscles.

SKELETAL MUSCLES

Skeletal muscles are arranged to move limbs or other body parts as efficiently as possible. Nearly all of them pull on bones, much like pulleys tugging on levers. The two ends of a muscle attach to different bones—one that moves a joint, and another that usually remains immobile. A muscle's "origin" is the site where it anchors to the stationary bone, and its "insertion" is where it attaches to the movable bone.

Neuron axon

Myofibrils
are the threadlike muscle fibers shown here in their bundles.

Axon endings
are in close proximity to the muscle fibers.

Nervous Contractions

When signals from the nervous system spark muscle contractions, the resulting force may move fingers on a keyboard, pucker lips for a kiss, or propel a runner's legs through a race. Whatever the outcome, the force that skeletal muscles exert is always a pull, never a push. These contractions also generate much of the body's heat.

Neuromuscular junctions

The branched endings of motor neurons (see pages 90–91) from the spinal cord deliver their commands, for the muscle fibers to contract, at neuromuscular junctions. At these points, a chemical signal —the neurotransmitter known as ACh (acetycholine)—travels from a neuron to a muscle cell across a narrow gap called a synapse (see page 93).

Muscle tears

Muscles are less likely to tear if they are strong from regular use, and properly warmed up before exercise. People playing sports or lifting weights need to be alert to signs of excess muscle stress, such as recurring aches and pains in one specific area. This image shows a torn calf muscle (shown in green).

Torn muscle

FIND OUT HOW THE BODY ACHIEVES *BALANCE* ON *PAGES 140–141.*

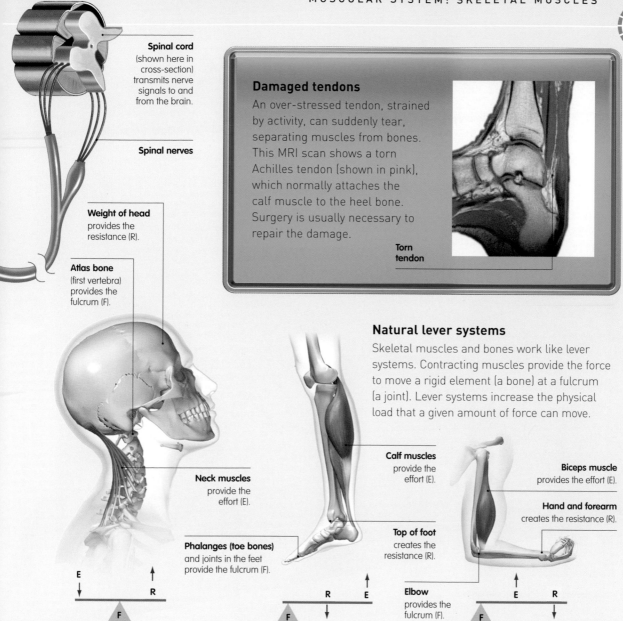

Spinal cord
(shown here in cross-section) transmits nerve signals to and from the brain.

Spinal nerves

Weight of head
provides the resistance (R).

Atlas bone
(first vertebra) provides the fulcrum (F).

Damaged tendons

An over-stressed tendon, strained by activity, can suddenly tear, separating muscles from bones. This MRI scan shows a torn Achilles tendon (shown in pink), which normally attaches the calf muscle to the heel bone. Surgery is usually necessary to repair the damage.

Torn tendon

Natural lever systems

Skeletal muscles and bones work like lever systems. Contracting muscles provide the force to move a rigid element (a bone) at a fulcrum (a joint). Lever systems increase the physical load that a given amount of force can move.

Calf muscles
provide the effort (E).

Biceps muscle
provides the effort (E).

Hand and forearm
creates the resistance (R).

Neck muscles
provide the effort (E).

Phalanges (toe bones)
and joints in the feet provide the fulcrum (F).

Top of foot
creates the resistance (R).

Elbow
provides the fulcrum (F).

E   R
F

R   E
F

E   R
F

Class one lever system

Here, the force lifts a load on the opposite side of a fulcrum. To lift the skull, neck muscles pull on the rear of the skull. The fulcrum is a joint where the skull and spinal column meet.

Class two lever system

In this movement, the load (the foot and the weight of the body upon it) is located between the force and the fulcrum. Standing on tiptoe requires calf muscles inserted on the heel bone to lift the body weight.

Class three lever system

Most body lever systems are of this type. The force is applied between the fulcrum and the load, as in this example of the biceps muscle lifting the hand and the forearm. The elbow joint is the fulcrum.

A MUSCLE AT WORK

Muscle contractions usually pull the moving bone toward the muscle's origin. Because muscles attach close to most joints, even a small contraction can produce a major movement. When a muscle contracts, it becomes shorter. Whole muscles consist of bundles of muscle fibers, which can be seen in more detail on these pages.

Muscle contraction: activation of myosin

A muscle contraction begins when nerve impulses cause sarcomeres in the muscle fibers to compress, lengthwise, like accordions. The impulses trigger chemical changes that activate filaments built of myosin, a protein with a rounded "head."

Sarcomere

Myosin head

Myosin "binding site" on actin

Actin thin filament

Attachment to actin filaments

Millions of activated myosin heads attach to filaments of a different protein, called actin, and slide them toward each other—making the sarcomere shorter. Repeated in hundreds or thousands of muscle fibers, this shortening of sarcomeres contracts the whole muscle.

"Cross bridges" now form at the binding sites.

Actin filaments slide toward each other.

The sarcomere itself now shortens.

Protein disengagement

A muscle relaxes when the myosin and actin proteins disengage (bottom left), so that the sarcomeres and other parts lengthen once again.

Sarcoplasmic reticulum

A lacy network of tubules around the myofibrils. The tiny tubes contain calcium, a necessary "chemical cue" for the steps of muscle contraction to occur.

Myosin

A myosin molecule has two rounded heads and a long tail. The heads attach to the actin protein, causing the inward sliding action that shortens a sarcomere.

Actin thin filament

Actin proteins are rounded, like miniature beads. Strands of them twist together, forming thin filaments that attach to sarcomeres.

Myosin thick filament

Myosin proteins, in a sarcomere, are organized into thick filaments. The twin heads of individual myosin molecules stick out from the filaments.

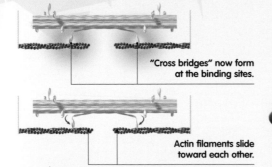

 MYOSIN IS A FIBROUS PROTEIN. IN CONJUNCTION WITH ACTIN, IT FORMS THE CONTRACTILE FILAMENTS OF MUSCLE CELLS.

Bulging biceps
The biceps muscle "inserts" on the radius bone of the forearm. When it contracts, the elbow joint flexes and the muscle bulges as it shortens.

Tendon
A band of fibrous, connective tissue that usually connects muscle to bone.

Epimysium
A sheath of tissue that covers an entire muscle.

Mitochondrion
These are organelles (see page 19) that create energy for the muscles.

Muscle bulk
Depending on its size and function, a skeletal muscle may contain hundreds to thousands of individual cells, known as muscle fibers.

Sarcomeres
are the basic, structural units of myofibrils.

Muscle fibers
Each fiber is a single muscle cell containing numerous myofibrils.

Myofibril
Viewed under a microscope, a myofibril has light and dark bands. The dark bands mark the boundaries between sarcomeres, the basic units of muscle.

Nucleus
Just like most other body cells, muscle cells contain a nucleus (see pages 18–19).

Perimysium
A delicate web that encloses bundled fibers of voluntary (consciously controlled) muscle.

Fascicle
The fibers in a whole muscle are bundled into fascicles, which are aligned—in parallel—along the full length of the muscle.

The working parts

Each fiber in each bundle is built out of myofibrils, which are threadlike strands subdivided into units called sarcomeres. Sarcomeres are the microscopic working parts that launch the shortening process (see page 74). All of these components run in parallel along the entire length of a muscle. This arrangement focuses the force of a contracting muscle in one specific direction.

FACIAL MUSCLES

More than 15 different muscles form the sheetlike "flesh" of the face. Most of these muscles play a part in our non-verbal communication—expressions such as smiles, frowns, raised eyebrows, and furrowed brows. Unlike most other skeletal muscles, which connect "bone to bone" to move joints, those used to make facial expressions connect skin to bone—or skin and muscles to bone. The muscles move the skin, or other muscles, when they contract.

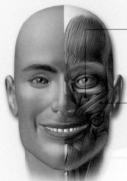

Levator labii superioris
This muscle opens the lips, and can also elevate the upper lip to form a snarl.

Zygomaticus minor and major
These paired "smiling" muscles draw the upper lip and mouth upward.

Orbicularis oculi
This circular muscle closes the eye. It is used for blinking and squinting.

Zygomaticus major
Running diagonally from the cheekbone, this muscle draws up the corners of the mouth when a person smiles or laughs.

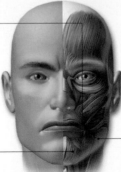

Risorius
Drawing the lips down and to the side, as in a grimace, uses this muscle.

Depressor labii inferioris
When a person pouts, this small muscle pulls the lower lip downward.

Platysma
This broad, flat muscle attaches to the lower jawbone and to the skin of the lower face. Its actions include pulling the lower lip downward, as in a "sad" or "pouting" expression.

Depressor anguli oris
This muscle draws down the corners of the mouth, as in a "sad" expression.

Smiles and frowns

Common expressions, such as smiling and frowning, involve muscles that pull the lips or corners of the mouth up, down, or sideways. Muscles such as the orbicularis oculi, which wrinkle or crease the skin around the eyes, often contribute to these facial expressions, too.

 STUDIES HAVE IDENTIFIED 20 DISTINCT FACIAL EXPRESSIONS THAT COMPUTERS COULD RECOGNIZE.

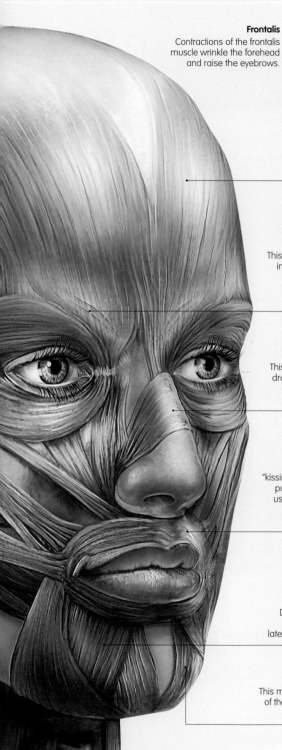

Frontalis
Contractions of the frontalis muscle wrinkle the forehead and raise the eyebrows.

Corrugator supercilii
This muscle pulls down the inner brow and vertically wrinkles the skin, both in between and above the eyebrows.

Nasalis
This is a small muscle that draws down the tip of the nose and helps to flare the nostrils.

Orbicularis oris
This circular muscle, sometimes called the "kissing muscle," closes and puckers the lips. It is also used to move and shape the lips during speech, and for whistling.

Depressor anguli oris
Draws the corner of the mouth downward and laterally (from side to side).

Mentalis
This muscle wrinkles the skin of the chin and enables the lower lip to stick out.

Cosmetic chemicals

Chemicals such as Botox® have become popular for smoothing facial lines. The chemical is injected to deliver a toxin created by Botulinum bacteria. The toxin prevents skeletal muscle contraction by blocking the release of neurotransmitter molecules at neurotransmitter junctions (see page 72). At low doses, the toxin relaxes the facial muscles that cause wrinkling.

Motor neuron nerve endings
connect with skeletal muscle fibers.

Incoming motor neuron impulse
reaches the neurotransmitter junction.

Neurotransmitter molecules released
in the natural, untreated muscle.

Neurotransmitter molecules blocked
in the muscle injected with Botox®.

OTHER FACIAL FUNCTIONS

Humans also use their facial muscles for a variety of activities related to opening, closing, and using some key openings in the head—namely the eyes and the mouth. Muscles around the mouth—and those linking the face and neck—assist with taking in, chewing, and swallowing food. Others open and close the eyelids, purse the lips for whistling, flare the nostrils in displeasure—or in preparation for inhaling a long, deep breath.

Extrinsic muscles
Constant tension in the "extrinsic" muscle oppositions, in the eye socket, mean that the eye can react and move very quickly—much faster than any other bodily movement.

Styloglossus
This muscle lifts and retracts the tongue toward the throat, an important movement in the process of swallowing.

Genioglossus
The main function of this muscle is to extend or "stick out" the tongue.

Hyoid bone

Hyoglossus
Attached onto one end of the hyoid bone (see pages 54–55), this muscle inserts on the side of the tongue and pulls it downward.

Muscles of the tongue

Contractions of the internal tongue muscles help to form speech sounds and move material around in the mouth. However, other types of tongue movements depend on muscles attached to the cranial (skull) bones (see page 77).

THE *HYOID* IS A U-SHAPED BONE. ITS NAME COMES FROM A GREEK WORD MEANING "SHAPED LIKE THE LETTER *UPSILON*" (U OR Y, IN ENGLISH).

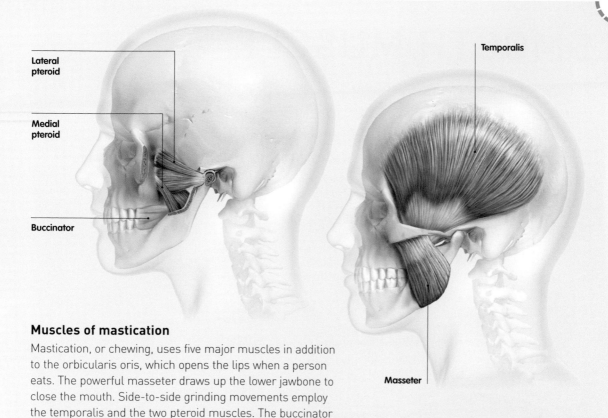

Lateral pteroid

Medial pteroid

Buccinator

Temporalis

Masseter

Muscles of mastication

Mastication, or chewing, uses five major muscles in addition to the orbicularis oris, which opens the lips when a person eats. The powerful masseter draws up the lower jawbone to close the mouth. Side-to-side grinding movements employ the temporalis and the two pteroid muscles. The buccinator muscles push food toward the rear teeth during chewing.

Eye movement

The muscles of the eye react incredibly quickly to track moving objects, focus the eye, and control the shielding eyelids. Each eye is held in place by three pairs of taut, elastic muscles called the "extrinsic" muscles. The superior rectus rolls the eye backward and upward—an action that is countered by the inferior rectus muscle. The lateral rectus pulls the eye to the side, while the medial rectus (on the opposing side) rolls it toward the nose. The clockwise and counterclockwise motion of each eye is controlled by two "oblique" muscles.

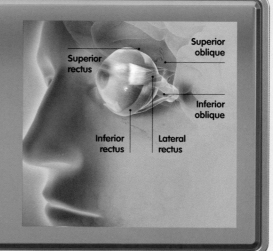

Superior rectus

Superior oblique

Inferior rectus

Lateral rectus

Inferior oblique

SMOOTH MUSCLE

Smooth muscle functions differently to skeletal muscle. Unlike skeletal muscle, its contractions do not help us to move around, and it is not under our conscious, voluntary control. Instead, smooth muscle forms much of the walls of hollow organs—such as the stomach, intestine, bladder, and uterus. It is also a key building material of body tubes including small blood vessels, the airways to the lungs, and the various types of ducts that transport substances from place to place in the digestive and reproductive systems.

Smooth muscle in the skin

In mammals, such as humans, threads of smooth muscle wrap around the base of hair follicles. These "arrector pili" muscles literally pull the hairs upright when they contract as part of the body's response to cold temperatures. This produces the raised areas we call "goose bumps." Cold temperatures also cause straps of smooth muscle to elevate the nipples and testicles.

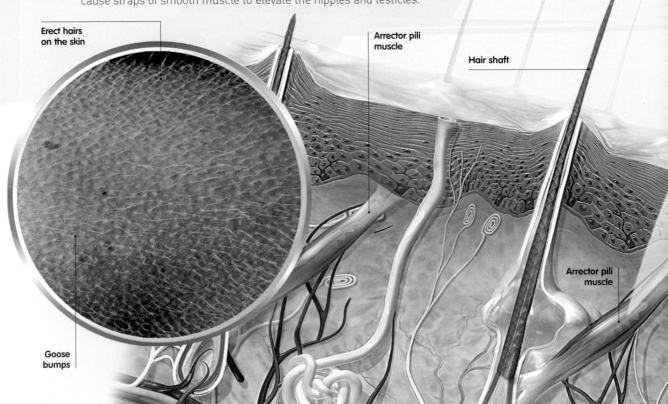

Erect hairs
on the skin

Arrector pili
muscle

Hair shaft

Arrector pili
muscle

Goose
bumps

 AUTOMATED, *BIOMETRIC IDENTIFICATION SYSTEMS* CAN RECOGNIZE HUMAN INDIVIDUALS BY THE UNIQUE PATTERNS IN THEIR IRISES.

Controlled activity

All of the functions of smooth muscle tissue are controlled by signals from the nervous system, from hormones, or from the smooth muscle fibers themselves. These signals trigger slow contractions that provide the steady force required to move food, blood, or urine from place to place—or even to bring a newborn baby into the world. Contractions can last for hours at a time, even when the muscle has been stretched, because smooth muscle is stimulated by the nervous system rather than motor neurones.

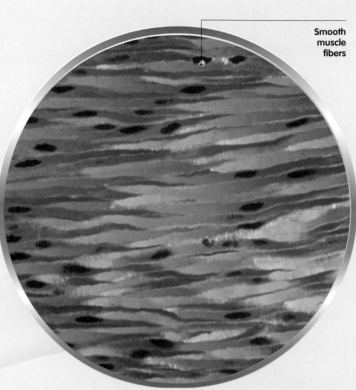

Smooth muscle fibers

Muscles of vision

In the eyes, tiny bands of smooth muscle perform fine adjustments that dilate (enlarge) or contract the pupils to change the amount of light entering the eye and focusing on the retina. The cillary muscles change the shape of the lens, in focusing, while the sphincter pupillae and dilator pupillae (in the iris) control the size of the pupil.

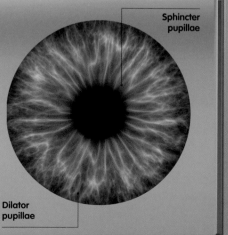

Sphincter pupillae

Dilator pupillae

EXPANDABLE ORGANS

Smooth muscle is remarkably stretchable and resilient, which is why it plays such a vital role in organs that need to expand or change their shape as part of their function. For example, it allows the stomach's walls to expand tremendously during a meal, store its contents for hours—while the food is slowly shifted into the small intestine—and then return the organ to its original size.

Slow but adaptable

Skeletal muscles contract rapidly. Their work is intensive and they tire quickly. By contrast, smooth muscle contracts slowly and uses far less energy. This allows most smooth muscles to contract steadily for long periods—in some cases, such as in the walls of blood vessels, for years on end.

Small intestine

Large intestine

In the uterus

Normally, the uterus is about the size of a pear, but during pregnancy its wall needs to stretch dramatically. A thick layer of smooth muscle, called the myometrium, is sandwiched between the other layers of the wall. As a fetus grows, increased levels of the hormone estrogen trigger the development of more smooth muscle cells—so the stretchy myometrium enlarges as well. When the baby is ready to come, powerful contractions of the myometrial muscles gradually push the baby out.

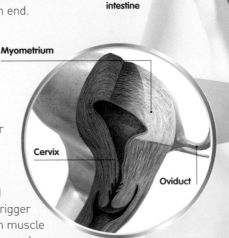

Myometrium

Cervix

Oviduct

FIND OUT HOW THE BODY CHANGES DURING LABOR ON *PAGES 272–273*.

Stomach lining

Stomach capacity
When completely full, an adult's stomach may contain roughly a gallon (3.75 liters) of food, bulging downward by up to three inches (8 cm) into the abdomen. After it has emptied, however, the stomach's volume may be less than one-quarter of a cup (60 milliliters).

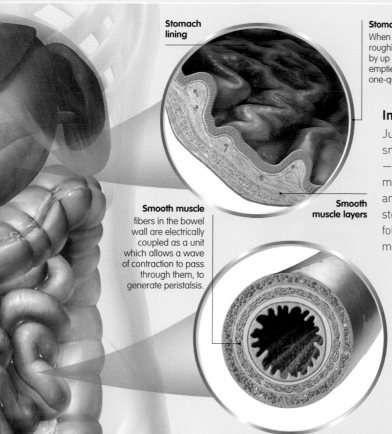

Smooth muscle layers

In the stomach
Just beneath the stomach's lining, layers of smooth muscle—arranged at different angles —form the stomach wall. Contractions of the muscles mix ingested food with digestive juices and shift the food into the intestines. As the stomach empties, the wall crumples into thick folds, only to expand again when the next meal arrives.

Smooth muscle fibers in the bowel wall are electrically coupled as a unit which allows a wave of contraction to pass through them, to generate peristalsis.

In the intestines
Like other parts of the gastrointestinal tract, the small and large intestines have a multi-layered wall that includes smooth muscle. As a result, both can stretch as food—in the process of being digested— moves through the tube and as unwanted residues accumulate. Contractions of the muscle layers also move the material along toward its destination.

Oviduct
Contractions of smooth muscle in the walls of the oviducts produce movements that can position the tube opening close to an ovulated egg.

Stretchy and expandable
Unlike other muscle types, smooth muscle can also put up with extended relaxation. The bladder, highlighted in orange in this colored X-ray, can expand for hours when the muscles relax and as it gradually fills with urine. The thick walls of an adult's bladder can hold up to just over 2 pints (about 950ml) of urine.

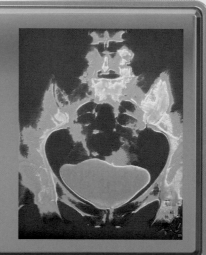

NERVOUS SYSTEM

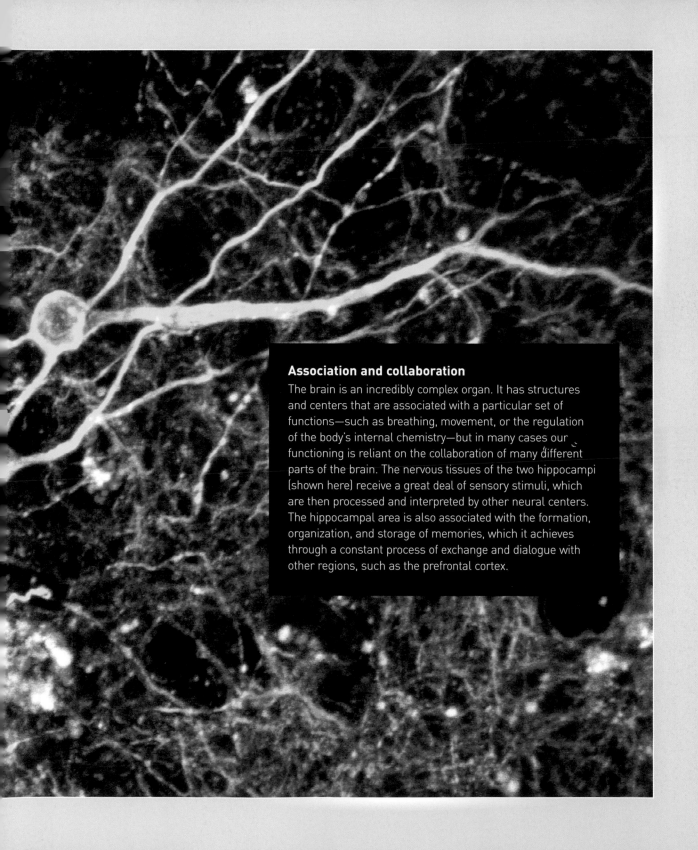

Association and collaboration

The brain is an incredibly complex organ. It has structures and centers that are associated with a particular set of functions—such as breathing, movement, or the regulation of the body's internal chemistry—but in many cases our functioning is reliant on the collaboration of many different parts of the brain. The nervous tissues of the two hippocampi (shown here) receive a great deal of sensory stimuli, which are then processed and interpreted by other neural centers. The hippocampal area is also associated with the formation, organization, and storage of memories, which it achieves through a constant process of exchange and dialogue with other regions, such as the prefrontal cortex.

NERVES IN CONTROL

The human nervous system is a sophisticated command and control center, rising to the challenge of three main functions. First, its basic parts—a complex brain and tens of billions of neurons—constantly monitor conditions within the body and in the outside environment. Secondly, the steady flow of arriving information is integrated and assessed. Lastly, the nervous system issues instructions for any necessary adjustments to the body's organs, tissues, or cells. A division of labor allows the system to meet all of these demands.

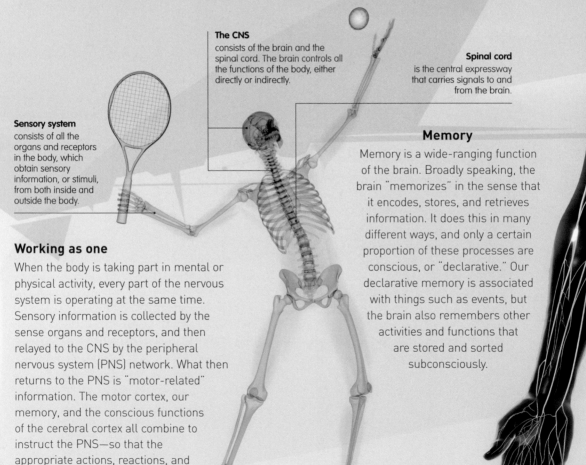

The CNS
consists of the brain and the spinal cord. The brain controls all the functions of the body, either directly or indirectly.

Spinal cord
is the central expressway that carries signals to and from the brain.

Sensory system
consists of all the organs and receptors in the body, which obtain sensory information, or stimuli, from both inside and outside the body.

Memory

Memory is a wide-ranging function of the brain. Broadly speaking, the brain "memorizes" in the sense that it encodes, stores, and retrieves information. It does this in many different ways, and only a certain proportion of these processes are conscious, or "declarative." Our declarative memory is associated with things such as events, but the brain also remembers other activities and functions that are stored and sorted subconsciously.

Working as one

When the body is taking part in mental or physical activity, every part of the nervous system is operating at the same time. Sensory information is collected by the sense organs and receptors, and then relayed to the CNS by the peripheral nervous system (PNS) network. What then returns to the PNS is "motor-related" information. The motor cortex, our memory, and the conscious functions of the cerebral cortex all combine to instruct the PNS—so that the appropriate actions, reactions, and changes are initiated in the body.

EXAMINE THE MANY DIFFERENT ASPECTS OF MEMORY ON PAGES 116–117.

Motor cortex
is a part of the cerebral cortex in the brain. Here, nerve impulses are generated to trigger our conscious muscular activities.

Cerebral cortex
is the outer layer of the larger portion of the brain. It is made up of folded layers of gray matter (see pages 94–95). Most of the brain's neural processing goes on here, including the functions of conscious human thought.

Brain stem
physically links the other regions of the brain to the spinal cord.

The CNS and the PNS

The brain and spinal cord form the central nervous system (CNS). Carrying signals to and from the CNS is the task of the peripheral nervous system (PNS). This is the elaborate network of nerves that services the rest of the body. Sensory receptors are the complex developments of nerve endings, which collect specific types of information for the PNS.

Pulsing signals
Constant electrical and chemical communication, between and among neurons, is the foundation for the operation of the CNS.

Spinal cord

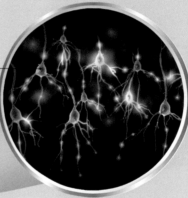

Neuron communications

Neurons (see page 16) are specialized cells that transmit nerve signals. They are the system's information carriers. Most neurons communicate with their "target cells" by releasing chemical neurotransmitters from the endings of long axons (see page 91). The cell body of each neuron is almost completely covered by axon endings, which extend toward it from other neurons.

THE MAJOR NERVES

As in others systems, such as the muscular system, there are different groups and circuits of nerves that serve the different parts of the body. Most of these groups are a part of the peripheral nervous system that feeds into the central nervous system.

Neural zones

Different spinal nerves convey signals between the spinal cord and specific areas of the skin. These are known as the cervical (C), thoracic (T), lumbar (L), and sacral (S) nerves. They get their names from the groups of vertebrae from where the spinal nerves emerge (from the spinal cord). The skin zones supplied, or "innervated," by these spinal nerves are called dermatomes.

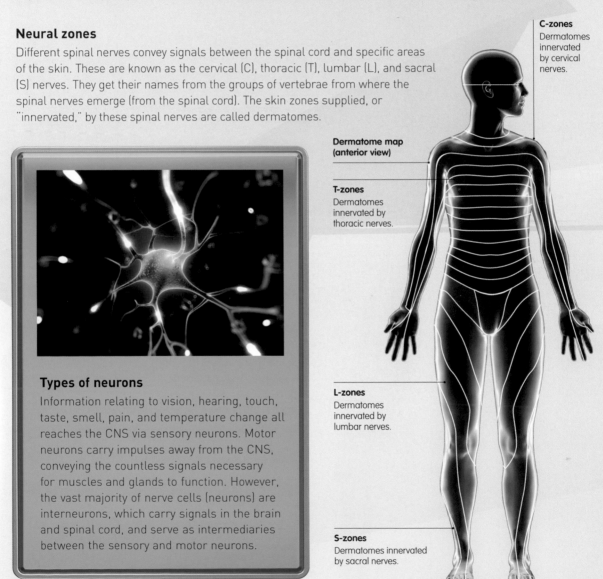

Types of neurons

Information relating to vision, hearing, touch, taste, smell, pain, and temperature change all reaches the CNS via sensory neurons. Motor neurons carry impulses away from the CNS, conveying the countless signals necessary for muscles and glands to function. However, the vast majority of nerve cells (neurons) are interneurons, which carry signals in the brain and spinal cord, and serve as intermediaries between the sensory and motor neurons.

C-zones
Dermatomes innervated by cervical nerves.

Dermatome map (anterior view)

T-zones
Dermatomes innervated by thoracic nerves.

L-zones
Dermatomes innervated by lumbar nerves.

S-zones
Dermatomes innervated by sacral nerves.

DOCTORS EVALUATE SPINAL CORD INJURIES BY TESTING TO SEE WHICH NEURAL ZONES ARE NOT AFFECTED.

Vagus nerves
are responsible for autonomic (unconscious) innervation, especially for the digestive tract, organs of the gut, and other organs such as the heart. They also carry motor and sensory impulses.

Radial nerve
helps control the muscles of the forearm, wrist, and fingers.

Intercostal nerves
supply the wall of the thorax, the pleura (in the chest cavity), and the peritoneum (in the abdominal cavity).

Median nerve
supplies several muscles of the forearm, wrist, and fingers.

Ulnar nerve
runs from the brachial plexus, through the forearm, to the muscles and skin of the ring finger and little finger.

Pudendal nerve
is a sensory, autonomic, and motor nerve that carries signals to and from the genitals, anal area, and urethra. Its sensory and motor role includes the erection of the penis and our voluntary control of the bowels and urination.

Common fibular nerve
transmits the motor signals that the muscles of the knee, calf, and foot respond to.

Deep fibular nerve
is a branch of the common fibular nerve. It supplies several foot muscles and the skin of the big toe.

Brachial plexus
is a group of nerves that service the shoulders and the arms.

Phrenic nerve
transmits signals associated with the movements of the diaphragm, which is a key muscle in breathing.

Iliohypogastric nerve

Genitofemoral nerve

Lumbar plexus
is a major nerve group. Nerves from this plexus service the abdominal muscles and most of the thigh.

Sciatic nerve
travels down the back of the legs and branches into other nerves such as the common fibular. It is the body's longest and thickest nerve. It has sensory and motor functions, supplying the buttocks and most of the lower limb muscles.

Tibial nerve

Superficial fibular nerve
carries signals to and from the lower legs and upper foot.

The dermatome map

Viewed from the rear (posterior), the dermatome map differs from the frontal (anterior) view. Lumbar nerves innervate skin on the front of the thighs and legs, but the rear areas of these limbs are served by the sacral nerves, which also innervate the genital area.

C-zones
Dermatomes innervated by cervical nerves.

T-zones
Dermatomes innervated by thoracic nerves.

Dermatome map (posterior view)

L-zones
Dermatomes innervated by lumbar nerves.

S-zones
Dermatomes innervated by sacral nerves.

NEURAL CIRCUITRY

The body's nerve cells are often organized into different types of circuits, described below, in which the neurons can connect. Nerve cells come in three basic types: sensory neurons, motor neurons, and interneurons, which are by far the most common. Neurons have a rounded cell body with two types of extensions: axons, which carry outgoing signals, and dendrites, which receive incoming ones.

Converging circuits

In a converging circuit, impulses from several sources converge in a single receiving neuron—which therefore receives a more powerful stimulus.

Diverging circuits

In a diverging circuit, a signal is passed to a widening number of receiving cells, relaying sensory impulses to multiple centers in the brain.

Reverberating circuits

A reverberating circuit may underlie the rhythmic muscle contractions of breathing. A "downstream" neuron in the circuit has a forking axon with two branches. As one branch passes the impulse onward, the other loops back to the starting neuron—and so the signal is recycled.

Microtubules

Mitochondrion

Cell nucleus

Myelin sheath
This is a fat-rich covering that electrically insulates the axons of motor neurons, and some other types of neurons, so that they can conduct nerve impulses much more rapidly.

Cell body

Synaptic knob
At the branched terminals of an axon, synaptic knobs house sacs of neurotransmitters—chemicals that convey the neuron's signal to a receiving cell.

 NO NEURON OPERATES ALONE. NEURONS INFLUENCE EACH OTHER AT ALL TIMES.

Neuroglial cells

As well as neurons, there are supporting cells called glial cells, or glia, which make up at least half the volume of the CNS. The most abundant glia are astrocytes—large, star-shaped cells that physically support neurons and also make chemical modifications in brain tissue. Among other functions, their adjustments help to maintain the chemical conditions that allow neurons to fire. Astrocytes may also foster the neural connections involved in learning and memory.

Glial cell
Called glia, for short, various types of these cells physically or chemically support neurons, produce cerebrospinal fluid, and defend against pathogens.

Astrocytes
Threadlike extensions from the main body of an astrocyte establish physical contact with neurons, blood capillaries, and other structures in the brain.

Dendrite
Much shorter than axons, dendrites are "little trees"—with many short branches—that receive impulses arriving on axons from other neurons.

Nucleus

Axon
Axons are bundled into long, cablelike structures to make up the body's nerves. The long projection of an axon carries impulses away from the cell body of a neuron and toward another neuron, a muscle cell, or a gland cell.

Nerve cell body

Like other body cells, a neuron must support itself biochemically at the same time as performing its specialized roles. It contains a nucleus with DNA to guide the generation of proteins, mitochondria (for forming fuel molecules), supportive microtubules, and membrane systems that make substances and channel them through the cell.

Nucleolus

NERVE IMPULSES

The fluid inside a neuron is negatively charged, but it is bathed in tissue fluid with a chemical make-up that conveys a positive charge. This electrical imbalance is called "resting potential," because—if it shifts sufficiently—it has the potential to fire off a nerve impulse, a signal that travels along a nerve. The stage is set for this kind of response while the neuron is inactive, resembling a living battery of stored potential.

Incoming signals
are received via dendrites. A neurotransmitter contacts the "post-synaptic" or receiving cell at this point. At some synapses in the brain, electrically charged particles (rather than chemical neurotransmitters) are the incoming signals.

Nerve cell body

Axon

Creating an action potential

The "resting potential" transforms into an "action potential"—a nerve impulse—when the chemical environment around the cell body shifts and briefly reverses the positive and negative electrical charges. The impulse then travels down the axon (shown above, right) to its branched tip.

Nucleus
of the nerve cell.

The trigger zone
is where the axon membrane first responds to an arriving stimulus. It then triggers an initial action potential.

Dendrites
are restricted to the immediate area around the cell body. They usually receive signals to the cell, while axons normally transmit them.

Depolarization

Repolarization

Resting potential (RP)

Action potential (AP)

Electrical nerve impulses

The cell body receives neurotransmitter signals, from other cells, via branched extensions called dendrites. In the trigger zone, channels open in a patch of the cell membrane, so that positively charged sodium can flow in. If the sodium shifts the electrical balance enough, it sparks a nerve impulse. Then the sodium level reduces and the membrane patch is once more at rest. Meanwhile, the impulse is traveling away down the axon as the chemical flux is repeated.

Receptors
are on a neuron's dendrite or at the surface of some other receiving cell. They can bind with one or more neurotransmitters, or with other substances that chemically mimic the neurotransmitters.

 THE BRAIN USES ABOUT 23 WATTS OF ELECTRICITY. THE SAME AMOUNT CAN POWER A LIGHT BULB.

Schwann cells
of the PNS are glial cells that wrap themselves around axons to create an insulating sheath of fatty myelin. In the CNS, other glial cells provide this service. Nerve impulses can move along a well-insulated axon as quickly as 400ft (120m) per second.

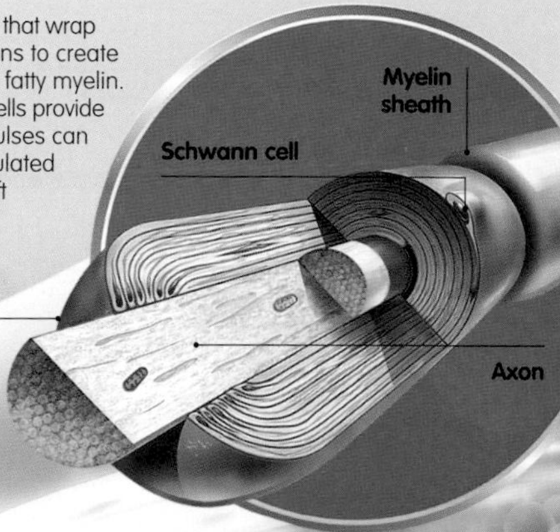

Myelin sheath

Schwann cell

Axon

Synapses

A synapse is a narrow gap between the end of a branch of an axon and a neighboring neuron—or some other type of cell. A signal arriving at the synapse prompts the release of neurotransmitter molecules into the gap, where they may pass across to the receiving cell and trigger a response.

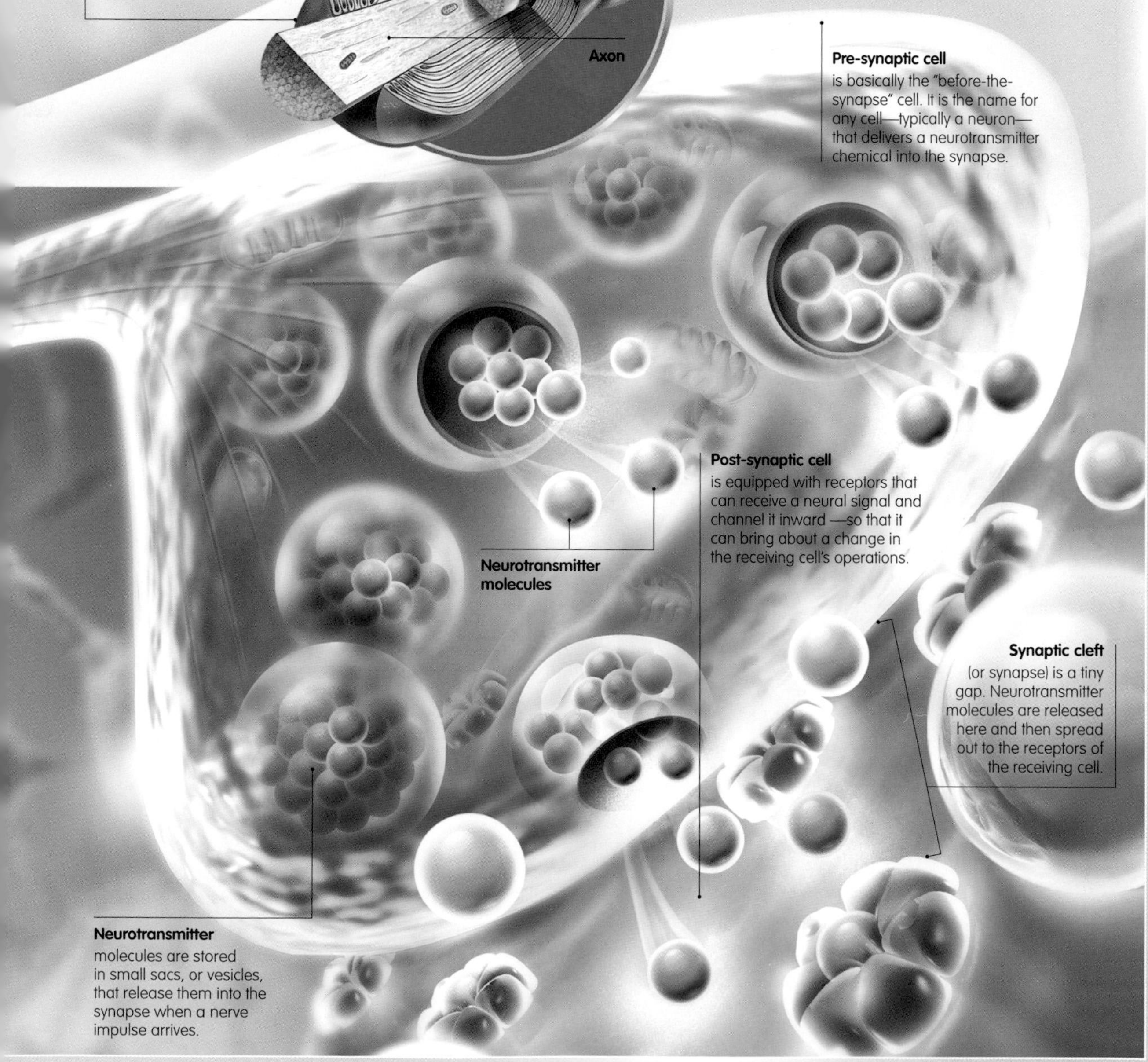

Pre-synaptic cell
is basically the "before-the-synapse" cell. It is the name for any cell—typically a neuron—that delivers a neurotransmitter chemical into the synapse.

Post-synaptic cell
is equipped with receptors that can receive a neural signal and channel it inward —so that it can bring about a change in the receiving cell's operations.

Neurotransmitter molecules

Synaptic cleft
(or synapse) is a tiny gap. Neurotransmitter molecules are released here and then spread out to the receptors of the receiving cell.

Neurotransmitter
molecules are stored in small sacs, or vesicles, that release them into the synapse when a nerve impulse arrives.

BRAIN ANATOMY

The brain is not only the master controller of the body's functions—it also provides humans with unrivaled mental abilities. Weighing 3–4lb (1.4–1.8kg) in an adult, this amazing organ's complex anatomy befits its sophisticated operations. The most advanced types of information processing take place in the upper, frontal parts of the brain.

Protective wrapping

In addition to the skull bones, membranes called the meninges protect the brain. They consist of three layers: the outer dura mater is thick and leathery, while the thin, innermost pia sheathes the brain tissue like a plastic wrapper. The arachnoid mater includes a shallow space containing cerebrospinal fluid. The meninges continue into the spine and wrap the spinal cord.

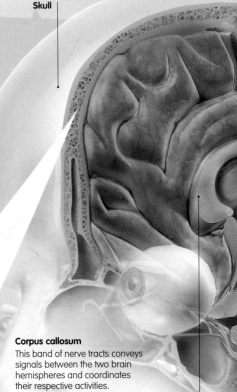

Skull

Corpus callosum
This band of nerve tracts conveys signals between the two brain hemispheres and coordinates their respective activities.

Hypothalamus
The neurons here adjust the physiological activities of internal organs. They also influence emotions, sexual behavior, hunger, and other basic human drives and motivations.

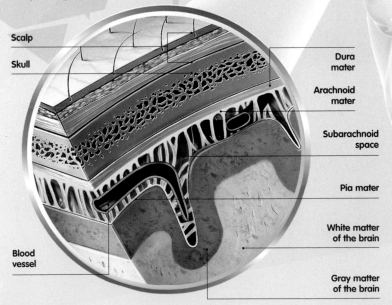

Scalp

Skull

Dura mater

Arachnoid mater

Subarachnoid space

Pia mater

White matter of the brain

Blood vessel

Gray matter of the brain

 SEE THE POSITION OF WHITE AND GRAY MATTER, IN CROSS-SECTION, ON *PAGES 99, 102,* AND *106.*

Cerebrum
The cerebrum's outer layer, the cerebral cortex, specializes in complex information processing and the management of motor responses to sensory signals.

Thalamus
This "switchboard" center routes information all around the brain. Clustered neuron cell bodies, called nuclei, process neural signals before forwarding them to "association areas" or other brain centers. The thalamus also plays a role in sleep, wakefulness, and consciousness.

Basal nuclei
These groups of neuron cell bodies play a vital role in relaying motor commands out from the cerebral cortex.

Brain stem
This region of brain tissue connects to the spinal cord. It includes the areas of the midbrain, pons, and medulla oblongata that control many basic operations, such as breathing.

Spinal cord

Midbrain
Neurons here receive raw visual and auditory signals and coordinate reflex responses—such as a startled response to a sudden, loud noise.

Cerebellum
The traditional idea that the cerebellum is purely a motor control device is no longer valid. Increasingly, it is recognized as a contributor to cognitive processing, intellect, and emotional control—in addition to its autonomic function and its role in motor coordination (see pages 98–99).

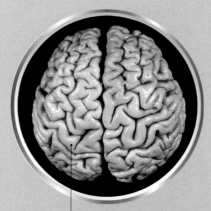

Surface of the brain
Although it is a dense organ, the brain's texture is soft. Cell bodies of neurons make up the cerebral cortex, the highly folded outer layer of the brain's gray matter.

Brain layers
Top to bottom, the brain has three tiers. The upper, complex forebrain is where the most sophisticated processing occurs. Deeper areas in the midbrain coordinate reflexes and provide the initial processing of information related to vision and hearing. Even deeper, the hindbrain—made up of the medulla oblongata and the pons—helps to control many basic reflexes and bodily functions.

The cerebral hemispheres
The upper three-quarters of the brain is divided into two sides, the right and left hemispheres of the cerebrum, which are linked by a thick band of nerve tracts called the *corpus callosum*. In each hemisphere, regions called the frontal, occipital, temporal, and parietal lobes are named after the skull bones above them.

STRUCTURE AND GROWTH

In the early life of an embryo, three basic tissues provide the foundation for organs and other future body parts. One of these, called ectoderm, gives the brain its initial form. After about three weeks of development, a portion of the embryo's ectoderm thickens into a "neural plate." This is the very basic foundation of what will become the most fundamental organ of the human body.

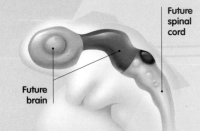

Future spinal cord

Future brain

Phase One: four weeks old

By the fourth week of life, the neural plate structure folds into a "neural tube"—which will eventually form the central nervous system— with the rudimentary brain at the upper end.

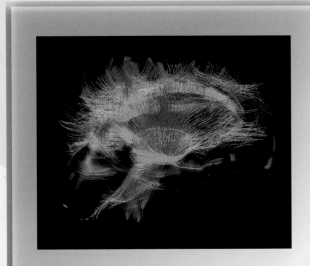

CEREBRAL WHITE MATTER

The myelin-coated axons of neurons make up much of the cerebrum's "white matter," below the "gray matter" of the brain's outer surface. These nerve fibers are bundled into nerve tracts that carry nerve impulses between the brain regions, and from the brain to the spinal cord. Horizontal tracts connect the brain's two hemispheres. Vertical tracts connect the brain stem and the motor and sensory association areas of the cerebral cortex.

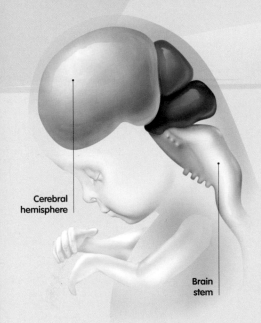

Cerebral hemisphere

Brain stem

Phase Two: sixteen weeks old

At 16 weeks, the fetus has defined cerebral hemispheres and other parts that will be fully formed before birth.

GRAY MATTER CARRIES SENSORY INFORMATION THAT ORIGINATES FROM THE BODY'S SENSORY ORGANS OR OTHER GRAY MATTER CELLS.

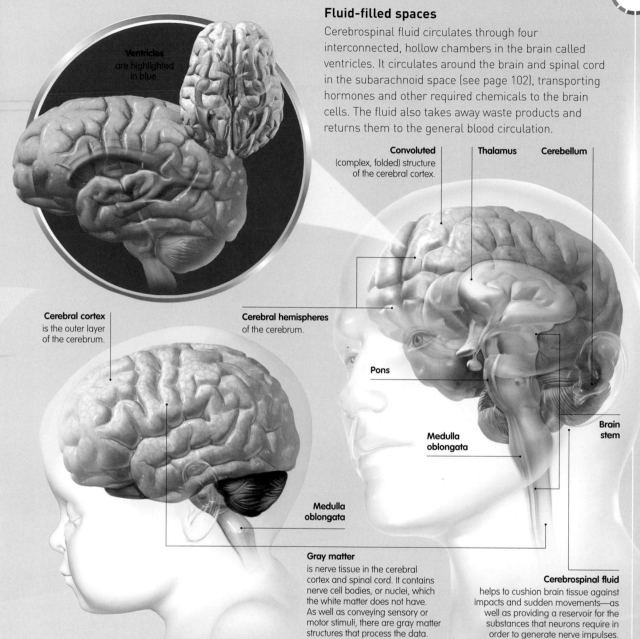

Ventricles are highlighted in blue.

Fluid-filled spaces

Cerebrospinal fluid circulates through four interconnected, hollow chambers in the brain called ventricles. It circulates around the brain and spinal cord in the subarachnoid space (see page 102), transporting hormones and other required chemicals to the brain cells. The fluid also takes away waste products and returns them to the general blood circulation.

Convoluted
(complex, folded) structure of the cerebral cortex.

Thalamus

Cerebellum

Cerebral cortex
is the outer layer of the cerebrum.

Cerebral hemispheres
of the cerebrum.

Pons

Medulla oblongata

Brain stem

Medulla oblongata

Gray matter
is nerve tissue in the cerebral cortex and spinal cord. It contains nerve cell bodies, or nuclei, which the white matter does not have. As well as conveying sensory or motor stimuli, there are gray matter structures that process the data.

Cerebrospinal fluid
helps to cushion brain tissue against impacts and sudden movements—as well as providing a reservoir for the substances that neurons require in order to generate nerve impulses.

Phase Three: the brain at birth

Initially, the brain hemispheres are smooth—but, as the cerebral cortex develops, it becomes deeply folded and convoluted. This folding helps to make the brain compact enough to fit inside the skull.

Phase Four: a fully-formed brain

The structure of the brain is now fully formed, but neurologically it will continue to develop and mature throughout life.

THE CEREBELLUM

Outwardly, the cerebellum—which sits behind the brain stem—resembles a layered, fan-shaped pad. Its name, meaning "little brain," reflects the fact that—just like the larger cerebrum—the cerebellum consists of two side-by-side hemispheres and that its outer layer is deeply convoluted. The cerebellum is a vital central processing unit, which has key connections with other parts of the brain.

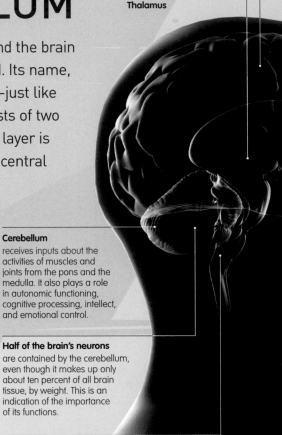

Premotor cortex

Thalamus

Cerebellum
receives inputs about the activities of muscles and joints from the pons and the medulla. It also plays a role in autonomic functioning, cognitive processing, intellect, and emotional control.

Half of the brain's neurons
are contained by the cerebellum, even though it makes up only about ten percent of all brain tissue, by weight. This is an indication of the importance of its functions.

Medulla oblongata

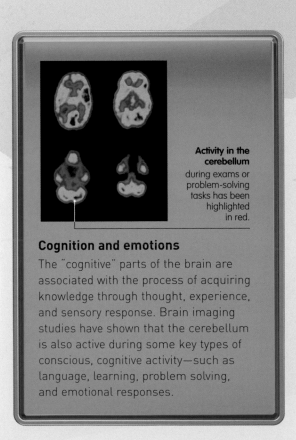

Activity in the cerebellum
during exams or problem-solving tasks has been highlighted in red.

Cognition and emotions

The "cognitive" parts of the brain are associated with the process of acquiring knowledge through thought, experience, and sensory response. Brain imaging studies have shown that the cerebellum is also active during some key types of conscious, cognitive activity—such as language, learning, problem solving, and emotional responses.

Motor functions

Operating below the level of conscious awareness, the cerebellum constantly assesses signals from sense receptors that detect changes in the position of body parts. It manages these, and other sensory data, to maintain the precise timing and patterns of skeletal muscle contractions. This enables humans to have the coordination and agility for rapid-fire movements associated with activities such as driving, playing video games, typing, and dancing.

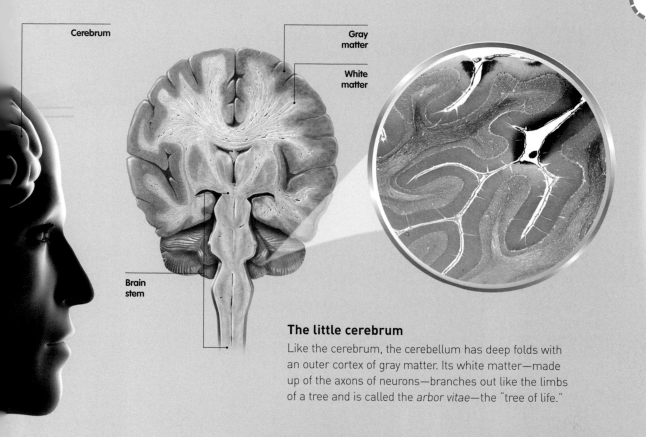

Cerebrum

Gray matter

White matter

Brain stem

The little cerebrum

Like the cerebrum, the cerebellum has deep folds with an outer cortex of gray matter. Its white matter—made up of the axons of neurons—branches out like the limbs of a tree and is called the *arbor vitae*—the "tree of life."

Complex coordination

The cerebellum receives inputs about the activities of muscles and joints from the pons and medulla. After assessing the position, balance, and momentum of body parts, it sends a message to the thalamus, which forwards the information to the premotor cortex (see page 110) to fine-tune the speed, force, and direction of muscle contractions. This ensures that all bodily postures and movements are precisely geared to the task in hand.

THE CEREBELLUM AND AUTISM

Recent studies of the cognitive role of the cerebellum have revealed that it is one of the key brain regions affected in people diagnosed with autistic spectrum disorder. There could be developmental differences in the cerebellum of the autistic brain, which would account for the language, learning, and emotional limitations that are indicative of the condition.

THE BRAIN STEM

Deep at the core of the brain, the brain stem controls many vital, unconscious functions—from consciousness to the beating of the heart and inflation of the lungs. Located between the top of the spinal cord and the cerebrum, it consists of the medulla oblongata, the pons, and the midbrain. So crucial are they in controlling essential activities, serious damage to these small structures may prove fatal.

The reticular formation

Running through the brain stem is a network of neurons called the reticular formation. With long axons that spread outward to other parts of the brain, these neurons are key to the spectrum of brain states we call human consciousness.

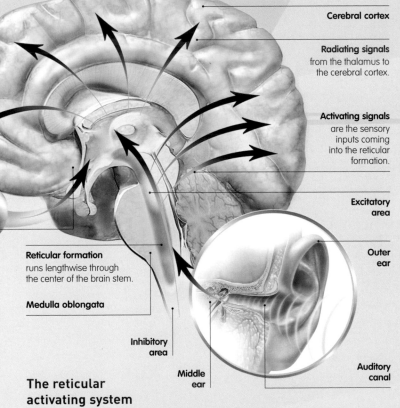

Cerebral cortex

Radiating signals from the thalamus to the cerebral cortex.

Activating signals are the sensory inputs coming into the reticular formation.

Excitatory area

Outer ear

Auditory canal

Middle ear

Inhibitory area

Reticular formation runs lengthwise through the center of the brain stem.

Medulla oblongata

Thalamus is not a part of the brain stem, although it does work in conjunction with it.

Unconscious control

The neurons of the reticular formation communicate with the spinal cord and many other parts of the brain. Some of these centers help to manage the automatic muscle contractions required for a wide range of body functions, such as breathing, heartbeat, balance, and posture.

The reticular activating system

Other neurons in this area form the reticular activating system (RAS), which helps to arouse the brain into alert consciousness. The RAS neurons become more active when sound, light, or other sensory inputs stimulate them. Their activity slackens during sleep.

The medulla oblongata

Called the medulla, for short, this brain stem region is a hub for sensory and motor signals passing between the spinal cord and other brain regions. It coordinates muscle movements involved in swallowing, sneezing, hiccuping, and vomiting. In association with other parts of the brain, it regulates the heartbeat, breathing, and the constriction and widening of blood vessels (to regulate blood pressure). It is also part of the pathway for reticular formation activities relating to arousal and consciousness.

Cranial nerves
These are 12 pairs of nerves that pass through the skull and carry signals directly to the brain. Ten of the pairs (labeled below, in italics) pass through the brain stem—carrying sensory or motor signals, or both, to and from the brain.

Thalamus
The thalamus receives and sorts sensory signals from the brain stem before passing messages on to the cerebral cortex. It also functions in arousal, memory, and awareness.

Occulomotor III
This nerve moves the eyeball and upper eyelid.

Midbrain
Neurons in the *substantia nigra*, in the midbrain, release a neurotransmitter called dopamine, which coordinates subconscious muscle movements. Loss of these neurons creates the tremors and other symptoms of Parkinson's disease.

Trochlear IV
The smallest of the cranial nerves, this moves the eyeball down and laterally (side to side).

Pons
The nerve cells here work with the medulla to control breathing, and to relay signals between the medulla and the midbrain.

Trigeminal V
This nerve carries motor and sensory impulses to and from the eyes, jaws, and face.

Abducens VI
This nerve "abducts" the eye (turns it outward).

Facial VII
Among other functions, this nerve controls most facial expressions.

Vestibulocochlear VIII
This auditory nerve carries impulses for hearing and equilibrium (balance).

Glossopharyngeal IX
This nerve serves the throat and back of the tongue—for tasting and swallowing.

Hypoglossal XII
This motor nerve carries impulses to the tongue for speech and swallowing.

Medulla oblongata

Spinal accessory XI
A nerve that conveys motor impulses to the shoulder and neck muscles.

Vagus X
This nerve branches from the head and neck to the thorax and abdomen. It is a complex nerve with the widest distribution of all the cranial nerves. It innervates areas such as the ear, larynx, heart, and digestive tract.

The pons and midbrain

Located toward the front of the medulla, the pons relays information between the cerebral cortex and the cerebellum. At the top of the brain stem, the midbrain coordinates and controls many of the sensory and motor functions of the body. Each of these vital structures is only about 1in (2.5cm) long.

THE SPINAL CORD

In the CNS, the spinal cord is the vital information expressway between the brain and the other parts of the body. It carries an unceasing flow of data—incoming sensory signals from the skin, muscles, and glands, as well as the brain's outgoing commands for body movements, the activity of the heart and other organs, and all the other essentials of bodily functions. The nerves of the PNS deliver incoming signals and receive and send on the responses.

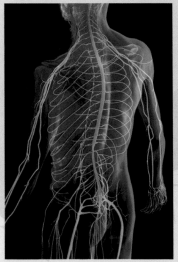

Somatic nerves

Threading throughout all body tissues, the communication lines of the PNS fall into two groups. Many are somatic ("of the body") nerves that directly link the spinal cord or brain with skeletal muscles and tendons. They transmit sensory information, as well as the motor impulses associated with the movements of the head, trunk, and limbs.

Autonomic nerves

Autonomic nerves make up the second group of PNS nerves. The CNS communicates with them indirectly by way of ganglia, which are located outside the spinal cord or brain stem. The ganglia are clusters of nerve cell bodies that serve as transfer points for signals from the CNS to muscles and glands.

Inside the cord

Neuron axons—sheathed in white, insulating myelin—make up the outer portion of the spinal cord (the "white matter"). Neuron cell bodies, dendrites, and synapses make up its interior of "gray matter." Membranes called meninges, plus the bony vertebrae, protect these delicate neural parts. Cerebrospinal fluid fills the central canal.

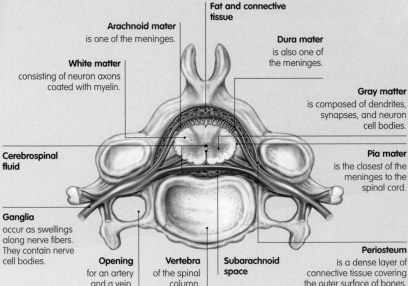

Fat and connective tissue

Arachnoid mater
is one of the meninges.

Dura mater
is also one of the meninges.

White matter
consisting of neuron axons coated with myelin.

Gray matter
is composed of dendrites, synapses, and neuron cell bodies.

Cerebrospinal fluid

Pia mater
is the closest of the meninges to the spinal cord.

Ganglia
occur as swellings along nerve fibers. They contain nerve cell bodies.

Opening
for an artery and a vein.

Vertebra
of the spinal column.

Subarachnoid space

Periosteum
is a dense layer of connective tissue covering the outer surface of bones.

 LEARN MORE ABOUT THE SPINE AND SPINAL INJURIES ON *PAGES 118–119.*

The tap of a surgical hammer
activates stretch-sensitive receptors in a tendon attached to the patella, sending nerve impulses along sensory axons to the spinal cord.

In the spinal cord
the signals pass to motor neurons that cause the quadriceps muscle to contract and briefly extend the lower leg.

The reflex arc

In a reflex arc, a sensory neuron communicates directly or indirectly with a motor neuron to trigger an automatic movement such as the "knee-jerk" caused by a tap at the base of the kneecap. The spinal cord is the hub for reflex arcs. These responses occur without signals passing up to the brain—resulting in fast reactions that automatically and instantly protect the body.

Spinal injuries

The spinal cord plays a fundamental role in the CNS. Injuries to the spine can result in paralysis if its bony protection is lost and the delicate nervous tissue is squashed or severed. However, quadriplegia (loss of control over all four limbs) may not be caused if the vertebrae alone are broken, and if the injured person is immediately immobilized and there are no harmful forces impacting on the spinal cord itself.

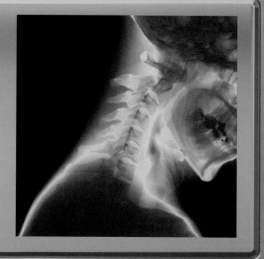

THE AUTONOMIC SYSTEM

The autonomic nerves of the peripheral nervous system subdivide into two types, which transmit counteracting signals to the heart and the smooth muscle of internal organs and glands. One type, the parasympathetic nerves, manages the "rest and digest" tasks that replenish the body's energy resources. Meanwhile, the sympathetic nerves manage changes associated with more demanding activities, such as our "fight or flight" response to stress or an impending threat. The shifting balance between these signals enables the fine-tuned control of the internal organs.

The sympathetic division

Generally speaking, this autonomic division prepares the body for exciting, stressful, or dangerous situations. Less urgent tasks such as digestion slow down, while the body's heart rate, breathing, and sweating increase as a person rapidly becomes excited or agitated.

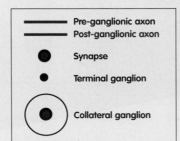

———	Pre-ganglionic axon
———	Post-ganglionic axon
●	Synapse
•	Terminal ganglion
⊙	Collateral ganglion

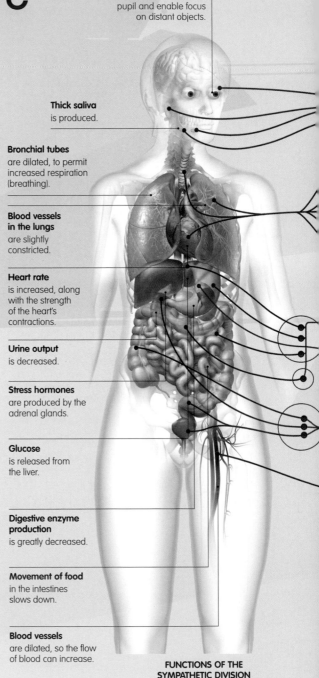

Ciliary muscle in the eye
is relaxed to dilate the pupil and enable focus on distant objects.

Thick saliva
is produced.

Bronchial tubes
are dilated, to permit increased respiration (breathing).

Blood vessels in the lungs
are slightly constricted.

Heart rate
is increased, along with the strength of the heart's contractions.

Urine output
is decreased.

Stress hormones
are produced by the adrenal glands.

Glucose
is released from the liver.

Digestive enzyme production
is greatly decreased.

Movement of food
in the intestines slows down.

Blood vessels
are dilated, so the flow of blood can increase.

FUNCTIONS OF THE SYMPATHETIC DIVISION

 THE WORD *AUTONOMIC* RELATES TO ANY NERVE-CONTROLLED BODILY FUNCTION THAT IS UNCONSCIOUS OR INVOLUNTARY.

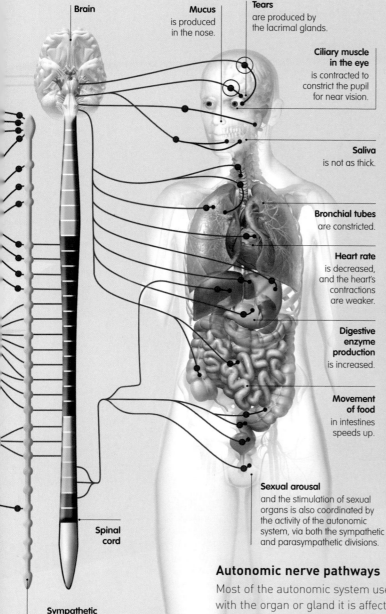

Brain

Mucus
is produced
in the nose.

Tears
are produced by
the lacrimal glands.

**Ciliary muscle
in the eye**
is contracted to
constrict the pupil
for near vision.

Saliva
is not as thick.

Bronchial tubes
are constricted.

Heart rate
is decreased,
and the heart's
contractions
are weaker.

**Digestive
enzyme
production**
is increased.

**Movement
of food**
in intestines
speeds up.

Sexual arousal
and the stimulation of sexual
organs is also coordinated by
the activity of the autonomic
system, via both the sympathetic
and parasympathetic divisions.

**Spinal
cord**

**Sympathetic
ganglion
chain**

**FUNCTIONS OF THE
PARASYMPATHETIC DIVISION**

The parasympathetic division

Signals from parasympathetic nerves stimulate routine operations such as food digestion and the elimination of wastes. Simultaneously, overall physical activity slows down.

Sympathetic responses

The activity signaled by the ANS is highly relevant to our survival. Sympathetic changes cause the pupils in the eyes to dilate, letting in as much light as possible so that more visual information can be gathered. The bronchial tubes in the lungs dilate, bringing in more oxygen to feed the muscles that are about to assist in an escape from danger. Among other changes, more glucose is released for the body to burn as a quick energy boost.

Autonomic nerve pathways

Most of the autonomic system uses a two-neuron chain to communicate with the organ or gland it is affecting. One of the nerve cells is in the brain stem or spinal cord and is connected by nerve fibers to the other cell, which is in an autonomic ganglion—a cluster of nerve cells (see page 102). Nerve fibers from the ganglia then connect with the internal organs. For the sympathetic division, the ganglia are sited just outside the spinal cord, while those of the parasympathetic division are nearer to the organs to which they connect.

THE HIGHER BRAIN

Many qualities associated with "humanness" stem from the activity of the cerebral cortex—the cerebrum's thin outer region of gray matter. Only a quarter inch thick, the cerebral cortex consists of several fine layers and is convoluted into deep, curving folds containing billions of neurons. In all, it accounts for approximately 40 percent of the brain's tissue. Signals from the cortex control our conscious behavior and thought, language, and understanding.

EEG tests

Electrodes can be placed on a person's head to monitor the brain's electrical activity as part of an electroencephalogram (EEG) test. The test is normally carried out while the person is working on a mental task or answering questions verbally. The electrodes positioned around the scalp record the electrical activity prompted by these mental or emotional challenges in various parts of the brain.

Thalamus

Hippocampus

Cerebellum

Amygdala

Cross-section
of the cerebral cortex.

Skull

Ventricles
are hollow cavities filled with cerebrospinal fluid.

White matter
is the paler tissue of the brain and spinal cord. It consists mainly of nerve fibers and their myelin sheaths.

Gray matter
is the darker neural tissue. It consists mainly of nerve cell bodies and their branching dendrites.

EPILEPSY IS A DISORDER ASSOCIATED WITH ABNORMAL ELECTRICAL ACTIVITY IN THE BRAIN. EEG TESTS CAN HELP TO REVEAL EPILEPSY IN A PERSON.

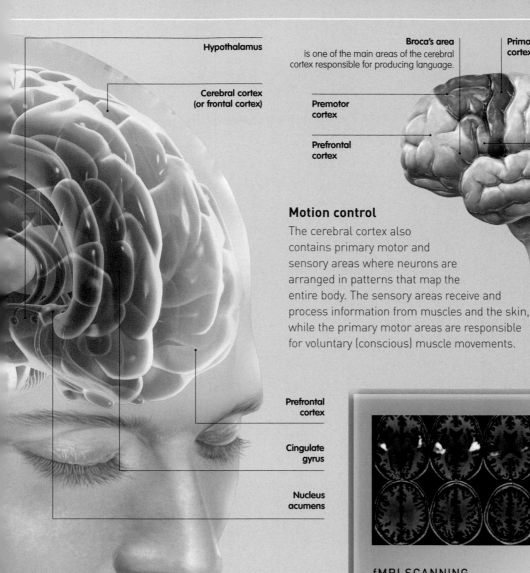

Hypothalamus

Cerebral cortex
(or frontal cortex)

Broca's area
is one of the main areas of the cerebral
cortex responsible for producing language.

Primary motor
cortex

Premotor
cortex

Prefrontal
cortex

Frontal eye
field

Prefrontal
cortex

Cingulate
gyrus

Nucleus
acumens

Motion control

The cerebral cortex also contains primary motor and sensory areas where neurons are arranged in patterns that map the entire body. The sensory areas receive and process information from muscles and the skin, while the primary motor areas are responsible for voluntary (conscious) muscle movements.

Conscious control

The complicated interactions among neurons—those that underlie reasoning and learning, planning, personality, judgement, aspects of memory, and the thought patterns of "conscience"—are centered in the prefrontal cortex. The prefrontal cortex communicates intimately with the limbic system (see pages 114–115), the seat of human emotions.

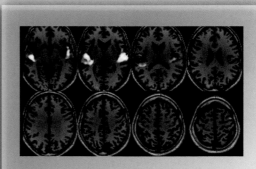

fMRI SCANNING

Functional magnetic resonance imaging (fMRI) of the brain is helping us to revolutionize our understanding of its cognitive functions. Highly active brain cells use more oxygen than less active ones do, and these differences are detected by the fMRI technology. This means that the activity levels of different regions of the brain can be measured while a person is performing a particular mental task.

LANGUAGE AND COMPREHENSION

The capacity to communicate using complex language is one of the traits that sets humans apart from their closest relatives in the animal world. In most people, this profoundly important aspect of humanness resides mainly in the brain's left hemisphere, where linked centers in the prefrontal cortex and temporal lobe play vital roles in our ability to produce and comprehend speech and the written word.

Auditory centers

Broca's area

Temporal lobe regions

Several different brain regions interact to coordinate our languange skills. They are not the product of independent "language centers."

LEFT CEREBRAL HEMISPHERE

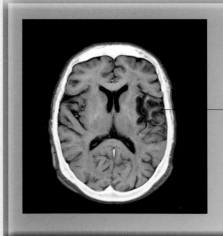

Stroke has occurred in a left-sided area of the brain, where the function of language is controlled.

TYPES OF APHASIA

Aphasia is the loss of the ability to produce or understand language, caused by damage to certain areas of the brain by disease or injury. In Broca's aphasia, the ability to produce speech is lost, but the sufferer may still understand spoken words. In Wernicke's aphasia, the ability to understand language is lost, and sufferers often speak in nonsensical words or sounds. This MRI scan (left) highlights the sudden onset of Broca's aphasia in the brain following a stroke.

Studying human language

PET (positron emission tomography) and functional MRI scans have expanded our scientific understanding of the roles different parts of the brain play in speaking and understanding language. By generating images that reflect the relative use of oxygen and other substances by metabolically active cells, researchers can track the shifting operations of brain neurons in real time.

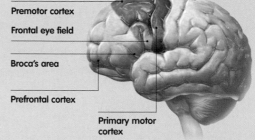

Premotor cortex
Frontal eye field
Broca's area
Prefrontal cortex
Primary motor cortex

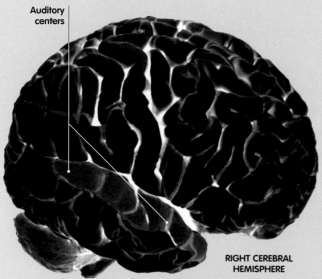

Auditory centers

RIGHT CEREBRAL HEMISPHERE

Roles of the left and right

While the left side of the brain dominates speech and comprehension for most people, the right cerebral hemisphere helps to process the emotional sense or components of language. These scans (left) show the activity of the brain while hearing and understanding language. On the left side of the brain, more areas are active—including the Broca's area and the temporal lobe areas dealing with comprehension. Auditory centers are active in both hemispheres.

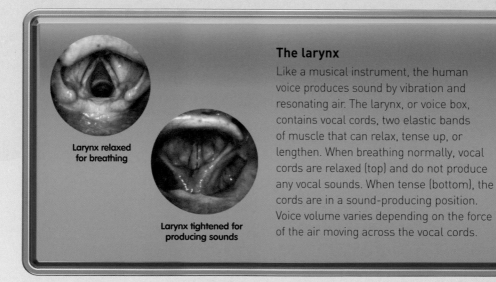

Larynx relaxed for breathing

Larynx tightened for producing sounds

The larynx

Like a musical instrument, the human voice produces sound by vibration and resonating air. The larynx, or voice box, contains vocal cords, two elastic bands of muscle that can relax, tense up, or lengthen. When breathing normally, vocal cords are relaxed (top) and do not produce any vocal sounds. When tense (bottom), the cords are in a sound-producing position. Voice volume varies depending on the force of the air moving across the vocal cords.

Interacting groups
of neurons in the motor cortex coordinate movements of opposing muscle groups, such as those used to flex and extend the forearms and legs.

Beyond the primary cortex

The premotor cortex, in front of the primary motor cortex, functions as a memory bank for operating muscles used in learned motor activities, such as writing. Such skills require muscles to contract in a specific, unvarying sequence. Nearby, neurons in the frontal eye field control voluntary eye movements. The Broca's area, in the left cerebral hemisphere, is active both when a person prepares to speak and when muscles move the lips, tongue, and other parts to make speech sounds.

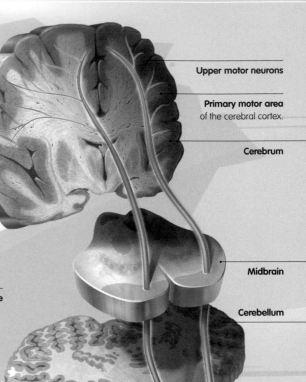

Upper motor neurons

Primary motor area
of the cerebral cortex.

Cerebrum

Midbrain

Cerebellum

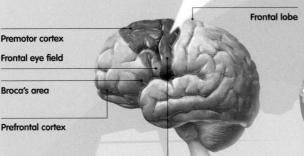

Frontal lobe

Premotor cortex

Frontal eye field

Broca's area

Prefrontal cortex

Primary motor cortex

DIRECT MOTOR
PATHWAYS

Pons

Medulla
oblongata

Pyramid

Cervical
spinal
cord

Lateral
corticospinal
tract

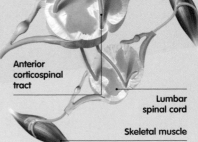

Anterior
corticospinal
tract

Lumbar
spinal
cord

Skeletal muscle

MOTOR
FUNCTIONS

The primary motor cortex is the director of all voluntary muscle movements. Occupying a broad, curving region at the rear of the frontal lobe, the motor cortex houses neurons that extend their axons directly to the spinal cord. The axons from each side of the cortex cross over, so that the right side of the cortex controls muscles on the left side of the body, and vice versa.

FIND OUT ABOUT MOTOR NEURONE DISEASE, OR AMYOTROPHIC LATERAL SCLEROSIS (ALS), AND ITS EFFECTS ON *PAGES 120–121*.

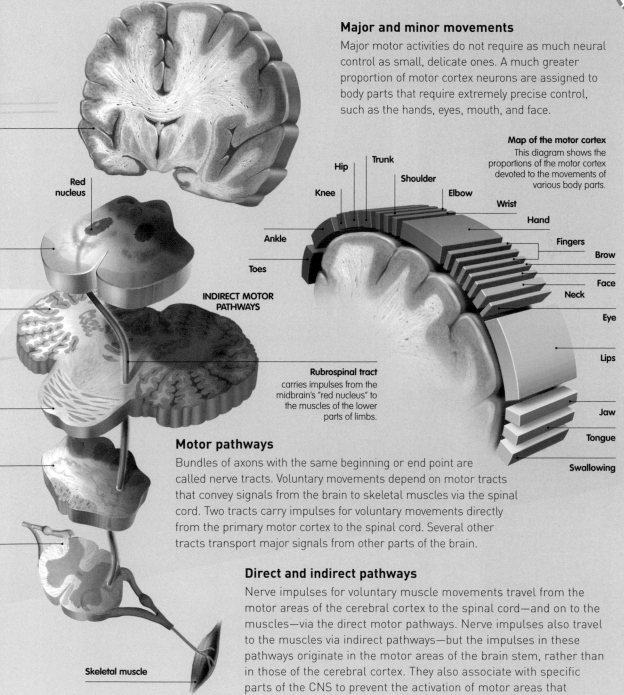

Major and minor movements

Major motor activities do not require as much neural control as small, delicate ones. A much greater proportion of motor cortex neurons are assigned to body parts that require extremely precise control, such as the hands, eyes, mouth, and face.

Map of the motor cortex
This diagram shows the proportions of the motor cortex devoted to the movements of various body parts.

Red nucleus

Trunk

Hip

Shoulder

Knee

Elbow

Wrist

Hand

Ankle

Fingers

Brow

Toes

Face

Neck

INDIRECT MOTOR PATHWAYS

Eye

Lips

Rubrospinal tract
carries impulses from the midbrain's "red nucleus" to the muscles of the lower parts of limbs.

Jaw

Tongue

Swallowing

Motor pathways

Bundles of axons with the same beginning or end point are called nerve tracts. Voluntary movements depend on motor tracts that convey signals from the brain to skeletal muscles via the spinal cord. Two tracts carry impulses for voluntary movements directly from the primary motor cortex to the spinal cord. Several other tracts transport major signals from other parts of the brain.

Direct and indirect pathways

Nerve impulses for voluntary muscle movements travel from the motor areas of the cerebral cortex to the spinal cord—and on to the muscles—via the direct motor pathways. Nerve impulses also travel to the muscles via indirect pathways—but the impulses in these pathways originate in the motor areas of the brain stem, rather than in those of the cerebral cortex. They also associate with specific parts of the CNS to prevent the activation of motor areas that would compete with the desired voluntary movement.

Skeletal muscle

THE UNCONSCIOUS BRAIN

Sleep is a state of altered consciousness that seems to be a biological essential. Centers in the brain stem's reticular formation (see page 100) govern both sleeping and waking, with different groups of neurons releasing neurotransmitters that either promote or inhibit sleep. As a person sleeps, the processing parts of the brain remain active, and may even perform functions such as stabilizing our memories, processing the information of the day, and solving problems.

NREM and REM sleep cycles

Non-rapid eye movement (NREM) sleep alternates with rapid eye movement (REM) sleep, when the eyeballs seem to be active. Every 90 minutes or so, the pattern typically shifts to REM sleep, when dreaming occurs. The first cycle of REM sleep may only last for a short time, and each subsequent cycle becomes longer. A long sleep maintains good health for the brain, which appears to need multiple cycles of both types of sleep.

Colored PET scans of unconscious brain activity

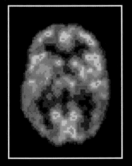 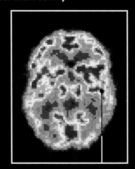

The brain in NREM sleep   The brain in REM sleep

Polysomnograph matching brain and eye activity during sleep

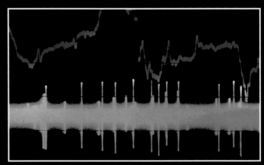

Blue graphic
shows data from an EEG tracking brainwaves.

Green graphic
shows the eye movements taking place at the same time as the brainwaves.

The stages of sleep

The stages of sleep are highly organized. NREM sleep has four stages that unfold in sequence. During NREM Stage One, a person sleeps lightly and is easily awakened. Sleep then progressively deepens. It is most difficult to rouse a sleeper during the deepest phase, NREM Stage Four. NREM sleep alternates with shorter periods of REM sleep, with dreams occurring almost entirely during the REM periods. The active parts of the cerebral cortex are highlighted in red in the above PET scans. In REM sleep, the activity is similar to that of the conscious brain, while in NREM sleep the brain is active—but in a different way.

 CHRONIC INSOMNIA (SLEEPLESSNESS) AFFECTS AS MANY AS ONE IN TEN ADULTS.

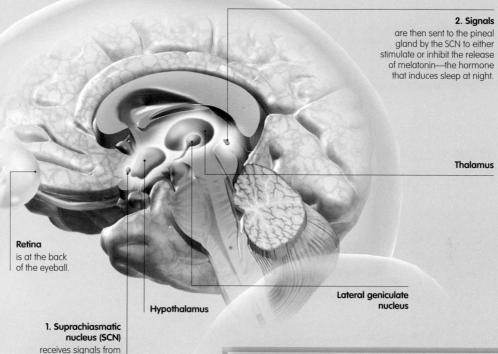

2. Signals
are then sent to the pineal
gland by the SCN to either
stimulate or inhibit the release
of melatonin—the hormone
that induces sleep at night.

Thalamus

Retina
is at the back
of the eyeball.

**Lateral geniculate
nucleus**

Hypothalamus

**1. Suprachiasmatic
nucleus (SCN)**
receives signals from
special photoreceptors in
the retina (see page 128)
that communicate rising
or falling light levels.

Circadian rhythm

The body's biological clock regulates sleep
and other physiological states in cycles—
of about 24 hours—that roughly follow
daily shifts in external light and dark
periods. The "clock" is a cluster of nerve
cell bodies, in the hypothalamus, called
the suprachiasmatic nucleus (SCN).

A TYPICAL SEQUENCE OF NREM SLEEP

- **Stage 1:** falling asleep—for five to ten minutes.
- **Stage 2:** body temperature drops; heart rate slows; some
  short periods of rapid brain activity—for about
  20 minutes, on average.
- **Stage 3:** the transitional shift between light sleep and
  very deep sleep—variable duration.
- **Stage 4:** deep sleep—lasting for about 30 minutes.
- **Stage 5:** the next cycle of REM sleep commences.

SLEEP STUDIES

Polysomnography is a way of monitoring the brain
during sleep. Such tests have revealed that during
REM sleep, when people usually dream, the limbic
system (see pages 114–115) and visual association
areas of the brain are highly active. This discovery
is consistent with the intense visual imagery and
charged emotions often associated with dreaming.

THE EMOTIONAL BRAIN

From infancy onward, the functions of emotions and other basic aspects of human life and experience rely on a ring of small structures collectively known as the limbic system—or more commonly as the "emotional brain." The system's parts include the almond-shaped amygdala, the hippocampus, the thalamus, the hypothalamus, and a curved fold of tissue called the cingulate gyrus.

Dealing with life

Looping around the upper brain stem, the parts of the limbic system collectively govern the full range of human emotions—feelings of joy, rage, fear, love, grief, desire, and empathy, among others. They also play key roles in memory and influence a person's capacity to perceive joy and pay attention to events in the outside world.

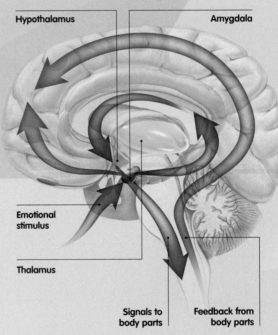

Hypothalamus

Amygdala

Emotional stimulus

Thalamus

Signals to body parts

Feedback from body parts

EMOTIONS AND STRESS
The limbic system's links with the hypothalamus may help to explain why negative pressures—such as money worries or a relationship problem—often manifest themselves in a physical illness. The hypothalamus secretes a hormone that indirectly causes the adrenal glands to release the "stress hormone" cortisol, a potent immune system suppressor that also heightens blood pressure.

Emotional pathways

Fear, joy, and other emotions are a mix of feelings and physiological responses, such as a racing heart, a burst of tears, or waves of nausea. These responses are coordinated by the amygdala, which processes the triggers and forwards them on to the hypothalamus, where signals are issued to evoke physical responses. As the affected organs "report back" to the frontal cortex, a person experiences both the emotion and its physical impacts.

 THE FEELING OF WHAT HAPPENS: BODY, EMOTION AND THE MAKING OF CONSCIOUSNESS BY ANTONIO R DAMASIO.

Neural traffic
in the frontal lobes can be imaged, using fMRI technology, to help scientists to understand how this area controls judgments and decision-making when under the influence of an emotional situation.

Cingulate gyrus
is a region that is active when a person feels frustrated or gestures to express an emotion of some kind.

Thalamus
is a part of the limbic system where clusters of neurons, called nuclei, manage the overall traffic of neural signals.

Hippocampus
is a C-shaped limbic system structure. It is involved mainly in the processes of memory, but it may also influence the "higher" brain centers associated with conscious thought.

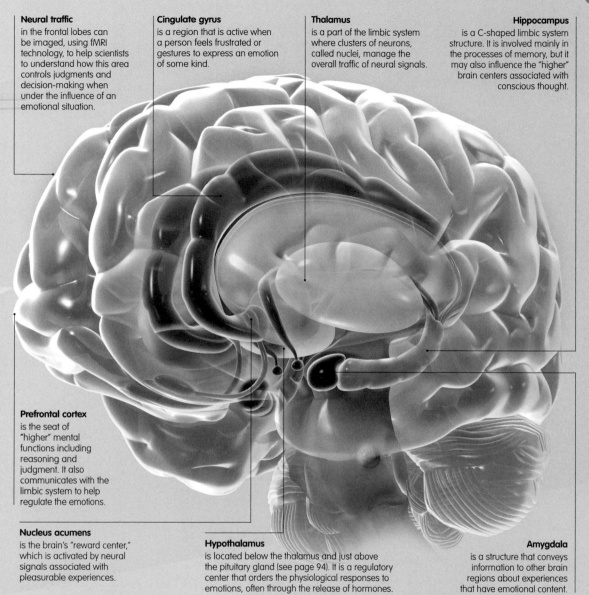

Prefrontal cortex
is the seat of "higher" mental functions including reasoning and judgment. It also communicates with the limbic system to help regulate the emotions.

Nucleus acumens
is the brain's "reward center," which is activated by neural signals associated with pleasurable experiences.

Hypothalamus
is located below the thalamus and just above the pituitary gland (see page 94). It is a regulatory center that orders the physiological responses to emotions, often through the release of hormones.

Amygdala
is a structure that conveys information to other brain regions about experiences that have emotional content.

Emotions and thoughts

Research in cognitive neuroscience suggests that the amygdala—and other parts of the limbic system—are involved in brain operations such as reasoning, judgment, and decision making. Investigators have used functional magnetic resonance imaging (fMRI) to see whether the emotional nature of a situation affected choices made by people taking part in the study. The images revealed "cross-talk" between the amygdala and parts of the prefrontal cortex.

MEMORY

Memory is the brain's capacity to store and retrieve information—a basic requirement for learning facts and skills, and for the human ability to modify behavior in response to experience. There is no single part of the brain that manages these processes. Instead, memories form as sensory processing areas of the cerebral cortex interact in complex ways with deeper brain structures, including the limbic system.

Making memories

Interacting circuits of neurons create memories. "Explicit" memories develop as stimuli from the eyes, nose—or some other sense organ—are delivered to an association area in the sensory cortex. From this area, signals pass to the amygdala and hippocampus, and are then routed to the thalamus and onward to the prefrontal cortex. Sensory input is only stored as a long-term memory when signals also enter a repeating pathway that loops between the hippocampus, basal ganglia, thalamus, and the sensory cortex.

Types of memories

Throughout life, the brain constantly sorts and assesses the sensory information it receives. Information such as a cab company's phone number is likely to be stored only briefly as a short-term memory, lasting a few hours at the most. More complex sensory input, such as the sights and sounds of an accident scene, become long-term memories that may be retained for decades.

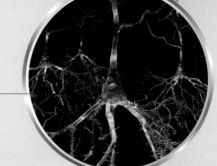

Prefrontal cortex

Frontal cortex

Visual stimulus sends sensory signals in to the receptors in the eye.

Dendritic spines are small, membranous branches on a neuron (nerve cell) that receive signals from synapses. They stick out from the dendrites of neurons (see pages 90–91). It could be here, in these tiny spines, that memories are stored.

Long-term memory

Depending on the circumstances linked to the sensory input, long-term memories are stored as facts or motor skills. They involve more complex neural circuitry and can be split into different categories, as follows:

- Explicit (declarative)
- Implicit (non-declarative)
- Episodic (to do with time and place)
- Semantic (to do with facts)
- Motor learning (to do with skills)

DEMENTIA IS A COLLECTIVE TERM FOR CHRONIC DISORDERS OF MENTAL PROCESSES, CAUSED BY BRAIN INJURY OR DISEASE.

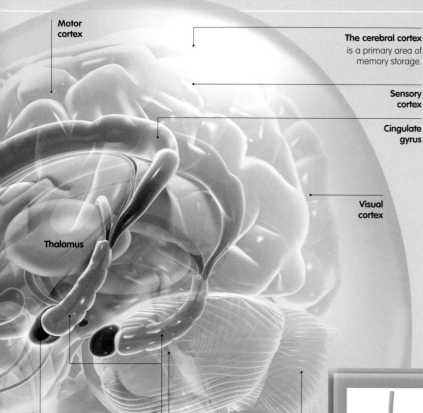

Motor cortex

The cerebral cortex
is a primary area of memory storage.

Sensory cortex

Cingulate gyrus

Visual cortex

Thalamus

Amygdala
Each of these has a "lateral subdivision" at its center, which has the role of creating our "fear memory." The amygdala's associated emotional function (see page 115) may explain the powerful link between our emotions and our memories.

Cerebellum

Hippocampi
are vital areas of the brain in terms of spatial awareness and memory. There are two of them—one on each side of the brain. The tissue of the hippocampi is where a lot of sensory stimuli are first received. It is possible that long-term memories relating to facts and events are stored in the these areas, initially, before they become a part of a more "generalized" system of storage throughout the brain.

Entorhinal cortex
is involved in fixing and consolidating memories, along with the basal ganglia (linked to the thalamus) and the cerebellum. The entorhinal cortex seems to have a specific role in spatial memory. It acts as a link between the memory-forming hippocampus and the neocortex, which deals with sensory perception.

Explicit memories
are also known as "declarative" memories—the conscious, intentional recollection of previous experiences and information.

Implicit memories
are long-term memories connected with skills, procedures, and routines.

Episodic memories
are the memories of "autobiographical" events—times, places, and any people and emotions associated with them.

Semantic memories
or "generic" memories are to do with the memory of meanings, understanding, and concept-based knowledge. They are vital to the recollection of factual knowledge.

Motor (skill) memories
are created by repeating a precise sequence of motor activities, such as dance steps. With time, that motor sequence becomes second nature and no longer requires conscious thought.

MEMORY RETRIEVAL

When we access our memories, the brain re-visits the nerve pathways that it formed when the memory was originally encoded and stored. The strength and stability of those pathways determines how quickly the memories can be recalled. People with forms of dementia, or Alzheimer's disease, often struggle with basic memory retrieval because these neural pathways may have broken down (see page 118).

NERVOUS SYSTEM DISORDERS

Wear and tear, injuries, disease, autoimmune disorders—these factors, and others, can prevent neurons from communicating normally. Examples of these disorders are shown on these pages. Multiple sclerosis (MS) and amyotrophic lateral sclerosis (ALS) are associated with the gradual destruction of neurons. Devastating physical injuries to the spine may result in partial or total paralysis, or even death.

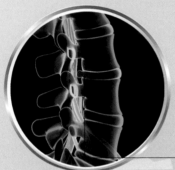

Spinal conditions

Countless people suffer from conditions such as spinal arthritis or a herniated disc, which puts pressure on the nerves issuing from the spine. Such a "pinched" nerve is not life threatening, but it can produce debilitating pain or numbness that disrupts normal life activities. Spinal cancer—often caused by metastasis (development of secondary growths) from a primary cancer elsewhere in the body—can mimic these same symptoms. Pressure on nerves exerted by vertebrae in the spine can also cause paralysis.

A ruptured disc of cartilage puts pressure on nearby spinal nerves.

A hollow needle is inserted into the CSF-filled space (above or below the fourth lumbar vertebra) to withdraw the CSF for testing.

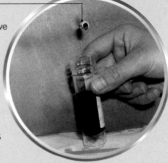

Testing for meningitis

Viruses and bacteria that invade the CNS can cause different types of meningitis, a dangerous but usually treatable inflammation of the meninges that surround the spinal cord and the brain (see pages 102–103). Using a procedure called a lumbar puncture, or spinal tap, a doctor can collect and analyze a sample of cerebrospinal fluid (CSF) to confirm whether a patient has meningitis. Blood tests and CT scans are also used to diagnose the disease.

(!) WORLDWIDE, *MORE THAN 2.3 MILLION PEOPLE* ARE AFFLICTED WITH MULTIPLE SCLEROSIS.

AMYOTROPHIC LATERAL SCLEROSIS

In amyotrophic lateral sclerosis, or ALS—also known as Lou Gehrig's disease—neurons in motor pathways of the spine and parts of the brain degenerate. The affected muscles quickly atrophy (waste away) and most patients die within five years of diagnosis. A remarkable exception is theoretical physicist Stephen Hawking (above), who has lived with ALS for decades.

Multiple sclerosis

Multiple sclerosis, or MS, is a progressive autoimmune disease in which the immune system mistakenly attacks neurons in both the central and peripheral nervous systems. A major symptom is muscle weakness that progresses to paralysis. Eventually, many patients are unable to walk and develop other symptoms related to the fading neural control of muscles.

Axon (nerve fiber)

Myelin sheath
insulates the long axon of a neuron (see pages 90 and 93).

Proteins
in the myelin sheath are attacked by the immune system of an MS sufferer.

Scleroses
are the scarlike patches that start to develop as MS progresses. They cause nerve impulses to travel more slowly down the axon. Eventually, the impulses come to a complete halt.

Myelin sheath breaking down

BRAIN DISEASES

Well-known disorders that affect the brain include concussion, Parkinson's disease, and forms of dementia such as Alzheimer's disease. One of the most common illnesses is stroke, which afflicts many millions of people every year and is a leading cause of disability and death. Benign and cancerous tumors may cause symptoms only when they begin to put pressure on brain tissue. In epilepsy, certain brain neurons malfunction. These disorders have far-reaching impacts on both mental and physical functions.

Brain hemorrhages

A subdural hematoma is a serious brain condition, often caused by a head injury, in which blood collects between the skull and the surface of the brain. Subarachnoid hemorrhages are an uncommon and very serious type of stroke caused by bleeding on the surface of the brain. An intracranial hemorrhage occurs when a blood vessel ruptures within the brain, or in between the skull and the brain. The pool of blood (the hematoma) then compresses on brain tissue.

Alzheimer's disease

This disease causes cell death, thus reducing the volume of brain tissue, which in turn leads to structural changes in the brain. As the cortex shrinks, damage is incurred to areas in charge of thinking, planning, and memory recall. The hippocampus is especially prone to shrinkage, impairing the formation of new memories. Sufferers therefore experience progressive memory loss and severe dementia.

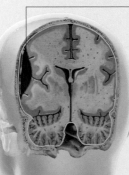

A subdural hematoma
forms between the two upper meninges (see page 94), the dura mater, and the arachnoid mater.

An epidural hematoma
is very rare. This is where blood collects in between the skull and the brain.

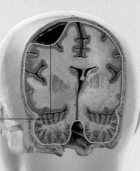

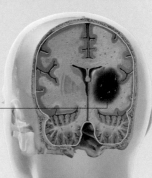

An intracranial hemorrhage
creates a clotted collection of blood inside the brain itself.

ISCHEMIC AND *ISCHEMIA* COME FROM A GREEK WORD. *ISKHEIN*, MEANING "TO RESTRICT."

A sudden stroke

A stroke is a sudden halt in the blood supply to some region of the brain. About 20 percent of strokes occur when a blood vessel bursts, causing a hemorrage. The vast majority are ischemic, occurring when a clot lodges in a blood vessel and blocks the flow of blood. Emergency treatment is crucial, because brain cells can only survive a few minutes without the oxygen that blood delivers.

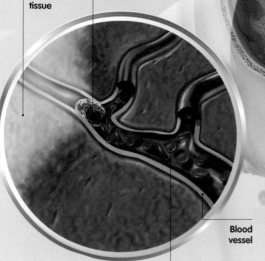

Ischemic tissue

Thrombus

Blood vessel

Blood cells

Clot-dissolving medication can help to restore the blood flow, if given in time, and limit any irreversible damage to the brain tissue.

Blood clots in the brain

Most ischemic strokes happen when a blood clot forms in the blood vessels of the brain. Called a thrombus, this clot may arise due to the build-up of fatty plaques in blood vessels—known as atherosclerosis—which encourages the formation of clots. Many of the clots originate in other parts of the bloodstream, most commonly in the atria (upper chambers) of the heart when the heart is beating irregularly in a condition known as atrial fibrillation.

Stroke: signs and symptoms

- Weakness in the face, with drooping on one side, and/or arms and/or legs (also typically one-sided)
- Problems with speech or other communication difficulties
- Loss or blurring of vision
- Numbness, usually on one side
- Dizziness and problems with balance or coordination
- Difficulty in swallowing
- An abrupt, severe headache
- Loss of consciousness, although this is less common

SENSORY SYSTEM

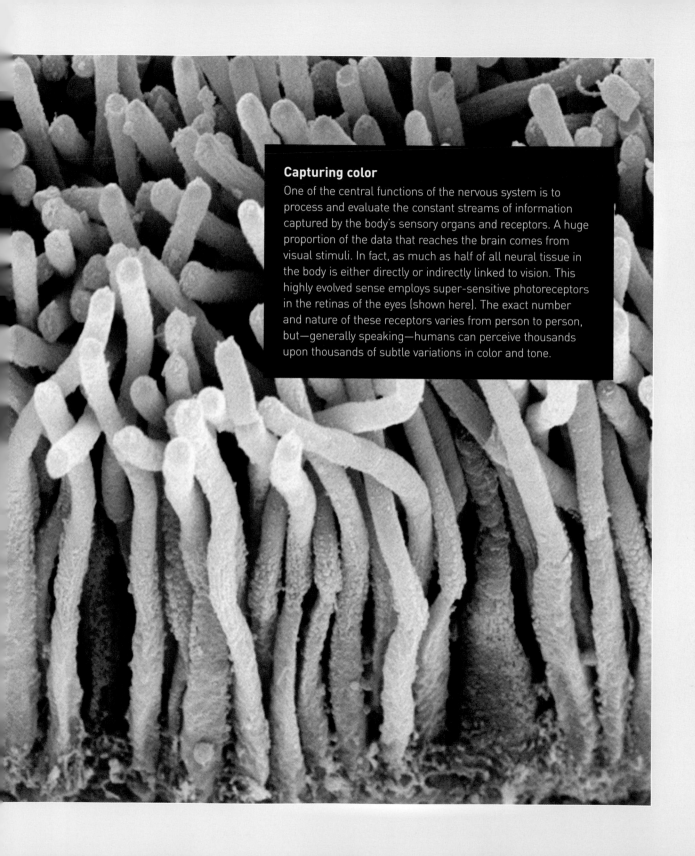

Capturing color

One of the central functions of the nervous system is to process and evaluate the constant streams of information captured by the body's sensory organs and receptors. A huge proportion of the data that reaches the brain comes from visual stimuli. In fact, as much as half of all neural tissue in the body is either directly or indirectly linked to vision. This highly evolved sense employs super-sensitive photoreceptors in the retinas of the eyes (shown here). The exact number and nature of these receptors varies from person to person, but—generally speaking—humans can perceive thousands upon thousands of subtle variations in color and tone.

BRAIN AND SENSING

The body's survival depends on a steady stream of sensory input into the central nervous system (CNS)—the brain and spinal cord. Sensory systems are crucial in allowing the CNS to receive, manage, and respond to changes within and outside of the body. The body's sensory apparatus includes millions of sensory receptors of varying complexity and arrangement. This complex, incredible system enables us to carry out everyday tasks such as playing the piano or writing a letter.

Perception and response

Sense receptors send nerve impulses speeding along sensory nerves to the brain. There, the specific processing center interprets the incoming signals. A person experiences a visual image of an apple, for example, when brain vision centers process signals from the optic nerves.

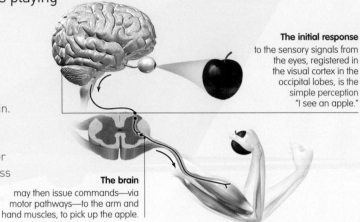

The initial response to the sensory signals from the eyes, registered in the visual cortex in the occipital lobes, is the simple perception "I see an apple."

The brain may then issue commands—via motor pathways—to the arm and hand muscles, to pick up the apple.

Cranial nerve	Nerve type	Functions
I. Olfactory nerve	Sensory	Smell (olfactory function).
II. Optic nerve	Sensory	Vision.
III. Oculomotor nerve	Primarily motor	Moves eyeball up, down, inward; raises eyelid; changes lens shape; constricts pupil.
IV. Trochlear nerve	Primarily motor	Moves eyeball.
V. Trigeminal nerve	Mixed	Sensory input about touch, temperature, and pain in the face, mouth, and scalp; movement of muscles of mastication (chewing).
VI. Abducens nerve	Primarily motor	Moves eye laterally (outward).
VII. Facial nerve	Mixed	Input from some taste buds; moves facial muscles; increases tear and saliva secretions.
VIII. Vestibulocochlear nerve	Sensory	Hearing and balance.
IX. Glossopharyngeal nerve	Mixed	Sensory input from the other taste buds; swallowing.
X. Vagus nerve	Mixed	Parasympathetic sensory innervation to various organs of the chest and abdomen; also involved in swallowing, heartbeat, breathing, and stomach secretions.
XI. Accessory nerve	Primarily motor	Moves some neck muscles and some pharynx muscles.
XII. Hypoglossal nerve	Primarily motor	Moves tongue muscles.

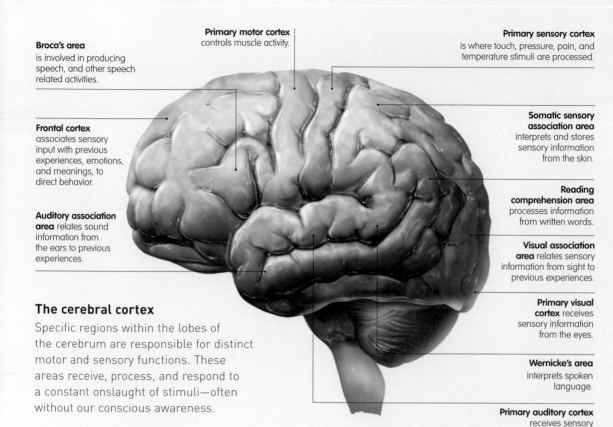

Broca's area
is involved in producing speech, and other speech related activities.

Primary motor cortex
controls muscle activity.

Primary sensory cortex
is where touch, pressure, pain, and temperature stimuli are processed.

Frontal cortex
associates sensory input with previous experiences, emotions, and meanings, to direct behavior.

Somatic sensory association area
interprets and stores sensory information from the skin.

Reading comprehension area
processes information from written words.

Auditory association area relates sound information from the ears to previous experiences.

Visual association area relates sensory information from sight to previous experiences.

Primary visual cortex receives sensory information from the eyes.

Wernicke's area
interprets spoken language.

Primary auditory cortex
receives sensory information about sounds from the ears.

The cerebral cortex

Specific regions within the lobes of the cerebrum are responsible for distinct motor and sensory functions. These areas receive, process, and respond to a constant onslaught of stimuli—often without our conscious awareness.

The cranial nerves

On the underside of the brain, twelve pairs of cranial nerves travel in from sensory organs, conveying signals into and out of the brain. Some, such as the optic nerve, carry only inputs from sensory receptors in the head. Most, however, carry a mix of sensory and motor signals. In addition to muscle contraction signals going out, these "mixed nerves" also convey information about the body's position, balance, and movements from signals coming in through receptors in the muscles (see pages 126–127).

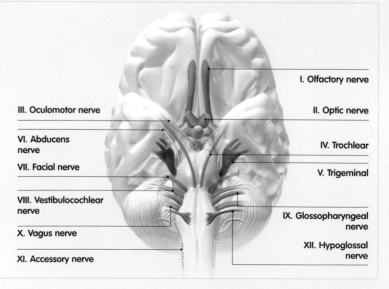

III. Oculomotor nerve

VI. Abducens nerve

VII. Facial nerve

VIII. Vestibulocochlear nerve

X. Vagus nerve

XI. Accessory nerve

I. Olfactory nerve

II. Optic nerve

IV. Trochlear

V. Trigeminal

IX. Glossopharyngeal nerve

XII. Hypoglossal nerve

THE SPECIAL SENSES

There are two categories of human senses. The "general senses" detect temperature, touch, pressure, and pain. Meanwhile, the "special senses" are associated with vision, hearing, smell, taste, and balance. Sensory receptors also fall into different groups, although all of them operate on the same principle. They detect a stimulus—such as light, mechanical pressure, or a stretching muscle—and convert it into a nerve impulse that speeds along sensory neurons to the CNS.

Different receptor groups

Exteroreceptors detect external stimuli such as touch, temperature, sound, and light. Interoreceptors detect stimuli that arise in the internal organs, such as blood pressure within the arteries. Proprioceptors—located mostly in muscles, tendons, joints, and ligaments—inform the brain about the body's position and movement.

Olfactory bulb
collects information from the olfactory nerves and is located on the underside of the brain. It transmits smell information from the nose to the brain.

Two eyes
are required for binocular vision.

Olfactory nerves
are associated with smelling.

Nasal cavity
contains two types of epithelial tissue. Olfactory epithelium aids the sense of smell, and respiratory epithelium acts as a protective surface.

Tongue
plays a major role in our ability to taste, as taste buds that are sensitive to chemicals from substances that dissolve in saliva, sit on its surface.

Taste cells
aid our understanding of what items we put into the body, and detect what may be good for us or harmful. The cells are organized into groups known as taste buds (shown here).

 STUDY THE UPPER AIRWAYS AND PASSAGES, AND THEIR ROLE IN BREATHING, ON *PAGES 194–195*.

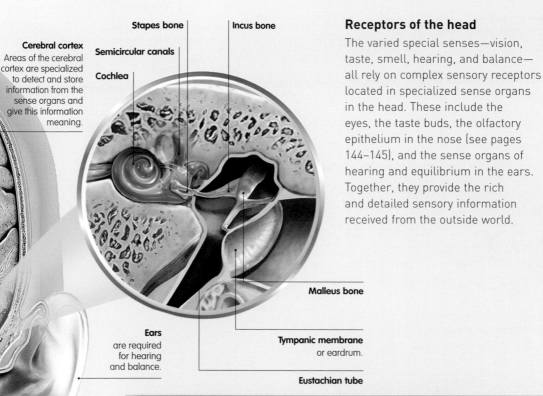

Cerebral cortex
Areas of the cerebral cortex are specialized to detect and store information from the sense organs and give this information meaning.

Stapes bone

Semicircular canals

Cochlea

Incus bone

Malleus bone

Ears
are required for hearing and balance.

Tympanic membrane
or eardrum.

Eustachian tube

Receptors of the head

The varied special senses—vision, taste, smell, hearing, and balance—all rely on complex sensory receptors located in specialized sense organs in the head. These include the eyes, the taste buds, the olfactory epithelium in the nose (see pages 144–145), and the sense organs of hearing and equilibrium in the ears. Together, they provide the rich and detailed sensory information received from the outside world.

COMBINED SENSING

Although we are most often aware of the general and special senses, there are a whole host of supporting senses that enable the body to function in response to internal bodily stimuli. Our nociception, for example, gives us a sensory awareness of tissue damage. Other senses work together or share information—such as when our vision, proprioception, and equilibrioception (see pages 136–137) combine to give us a sense of where our body parts are positioned and how they are balanced. Many of these sensory signals operate at a subconscious level.

THE EYE

The three-layered architecture of the eye is what makes sight possible. The outer layer includes the cornea and the white sclera—a tough, fibrous structure that protects the more delicate parts within. The middle layer includes blood vessels and muscles that move the lens, which focuses light onto the third, innermost layer at the back of the eyeball—the retina.

Fluids of the eye

A human eye is about one inch (2.5cm) in diameter. Tears moisten the cornea, while a watery fluid called aqueous humor lubricates both sides of the lens. Behind the lens is a glassy, jellylike tissue that fills the eyeball. This is known as the vitreous humor.

The curved cornea

Light rays strike the curved surface of the cornea at different angles. As they pass through the cornea the rays bend and come together at the back of the eyeball. These changes in trajectory cause the light rays to stimulate photoreceptors in a pattern that is reversed—right to left and upside down—relative to the source of the rays. Visual processing in the brain then corrects the orientation.

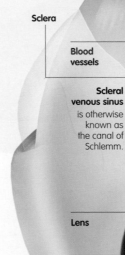

The retina
probably contains more than 125 million photoreceptors and support neurons. This number varies between individuals —some people have fewer red receptors.

Sclera

Blood vessels

Scleral venous sinus
is otherwise known as the canal of Schlemm.

Lens

Pupil

Iris

Cornea

This corneal strip
is a transparent piece of tissue that has been grown, in a lab, from stem cells removed from a human cornea. It can be used to replace a defective cornea.

THE TERM *RETINA* COMES FROM A LATIN WORD, *RETE*, MEANING "NET"—ALLUDING TO THE LIGHT-CATCHING NATURE OF THIS PART OF THE EYE.

Optic nerve
Signals from photoreceptors in the retina travel along nerve fibers into the optic nerve, which carries them to the visual processing area of the brain.

Lateral rectus
is one of the eye muscles housed inside the eye socket, or orbit.

Conjunctiva
is a mucous membrane that covers the surface of the eye, including the cornea. It also lines the inside of the eyelids.

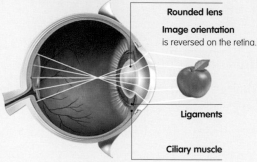

Ciliary muscle

Ligaments

DISTANT VISION

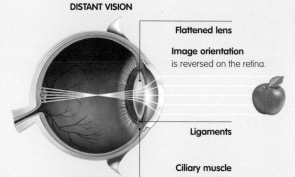

Flattened lens

Image orientation
is reversed on the retina.

Ligaments

Ciliary muscle

CLOSE VISION

Rounded lens

Image orientation
is reversed on the retina.

Ligaments

Ciliary muscle

Focusing images

Minute changes in the shape or position of the lens can focus visual stimuli onto the retina with great precision. A narrow ciliary muscle encircles each lens and is attached to it with ligaments. If light is initially focused behind the retina, the muscle contracts so that the lens bulges and the focal point moves forward. If the light is focused too far forward, the muscle relaxes and shifts the focal point farther back. These adjustments are known as "visual accommodation."

The unique iris

Smooth muscle fibers (see page 81) in the eye's iris radiate outward in a pattern that is unique to each person. This feature makes the iris an excellent personal identifier. Iris scanning is now used in some of today's security systems.

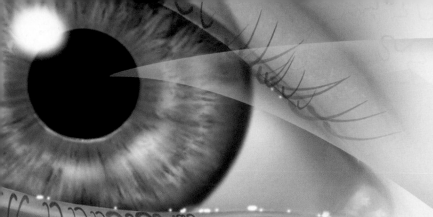

Photoreceptors
of the human retina, shown up
by a colored scanning electron
microscope (SEM) image.

VISUAL PROCESSING

Seeing is a complex process that requires chemical reactions to convert light into nerve impulses. The process begins in the photoreceptors of the retina, where photopigments intercept the light focused onto the retina by the lens. The light energy temporarily reconfigures these colored proteins, molding them into a new shape. The change quickly reverses, but it allows the neurons next to the photoreceptors to fire. This is where the process of visual perception truly begins.

Visual pigments

Without the visual pigments in rods and cones, the human eye would not be able to send impulses along the optic nerves. Each cone contains one of three pigments sensitive to blue, green, or red light. Rods contain the pigment rhodopsin (right), which absorbs the blue-green light wavelengths that are typical of dimly-lit environments.

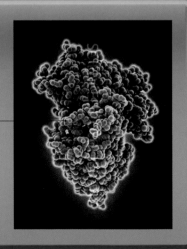

Rhodopsin molecule
is a combination of the proteins opsin and cis-retinal, a compound formed from vitamin A. This is why visual impairments—such as poor night vision—are sometimes the result of a vitamin A deficiency.

 ROD CELLS COVER APPROXIMATELY *94.5 PERCENT* OF THE RETINA'S SURFACE AREA, WHILE *CONE CELLS* OCCUPY THE REMAINING *5.5 PERCENT*.

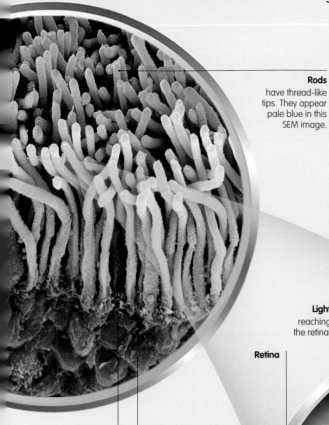

Rods
have thread-like tips. They appear pale blue in this SEM image.

Photoreceptors

Extremely sensitive to light, the photoreceptors in the retina consist of tapered "cone" cells that respond to bright light, and blunt-ended "rod" cells, which respond to dim light levels. Both types of photoreceptors contain photopigments, proteins that absorb different wavelengths, or colors, of light. This, ultimately, is what produces our color vision.

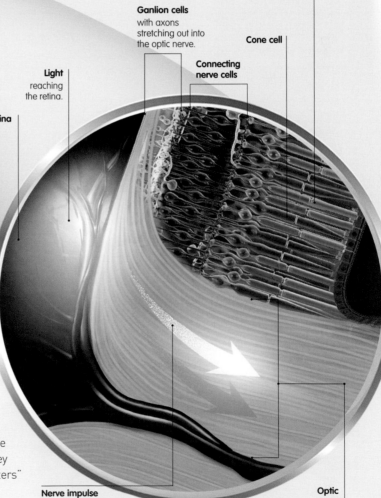

Rod cell

Ganlion cells
with axons stretching out into the optic nerve.

Cone cell

Connecting nerve cells

Light
reaching the retina.

Retina

Cones
have tapered tips. They are purple in the above image.

Outer nuclear layer
is brown in this image. The rounded structures are the cell bodies of rods, cones, and neurons.

Ganglion cells

Once the neurons at the back of the eye have fired up, the newly generated visual signals converge onto a number of other neurons called ganglion cells. The ganglion cells process the signals and then send nerve impulses speeding along their axons, which come together to form the optic nerve. This nerve delivers the signals to the primary visual cortex, but they swiftly move on to nearby "association centers" where the raw visual data is processed.

Nerve impulse
traveling to the brain.

Optic nerve

OPTICAL ILLUSIONS

Simple organisms, such as worms, are able to detect light—but human vision is a sophisticated sense that can determine the shape and position of visual stimuli, as well as their brightness, movement, and distance from the viewer, and gives them meaning. This versatility comes from different fields in the retina, where photoreceptors supply signals to various groups of impulse-firing neurons. Each group responds best to a specific category of stimuli: spots of light ringed with dark, hard-edged lines, motion, or some other attribute.

Confused images

Optical illusions result from the brain's efforts to sort confusing or unusual visual stimuli into its pre-programed categories and associations. The association centers try to make the visual input fit the patterns the brain commonly encounters. The resulting illusions may seem like a defect, but in fact they show exactly how resourceful the brain can be when it tries to resolve a visual problem.

Sorting sights

The brain's preset visual patterns include broad classes, such as "shadow," "sharp edge," and "tilted line." Many intriguing optical illusions exploit neurological processes geared to fit visual phenomena into one of these standard groupings. Neural processing also equalizes any perceived size differences between shapes that are close to each other, such as a circle inside a square (below).

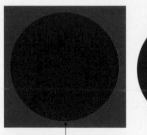

Assimilation
is the optical effect whereby the perceived difference between neighboring objects is reduced. The brain interprets each circle as being closer in size to its square than it really is. This is why the red circle on the left "appears" to be bigger.

A "peripheral drift"
illustration appears to rotate when the eyes take in the outer parts of the image, using peripheral vision. When the eyes focus on the central part of the illustration, the rotation effect ceases.

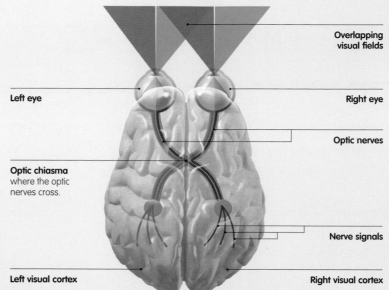

Overlapping
visual fields

Left eye

Right eye

Optic nerves

Optic chiasma
where the optic
nerves cross.

Nerve signals

Left visual cortex

Right visual cortex

Overlapping visual fields

Light is reversed as it passes through the lens of each eye (see pages 128–129), so signals from the left visual field are detected by the right side of the retina, and then transmitted to the right visual cortex in the brain—and vice versa. The two visual fields overlap greatly. The only "blind spot" that is encountered by our binocular (double-eye) vision is a small area blocked by the nose.

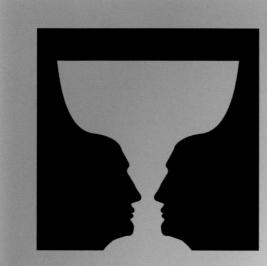

DIFFERENT INTERPRETATIONS
In this one image (above), the viewer may see hard-edged lines as either a goblet or two faces, which are both valid interpretations. When given the choice of different (yet equally possible) interpretations, the brain may continue to switch between the two.

CONTRASTING SIGNALS
This illusion (below), first noticed on the tiled wall of a cafeteria, shows contrasting black and white tiles. The tiles produce visual signals of contrasting intensity. The lines between the tiles are, in fact, perfectly parallel—but the brain's effort to manage the contrasting inputs makes them appear jagged and uneven.

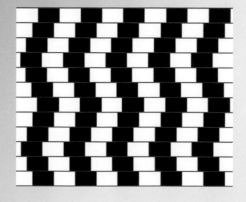

EYE DISORDERS

The most common and easily treatable eye conditions include myopia (short-sightedness), hypermetropia (long-sightedness), and astigmatism, in which the cornea is misshapen and does not bend light rays properly. Infectious eye diseases such as conjunctivitis affect millions. Other common eye problems—including glaucoma, cataracts, and macular degeneration—often develop as people get older.

Correcting vision problems

Myopia and hypermetropia can be corrected by adjusting how light rays are bent in the eye. Prescription eyeglasses and contact lenses are the simplest, least expensive strategies. For mild to moderate short-sightedness, an intracorneal ring (a removable plastic device) can be inserted to slightly flatten the cornea and focus light on the retina. In cases of extreme refractive defects, the lens may be replaced with an implant.

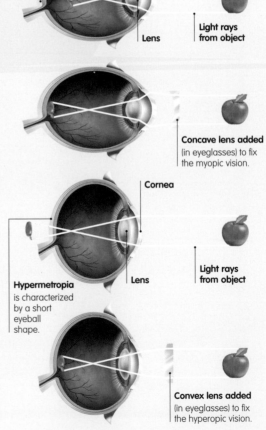

Myopia is characterized by a long eyeball shape.

Cornea

Lens

Light rays from object

Concave lens added (in eyeglasses) to fix the myopic vision.

Cornea

Hypermetropia is characterized by a short eyeball shape.

Lens

Light rays from object

Convex lens added (in eyeglasses) to fix the hyperopic vision.

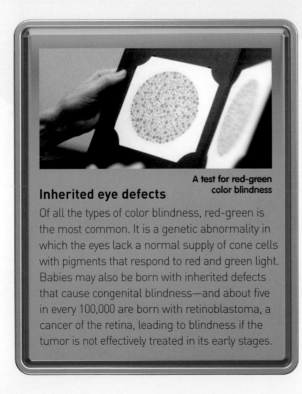

A test for red-green color blindness

Inherited eye defects

Of all the types of color blindness, red-green is the most common. It is a genetic abnormality in which the eyes lack a normal supply of cone cells with pigments that respond to red and green light. Babies may also be born with inherited defects that cause congenital blindness—and about five in every 100,000 are born with retinoblastoma, a cancer of the retina, leading to blindness if the tumor is not effectively treated in its early stages.

A RECENT STUDY OF MORE THAN *45,000 EUROPEANS AND ASIANS* HAS IDENTIFIED *24 GENES* THAT MAY BE INVOLVED IN TRIGGERING THE ONSET OF MYOPIA.

Laser correction surgery

Eye surgeons can use a tiny laser to reshape the cornea, to correct conditions such as myopia. In LASIK (laser in situ keratomileusis) surgery, instruments called "spreaders" hold the patient's eyelids open. After applying an anaesthetic, the physician performs the laser correction and monitors progress on a screen. Usually, only one eye is corrected at a time.

The LASIK correction procedure

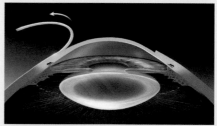

Phase One: a flap is cut into the cornea.

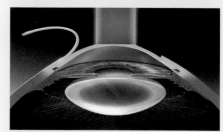

Phase Two: the exposed surface of the cornea is reshaped using an excimer ("excited molecule") laser.

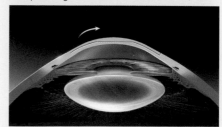

Phase Three: the flap of tissue is put back into place.

Cataract removal

The clouding of the lens, known as a cataract, causes progressive vision loss in millions of people—and is the major cause of vision loss worldwide. As well as aging, the most common causes are over-exposure to sunlight, eye injuries, tobacco use, and diabetes. Cataracts can be removed before they become severe, often using pulses of ultrasound to break up the clouded areas of the lens. The lens can also be replaced, surgically, or an intraocular lens can be implanted.

THE EAR

The ears detect sound waves and convert them into nerve impulses that travel to the auditory cortex in the brain. The ear's outer flap, the pinna, receives the sound waves and channels them into the middle ear—where tiny, interlocking bones amplify the wave energy and transfer it to a fluid-filled structure in the inner ear. Within this structure, the waves literally create a "ripple effect" that is the force behind hearing.

Sound waves

Hearing is the result of a biological domino effect. When you clap your hands, the air between them forms invisible sound waves. Speeding through the air at about 1,000ft (305m) per second, the waves provide the force that makes the inner ear fluid vibrate. Those vibrations set up pressure waves that bend the ear's sensory hairs (see page 139).

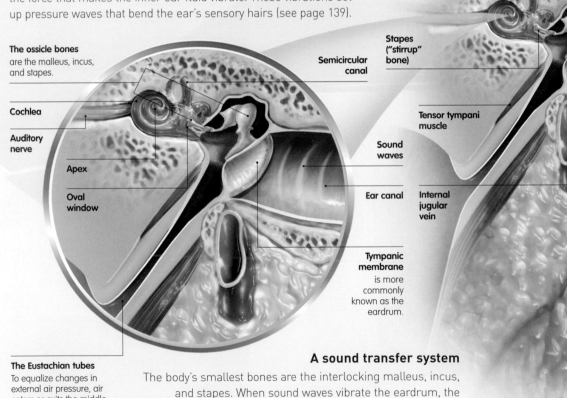

The ossicle bones are the malleus, incus, and stapes.

Cochlea

Auditory nerve

Apex

Oval window

Stapes ("stirrup" bone)

Semicircular canal

Tensor tympani muscle

Sound waves

Ear canal

Internal jugular vein

Tympanic membrane is more commonly known as the eardrum.

The Eustachian tubes To equalize changes in external air pressure, air enters or exits the middle ear—often with a sudden "pop"—via the Eustachian tubes, which lead to the upper throat.

A sound transfer system

The body's smallest bones are the interlocking malleus, incus, and stapes. When sound waves vibrate the eardrum, the malleus begins vibrating at the same frequency. Its motion transfers to the incus, the stapes, and finally to the "oval window," creating pressure waves in the cochlear fluid (see pages 138–139).

BARTOLOMEO EUSTACHIO (C. 1524–74) WAS A PIONEERING ITALIAN ANATOMIST WHO IDENTIFIED AND DESCRIBED THE *EUSTACHIAN TUBE*.

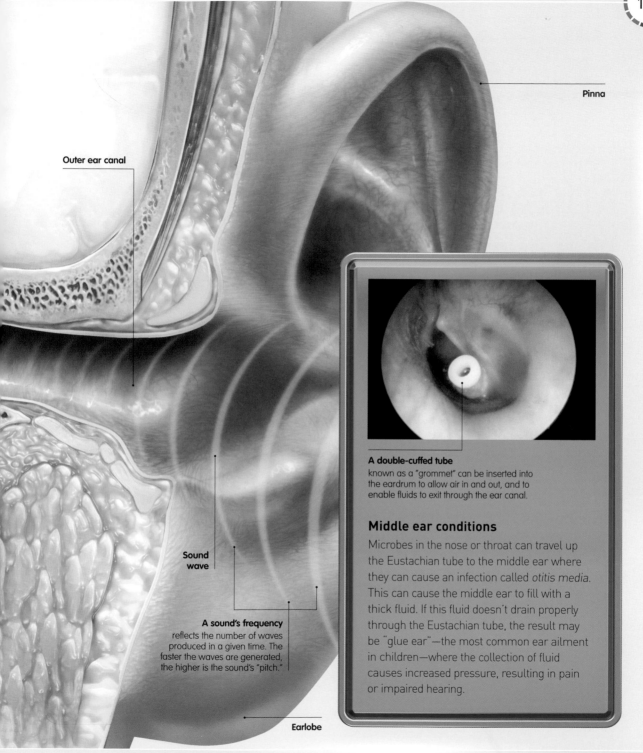

Pinna

Outer ear canal

Sound wave

A sound's frequency
reflects the number of waves
produced in a given time. The
faster the waves are generated,
the higher is the sound's "pitch."

Earlobe

A double-cuffed tube
known as a "grommet" can be inserted into
the eardrum to allow air in and out, and to
enable fluids to exit through the ear canal.

Middle ear conditions

Microbes in the nose or throat can travel up
the Eustachian tube to the middle ear where
they can cause an infection called *otitis media*.
This can cause the middle ear to fill with a
thick fluid. If this fluid doesn't drain properly
through the Eustachian tube, the result may
be "glue ear"—the most common ear ailment
in children—where the collection of fluid
causes increased pressure, resulting in pain
or impaired hearing.

AURAL PROCESSING

Once they have been transferred through the middle ear by the three small ossicle bones, sound waves reach the tiny, curling cochlea in the inner ear. Inside this spiral-shaped structure, the waves create vibrations in a membrane that presses on the ear's mechanoreceptors. These receptors are cells with delicate, hairlike structures—called stereocilia—sticking out from them. As incoming vibrations bend the stereocilia, the hairs generate volleys of nerve impulses that move to the brain via the cochlear nerve.

Cochlear nerve

COCHLEAR IMPLANTS

Special implants can provide hearing for people with deafness or serious aural impairment. A transmitter, attached to the scalp, passes sound signals to a receiver implanted below the skin of the scalp. Electrodes attached to the receiver run deep into the cochlea of the inner ear. This ensures that the sound signals stimulate the cochlea's sensory structures, enabling nerve impulses to reach the brain. Even if a person is profoundly deaf, such implants provide an awareness of sounds and speech, which makes lip-reading much easier.

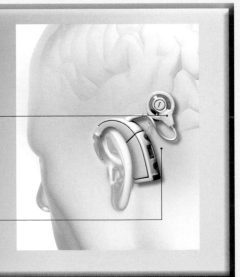

Transmitter

Receiver
is surgically implanted beneath the scalp layer.

 PRESBYCUSIS IS AGE-RELATED HEARING LOSS. MOST PEOPLE BEGIN TO LOSE A SMALL AMOUNT OF THEIR HEARING BETWEEN THE AGES OF 30 AND 40.

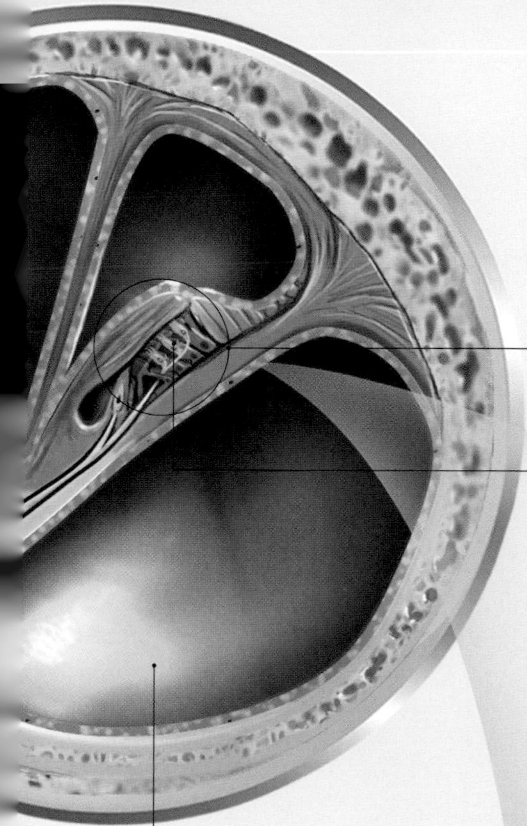

The ear's sensors

The coiled cochlea contains the ear's sound sensors—rows of hair cells in a ribbon of tissue called the organ of Corti.

Organ of Corti

Mechanoreceptors

Consistent vibrations

Although the vibrating cochlear fluid is the direct trigger for auditory signals, the vibrations physically track the nature and frequency of the original sound waves—so a person perceives sounds exactly as they were produced in air.

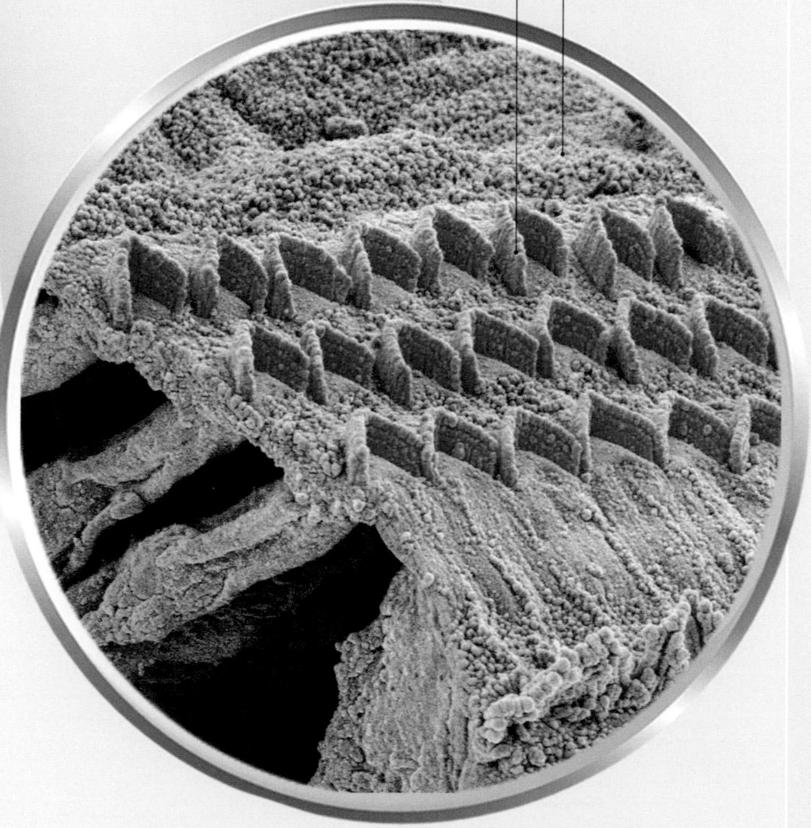

Hairlike stereocilia

Mechanoreceptor cells

Cochlear fluid

Stereocilia

The cochlea's 16,000 hair cells each have approximately 100 sterocilia protruding from them. When pressure waves traveling in the cochlear fluid bend the stereocilia, it stimulates a hair cell to fire nerve impulses. When the pressure ceases, the hairs straighten and the nerve impulses stop.

BALANCE

When standing up straight, the body's position feels stable—but when riding on a roller coaster the body instantly senses when the car drops sharply or achieves great speed. The sense of natural body position is known as equilibrioception—or simply as equilibrium, or balance. Our organs of equilibrium are located in the inner ear, in a system of fluid-filled sacs and looping channels called the vestibular apparatus.

The vestibular apparatus

In the structures of the apparatus, sensory hair cells register changes in the head's position. This includes linear movements, as in normal walking, and more complex motions that combine acceleration or deceleration with rotation, such as when twirling across a dance floor.

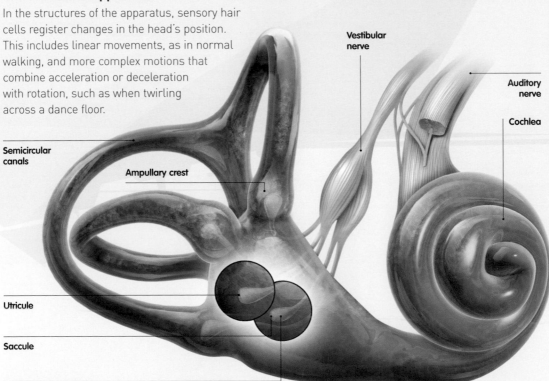

Vestibular nerve

Auditory nerve

Cochlea

Semicircular canals

Ampullary crest

Utricle

Saccule

Chambers in the sacs
contain otoliths, shards of calcium carbonate that slide when the head tilts, bending hair cells that trigger nerve impulses, that pass to the brain along the vestibular nerve.

Balance organs

The orientation of the semicircular canals corresponds to the three planes of space: height, width, and depth. Their hair cells respond to movement in fluid in the canals from the vertical or horizontal rotation of the head. Receptors in sacs called the utricle and saccule assess "static" equilibrium, the head's position relative to the ground (and the pull of gravity).

COCHLEA COMES FROM A LATIN WORD MEANING "SNAIL SHELL" OR "SCREW." IT DERIVES FROM A GREEK WORD, KOKHLIAS.

Combined inputs

As well as from the vestibular system, the brain gathers input from other sensory systems as it monitors the body's position. The eyes provide visual clues about the direction of movements, while proprioceptors in skeletal muscles, joints, tendons, and ligaments convey information about the degree of stretching in those tissues. This sensory feedback assists the brain in its task of maintaining equilibrium.

Complex balancing

Balancing on a surfboard challenges the brain to integrate an influx of sensory signals from the inner ear, eye, and muscle proprioceptors. The resulting muscle activity seeks to maintain upright posture despite the downward pull of gravity.

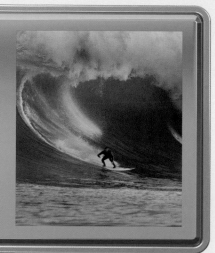

These four illustrations show the action of sensory hair cells in the vestibular apparatus—in response to different types of motion.

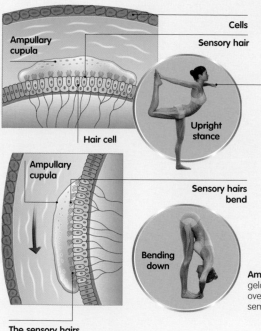

Ampullary cupula

Cells

Sensory hair

Hair cell

Upright stance

Ampullary cupula

Sensory hairs bend

Bending down

The sensory hairs in the vestibular apparatus resemble those in the cochlea (see page 139)—but here they contribute to automatic adjustments in skeletal muscle contractions, which maintain balance and equilibrium.

Proprioceptors are sensors in synovial joints, skeletal muscles, and connections between muscles and tendons. They include "muscle" spindles, which detect the length or "stretch" of the muscles, so that the brain can adjust muscle contractions to match the demands of the physical activity.

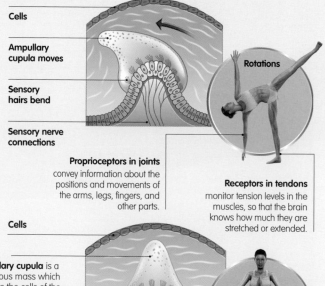

Cells

Ampullary cupula moves

Sensory hairs bend

Sensory nerve connections

Rotations

Proprioceptors in joints convey information about the positions and movements of the arms, legs, fingers, and other parts.

Receptors in tendons monitor tension levels in the muscles, so that the brain knows how much they are stretched or extended.

Cells

Ampullary cupula is a gelatinous mass which overlays the cells of the semicircular canals.

Sensory hairs

Stationary position

TASTING

Taste, or gustation, is one of the body's two "chemical" senses. Taste is the province of the estimated 10,000 taste buds clustered in different areas of the tongue's surface and scattered across the palate and throat. Within taste buds are chemoreceptors that are sensitive to chemicals from substances—such as those in our food—that dissolve in saliva.

Hard palate
The membrane covering this bony roof of the mouth also contains some taste receptors.

A sense for survival

This sensory ability has a survival value for humans. When a person first tastes or smells food, the digestive system increases its secretion of digestive enzymes required to break down ingested food and extract its nutrients. In addition, many toxic substances taste bitter—and spoiled food often has a distinctive flavor, which signals that it may be harmful.

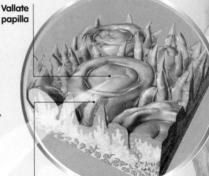

Vallate papilla

Conelike papillae

Vallate papillae

These raised, circular, fleshy areas are located at the back of the tongue. They contain clusters of taste buds.

Fungiform papillae
These mushroom-shaped papillae are located mainly on the tongue's sides and top.

Taste buds

Taste buds are mainly sited on the papillae (or tiny protrusions) of the tongue's surface—but they can also be scattered across other areas, such as the palate, pharynx, and epiglottis. No matter where they are located, taste buds always have the same structure.

Filiform papillae
Most tongue papillae are of this type. They do not contain any taste buds.

Categories of taste

Physiologists recognize five primary tastes: sweet, sour, salty, bitter, and umami—the savory taste associated with protein-rich foods, such as meat and pungent cheeses. Each category is associated with particular chemicals, such as the sodium that stimulates salt-sensitive receptors, and the sugars, amino acids, and alcohols that stimulate sweet-sensitive receptors. All of these chemoreceptors steadily wear out and are replaced.

SMELLING ASSISTS TASTING. WITHOUT THE SENSE OF SMELL, HUMANS WOULD FIND FOOD ABOUT 80 PERCENT LESS FLAVORSOME.

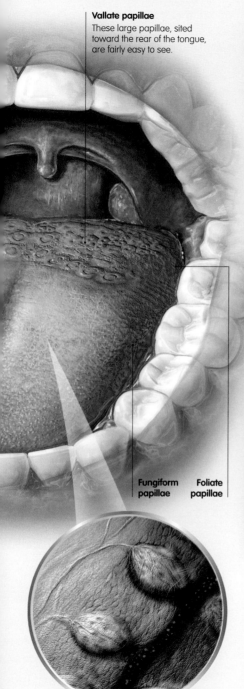

Vallate papillae
These large papillae, sited toward the rear of the tongue, are fairly easy to see.

Fungiform papillae **Foliate papillae**

Taste preferences

Research shows that individual taste preferences are shaped by genetic variations in taste bud receptors, and by the particular flavors people are exposed to during infancy and childhood. Those differences help to explain why some people prefer or strongly dislike certain foods or flavors.

Super-tasters

Our genes determine the capacity of taste receptors in taste buds to detect particular chemicals. People who inherit certain genes, especially those coding for bitter tastes, are especially sensitive to some substances. Common examples are PTC (phenylthiocarbamate), a chemical in cruciferous vegetables such as cabbage and broccoli, and naringin, a bitter-tasting component of grapefruit juice.

Chemoreceptors

Taste chemoreceptors, within the taste buds, are located on the papillae. Each papilla contains epithelial receptor cells that have taste-sensitive hairs (cellular structures) sticking out into a pore. Every week or so, new receptor cells replace the old ones. This renewal process slows with age, which may explain why some older adults perceive that certain foods have "lost their flavor."

SMELLING

Research suggests that humans can detect over a trillion different smells. We possess an estimated five million olfactory receptors of various types, that are sensitive to thousands of odor molecules. This diverse array of receptors may also be responsible for as much as 80 percent of the experience of taste. Perceived flavors are generally a blend of the five primary tastes (see page 142), the texture of food, and cues from odor molecules that make their way into the nasal passages.

The ancient art of sniffing

The action of sniffing objects and foods draws their odor molecules into the upper nasal passages more rapidly than they would arrive during normal breathing. This is another process that links us to our early ancestors and to other mammals. Early vertebrate animals of around 400 million years ago had brains with massive olfactory bulbs. This reflects the high survival value associated with a keen sense of smell.

Epithelial cells form the lining of the nasal cavity.

ANIMAL PHEROMONES

A pheromone is a distinctive chemical used to influence the behavior of other animals of the same species. Pheromone signals can be essential to locating a mate or communicating danger or the presence of food. In humans, pheromones could be linked to the synchronization of menstrual cycles among women living or working in the same place. They may also influence sexual attraction among humans.

Nasal cavity lining

This SEM image (above) shows the cells that line the nasal cavity. The lining also has cells that secrete moisture and mucus. The mucus traps bacteria, dust, and other particles—and prevents them from entering the lungs.

 THERE ARE AROUND 12 MILLION OLFACTORY RECEPTOR CELLS IN THE NASAL PASSAGES.

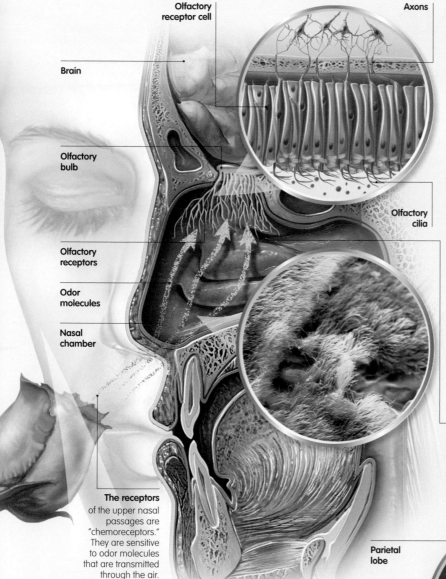

Olfactory receptor cell

Brain

Olfactory bulb

Olfactory receptors

Odor molecules

Nasal chamber

Axons

Olfactory cilia

Olfactory receptors

Olfactory receptors are specialized sensory neurons that can fire off nerve impulses directly to the brain. The signals travel along axons that pass through openings in the skull to reach the olfactory bulbs (extensions from the brain). The processing of these signals by the bulbs—signals received from millions of olfactory receptors—is what enables humans to distinguish between thousands of different odors.

Olfactory cilia

These tiny hairs, revealed by this SEM image (left), stick out from the dendrite of an olfactory receptor cell, protruding into the mucus covering the epithelium of the upper nasal passages. They collect chemical information from the circulating odor molecules (far left).

Mucus coating
in the olfactory epithelium becomes thicker than usual when a person develops a head cold. This reduces the contact between odor molecules and olfactory receptors, which can make food taste bland.

The receptors
of the upper nasal passages are "chemoreceptors." They are sensitive to odor molecules that are transmitted through the air.

Parietal lobe

The limbic system

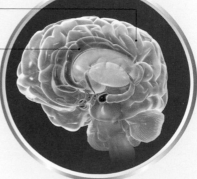

Odor processing

Signals related to both taste and smell are split when they reach the brain. Some taste signals are relayed to centers in the parietal lobe, while others travel to the "emotional brain" in the limbic system (see pages 114–115). Likewise, the processing in the olfactory bulbs provides our immediate perception of odors, but neural connections with the limbic system can link particular odors with lifelong memories and emotions.

TOUCHING

The somatic—or "body"—senses of touch, pressure, and vibration depend on receptors in and just below the skin and in the mucous membranes. Some of these sensors are free nerve endings, such as those that wrap around the base of a hair follicle and fire nerve impulses when something moves the hair shaft. Others are more elaborate mechanoreceptors, embedded in a capsule.

Detecting tactile differences

When "tactile receptors" are activated, the brain receives information about the location, shape, size, and texture of whatever has touched the skin. Such signals convey the tactile difference between, for example, a rubber ball in the hand and a drop of water dribbling down the arm.

Epidermis
is the uppermost skin layer. It is supplied with several types of free nerve endings.

Inflammation of the skin
is often caused by the release of chemicals such as the protein bradykinin, for example after a bug bite. Free nerve endings are sensitive to these stimuli, which cause itchy sensations.

Meissner's corpuscle
is a sensor attuned to light pressure and vibration. Hairless areas of skin usually contain this type of receptor.

Dermis
is the second layer of skin. It contains free nerve endings wrapped around hair follicles, as well as receptors that are sensitive to deep pressure and the stretching of the skin.

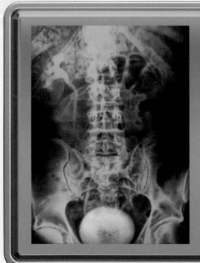

Internal sensations

Blood vessels and many internal organs contain interoceptors—sensors that respond to events below the body's surface—such as the stretching of tissue or a chemical change. Usually, the brain monitors these signals below the level of consciousness. However, interoceptor signals are sometimes felt as internal pressure or pain—for example, if the stomach is distended after a large meal or the bladder is stretched after filling with urine (left).

 THE HEAD AND HANDS CONTAIN THE GREATEST CONCENTRATION OF RECEPTORS THAT RESPOND TO HEAT.

Basal cell layer
is the lowest epidermal layer. Merkel disks are found here, which respond to light pressure.

Merkel disks
are flattened structures in the basal cell layer. They respond to sustained, light pressure.

Free nerve endings
are the exposed endings of sensory neurons that are stimulated by heat, cold, and pain. They also detect most of the stimuli responsible for itchy and tickly sensations.

Receptors in the dermis
are sensitive to thermal stimuli at 90–118°F (32–48°C). Receptors for stimuli of about 50–105°F (10–40°C) lie closer to the skin's surface. Colder temperatures activate pain sensors (see pages 148–149).

Pacinian corpuscle
is a type of sensor found in the dermis, the subcutaneous ligaments, and elsewhere. It is stimulated by rapid vibrations and deep pressure.

Ruffini's corpuscle
is a sensor located in the dermis and subcutaneous tissue. It detects deep, sustained pressure.

Subcutaneous layer
is also known as the hypodermis. It is a fat-rich layer that loosely anchors the skin to the underlying tissue.

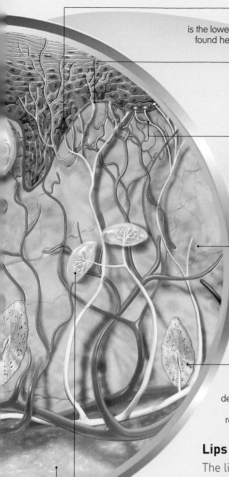

Sensory receptors

Various types of sensory receptors are distributed widely throughout the body—but familiar touch sensations rely on those in the skin's epidermis, the dermis below it, and even in subcutaneous tissue. Free nerve endings are the most common. The receptors depicted in this illustration (left)—such as the Ruffini's corpuscle—are not shown at their true scale.

Lips and tongue

The lips and tongue are sensitive to heat and cold as well as to pressure. Per unit of area, they have more free nerve endings and other sensory receptor types than any other part of the body.

Evolving receptors

Most tactile receptors adapt, either rapidly or slowly, and gradually become less sensitive to stimuli. The rapid adaptation of sensors that detect fine touch and skin pressure explains why people quickly become less aware of wearing eyeglasses or clothing.

SENSING PAIN

Pain is a natural warning of bodily damage, information that is crucial to avoiding or combatting injuries. For this reason, the body's pain detectors—millions of free nerve endings called nociceptors—are present everywhere except the brain. Nociceptors produce two general forms of pain. One of these is the sharp, "fast" pain—such as a pin prick—that is felt within a tenth of a second after damage occurs. The other is the aching or throbbing "slow" pain that takes longer to register—and lasts longer.

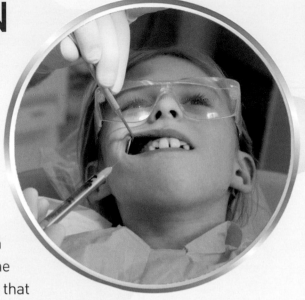

Dentists often use local anaesthetic to block sensation in a area of the mouth so that the patient doesn't feel pain.

The stimuli of pain

The prompt for pain signals may be an injury, the chafing or chemical irritation of a tissue, over-stretching, reduced blood flow, muscle spasm, or intense heat or cold. The affected cells release prostaglandins and other chemicals involved in inflammation.

Natural pain relief

The body produces several chemicals that help to make pain more bearable. These natural painkillers—endorphins and enkephalins—work by slowing down the release of a pain-signaling chemical called "substance P" in the brain. Endorphins also function in the brain's "pleasure responses" (see page 115), producing the euphoria some people experience during long bouts of exercise.

PAIN TOLERANCE

Everyone's pain receptors have the same sensory threshold—the stimulus intensity that triggers a nerve impulse. Individuals do differ, though, in their tolerance and ability to cope with pain. Cultural norms, emotional states, age, and other factors all shape our responses to painful episodes. When pain is prolonged, however, even a higher degree of tolerance fades.

SUBSTANCE P IS ASSOCIATED WITH THE TRANSMISSION OF PAIN AND OTHER NERVE IMPULSES.

FRONT VIEW OF BODY

REAR VIEW OF BODY

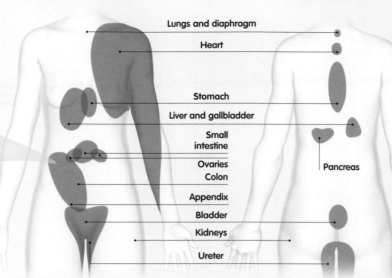

Lungs and diaphragm

Heart

Stomach

Liver and gallbladder

Small intestine

Ovaries

Colon

Appendix

Bladder

Kidneys

Ureter

Pancreas

Referred pain

A quirk of the body's pain signaling system causes "referred pain." This is where the brain associates pain sensations from an internal organ with a specific region of the skin. A good example is the pain from a heart attack, which is felt in the skin of the left arm or shoulder, or between the shoulder blades. Similarly, pain from the ovaries may be felt in the skin of the upper abdomen, and pain from the bladder is perceived in the skin of the buttocks.

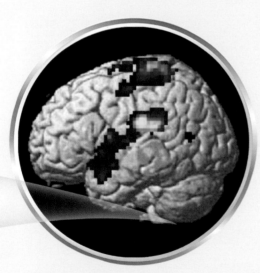

Central control of pain

The MRI scan above shows the areas of the brain that are activated (the red and yellow areas) in response to pain. Developments in research now mean that the intensity of pain can be measured and scientists can tell whether a drug is relieving it.

ACUPUNCTURE

The ancient Chinese practice of acupuncture employs slender needles to relieve pain by stimulating certain body "pressure points." The points correspond to different body organs and are situated along specific pathways, or channels. There are six primary "yin" and "yang" channels on each arm, and six on each leg.

CHAPTER SEVEN

ENDOCRINE SYSTEM

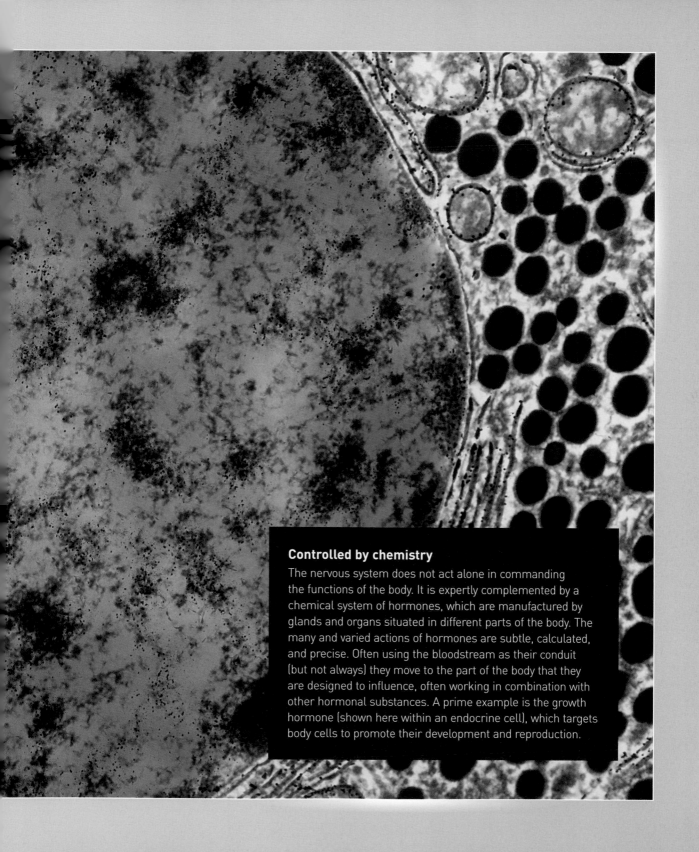

Controlled by chemistry

The nervous system does not act alone in commanding the functions of the body. It is expertly complemented by a chemical system of hormones, which are manufactured by glands and organs situated in different parts of the body. The many and varied actions of hormones are subtle, calculated, and precise. Often using the bloodstream as their conduit (but not always) they move to the part of the body that they are designed to influence, often working in combination with other hormonal substances. A prime example is the growth hormone (shown here within an endocrine cell), which targets body cells to promote their development and reproduction.

CHEMICAL MESSENGERS

Hormones are chemicals which are produced in one organ and travel through the body to work alongside the nervous system to control and adjust bodily functions. Organs and cells of the endocrine system—such as the pituitary gland, the thyroid, the ovaries, and testes—generate these substances. Often, several different hormones influence the same process, but, unlike the fleeting nature of nerve impulses, hormones usually act more slowly, and many move in the bloodstream to the site where they will act.

Hormone activity

Some hormones stimulate activity in "target cells" while others inhibit the activity. Proper body functioning requires a steady supply of certain hormones, some "on-demand" bursts from certain others—as well as cyclical spurts of other hormone types. The cyclical types include estrogen, which is a steroid sex hormone, and is present during the female menstrual cycle.

Hypothalamus gland

produces the most hormones of any endocrine gland. It is the endocrine system's master controller, as it releases hormones which control the release of hormones from other glands.

Pituitary gland

has two lobes. The anterior lobe produces several hormones, while the posterior lobe stores and releases two different hormones made by the hypothalamus.

Thyroid gland
creates three hormones that have major impacts on metabolism.

Targeting cells

A hormone is basically a chemical message that is "readable" only by the receptors on specific target cells. When the signal arrives it affects the target cell's internal operation—for example, body cells may begin to take up blood sugar, muscle cells may start dividing, or some other change might be launched in this ever-shifting internal landscape.

Feedback loops

Hormones are regulated by a "negative feedback" process. As target cells and tissues respond to a hormone, their activities change in ways that eventually reverse the triggering signal—so that the secretion of the hormone shuts down.

Thymus gland
is the main organ of the lymphatic system, and is active in young life. It produces the hormones necessary for the development of T lymphocytes, or T cells, that will operate in the immune system's defenses.

The stomach
contains cells that secrete hormones to aid the control of hunger and food digestion.

Ovaries
create hormones related to the reproductive characteristics and functions in females.

The heart
produces a hormone that helps to reduce blood pressure (see pages 166–167).

Adrenal glands
have outer and inner regions that produce different types of hormones. These include several steroids that have diverse roles in the body (see pages 164–165).

The kidneys
secrete hormones such as erythropoietin, which stimulates bone marrow to produce red blood cells.

The pancreas
contains cells that produce the hormones for adjusting blood sugar levels.

The small intestine
produces at least half a dozen hormones that regulate different aspects of food processing.

Vas deferens
is a duct that conveys sperm from the testes to the urethra (see page 263).

Epididymis
is a duct, behind the testis, that carries sperm to the vas deferens.

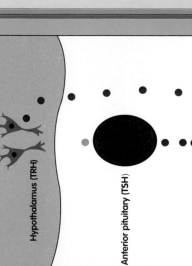

Hypothalamus (TRH)

Anterior pituitary (TSH)

Thyroid gland

The male testes

The testes produce the male sex hormones (primarily testosterone) that are necessary for sperm production (see pages 262–263).

Seminiferous tubules
are coiled tubes, which contain the cells that generate male sperm.

KEY ENDOCRINE GLANDS

Normal body growth, the day-to-day metabolic activities of cells, the development and functioning of the reproductive organs, bodily responses to stress—all of these processes depend on the two major glands of the endocrine system. They are the hypothalamus and its much smaller subsidiary, the pituitary gland.

The hypothalamus

The hypothalamus is a dual-purpose organ. Some of its neurons regulate specific bodily states—such as temperature, hunger, and thirst—that are vital for keeping our internal conditions constant and stable (a state known as homeostasis). Other hypothalamus neurons function in the endocrine system and produce hormones.

Hypothalamus is the main link between the endocrine and nervous systems.

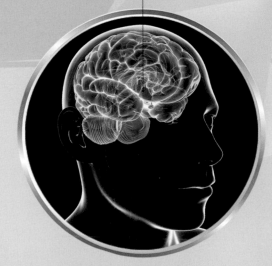

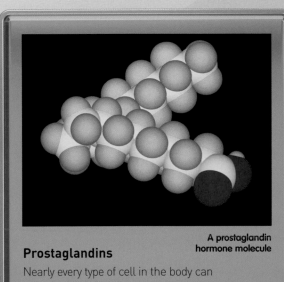

A prostaglandin hormone molecule

Prostaglandins

Nearly every type of cell in the body can manufacture the chemical messengers called prostaglandins. These are "local" messengers that act at or near the site where they are released. Their potent impacts include causing smooth muscle in blood vessels and the uterus to contract. This effect can be felt in the menstrual cramps experienced by women.

Controlling the pituitary

Among the chemical messengers created by hypothalamus neurons, there are several hormones that actively control the pituitary gland. The other hormones influence tissues elsewhere in the body, and are merely stored in the pituitary until they are secreted into the bloodstream to reach their particular destinations.

PROSTAGLANDINS PLAY A ROLE IN LABOR AND CHILDBIRTH. FIND OUT MORE ON *PAGES 272–273.*

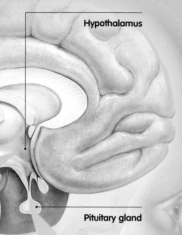

Hypothalamus

Pituitary gland

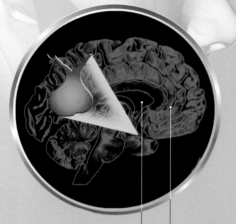

EXCESSIVE GROWTH

When too much growth hormone is secreted from the pituitary in adulthood, the result is acromegaly. This is a condition in which epithelial tissue in the skin, nose, tongue, and lips thickens abnormally. Bones, cartilage—and other connective tissues in the jaw, feet, and hands—are also affected in the same way.

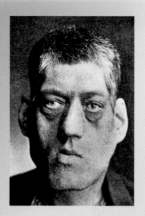

Forward, or anterior, lobe
is a true endocrine gland that produces six hormones, all of which have major effects on tissues and organs.

Rear, or posterior, lobe
of the pituitary houses the axons of hormone-secreting hypothalamus neurons.

The pituitary

This tiny gland is just half an inch (1cm), in diameter—roughly the size of a pea. It is located in a hollow of the sphenoid bone, which is part of the floor of the skull (see page 57). Networks of small arteries and veins transport hormones from the hypothalamus to the anterior part of the pituitary. These vessels also carry other hormones out of the pituitary and into the general circulation.

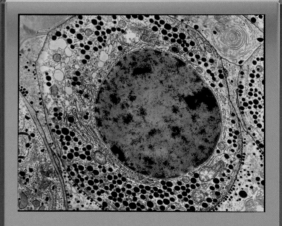

Growth hormone

This anterior pituitary cell has growth hormone (GH) stored inside its small vesicles (shown above in brown). As its name suggests, GH stimulates the growth of muscle, bones, and other tissues. In the young, GH targets the majority of body cells to promote development. It builds proteins and influences the use of sugars and proteins in the body's metabolism.

ENDOCRINE CONTROL CENTER

Linked by just a slender stalk, the hypothalamus and pituitary are located at the base of the brain and operate jointly as an endocrine command center. Regulator hormones from the hypothalamus govern the release of anterior pituitary hormones. The anterior pituitary's chemical messengers include growth hormones—which affects virtually all body cells—and hormones that stimulate other endocrine organs, such as the thyroid, adrenals, ovaries (in females), and testes (in males).

TSH
This anterior pituitary hormone is also known as thyrotropin. It stimulates the thyroid gland to release the hormones T3 and T4, which both play a role in growth and metabolism.

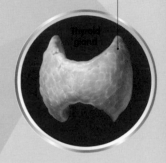

Hormones for "on" and "off"

Certain neurons in the hypothalamus, known as neurosecretory neurons, secrete hormones that strictly control the release of hormones from the anterior pituitary. "Releasing" hormones switch the anterior pituitary hormones on, while "inhibiting" hormones turn them off.

ACTH
This anterior pituitary hormone is otherwise known as corticotropin. It stimulates the cortex (outer region) of the adrenal glands to release adrenal steroid hormones.

BREASTFEEDING
Nursing an infant may seem like a simple process, but in fact it requires the interaction of two maternal hormones. Prolactin, from the pituitary gland, triggers the natural formation of milk in the female mammary glands, or breasts. Meanwhile, oxytocin, from the hypothalamus, stimulates the flow of milk into the ducts that open at the nipple.

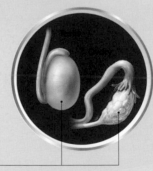

LH and FSH
Luteinizing hormone (LH) and the follicle-stimulating hormone (FSH) are known as "gonadotropins," because they stimulate the gonads—the male testes and female ovaries (see pages 260–263). They prompt these reproductive organs to form gametes, or eggs and sperm.

GO TO *PAGES 260–263* FOR MORE INFORMATION ON THE PRODUCTION OF MALE AND FEMALE *GAMETES* (GERMS CELLS).

HYPOTHALAMUS

Oxytocin and ADH

(antidiuretic hormone) are manufactured by neurons in the hypothalamus. They are released from the terminals of the neurons' axons, which are clustered together in the posterior pituitary.

ADH

Short for antidiuretic hormone, ADH targets the kidneys, causing them to conserve water in the body by producing more concentrated urine. This maintains the amount of fluid circulating in the blood..

Axons

extend from the thousands of neurons in the hypothalamus. The axons reach into the posterior lobe of the pituitary.

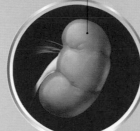

Kidney

Anterior pituitary lobe

Posterior pituitary lobe

Oxytocin

This is a hypothalamic hormone that triggers contractions of the uterus during the labor stages of childbirth. It also stimulates the "letdown" of milk in a mother's breasts.

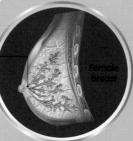

Female breast

Axon terminals

are where the hormones (created by hypothalamus neurons) are released.

Blood vessels

transmit the bloodstream in which hormones are carried to their target tissues through the body.

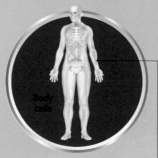

Body cells

Prolactin

A hormone that stimulates and sustains the production of breast milk in a lactating woman.

Growth hormone

Targeting most body cells, GH stimulates growth in the young. It builds proteins and influences the use of sugars ands proteins in metabolic processes.

Neurotransmission of pain signals

Endorphins

The body produces many types of endorphins which have hormonal effects, and also pain relieving effects, through the neurotransmission of pain signals. Beta-endorphins (the most powerful type) are primarily stored in the pituitary gland.

Female reproductive cycle

The ovaries produce the hormones estrogen and progesterone, which drive a monthly cycle of supplying eggs and preparing the uterus for a possible pregnancy.

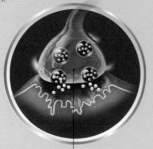

Female breast

THE THYROID

Few of the body's endocrine glands make hormones that influence cells and tissues throughout the body. One of these exceptional organs is the thyroid, a gland located below the shield-shaped thyroid cartilage of the larynx (the "Adam's apple"). Flaring out around the base of the trachea, the thyroid makes three hormones.

The thyroid hormones

Two of the hormones produced by this gland, triiodothyronine (T3) and thyroxine (T4), are jointly known as "thyroid hormone" (TH). Nearly every cell in the body has TH receptors—so, unlike most other hormones, TH affects the majority of body tissues, helping to regulate their metabolism, growth, and development. The third thyroid messenger is calcitonin. This hormone helps to maintain sufficient calcium in the blood for the processes that need it, such as muscle contraction.

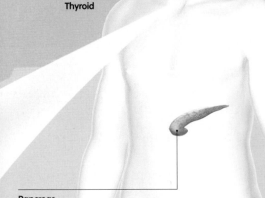

Thyroid

Pancreas

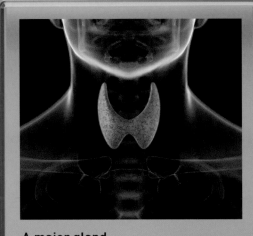

A major gland

The thyroid, highlighted here in relation to the front of the neck and larynx, is one of the body's largest endocrine glands. It has two lobes that connect in front of the trachea. These lobes contain numerous round, hollow sacs where cells produce the thyroid's three hormones.

Hormone functions (thyroid)	
Calcitonin	lowers the level of calcium in the blood.
Triiodothyronine (T3)	regulates (controls the rate of) the metabolism.
Thyroxine (T4)	stimulates the metabolism.

 NO APPLE IS MENTIONED IN THE BIBLICAL STORY OF *ADAM AND EVE*. THE TERM *ADAM'S APPLE* MAY DERIVE FROM A LATIN OR HEBREW DESCRIPTION.

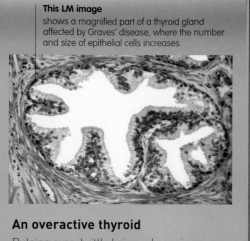

This LM image shows a magnified part of a thyroid gland affected by Graves' disease, where the number and size of epithelial cells increases.

An overactive thyroid

Bulging eyes, brittle hair, and a racing metabolism are the classic signs of Graves' disease, which is caused by an overactive thyroid. This relatively common disorder is normally classified as an autoimmune condition, in which antibodies of the immune system stimulate thyroid gland cells to generate a constant oversupply of TH. Radiation therapy or surgery can eliminate the malfunctioning tissue.

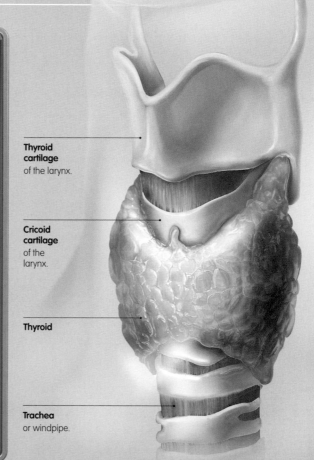

Thyroid cartilage of the larynx.

Cricoid cartilage of the larynx.

Thyroid

Trachea or windpipe.

AN ENLARGED THYROID

A goiter (right) is an extreme enlargement of the thyroid gland. A dietary deficiency of iodine may be the cause, but more often the growth is due to the failure of the thyroid to release TH in response to a stimulating hormone, TSH, from the pituitary (see page 156). Over time, continued stimulation by TSH causes the thyroid to enlarge to an excessive degree.

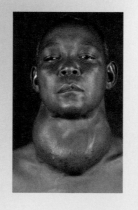

Metabolic control

Thyroid hormone (TH) is involved in many metabolic processes. It regulates our cells' use of blood sugar and oxygen to manufacture ATP, the chemical fuel that cells use to power their activities. It also adjusts body temperature by setting the "basal metabolic rate," or BMR. BMR is the amount of energy used to sustain our basic body operations. Without TH, virtually no major body system can function normally.

THE PARATHYROIDS

Like most other endocrine glands, the parathyroids respond to control signals from the pituitary gland. They consist of four tiny, bean-shaped masses of tissue—two of which are positioned on either side of the rear of the thyroid. Along with the thyroid, they contribute to a never-ending balancing act that helps to maintain the correct level of calcium in the blood.

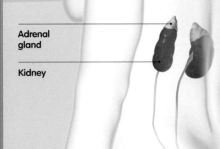

Pituitary gland

Thyroid gland

Parathyroids

Adrenal gland

Kidney

Bladder

Supplementing minerals

Nearly all body cells require a steady, blood-borne supply of calcium in order to function properly. The calcium consumed in a person's diet does not always meet this demand, which is why the PTH hormone is required to trigger the process of breaking down, or "digesting," the bone matrix to release supplementary minerals. These minerals also include phosphate, which is required for the growth and repair of cells.

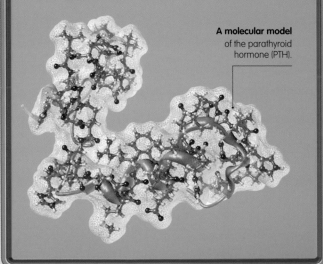

A molecular model of the parathyroid hormone (PTH).

SOMATOSTATIN IS A HORMONE THAT INHIBITS THE RELEASE OR ACTIVITY OF OTHER PANCREATIC AND GASTROINTESTINAL HORMONES.

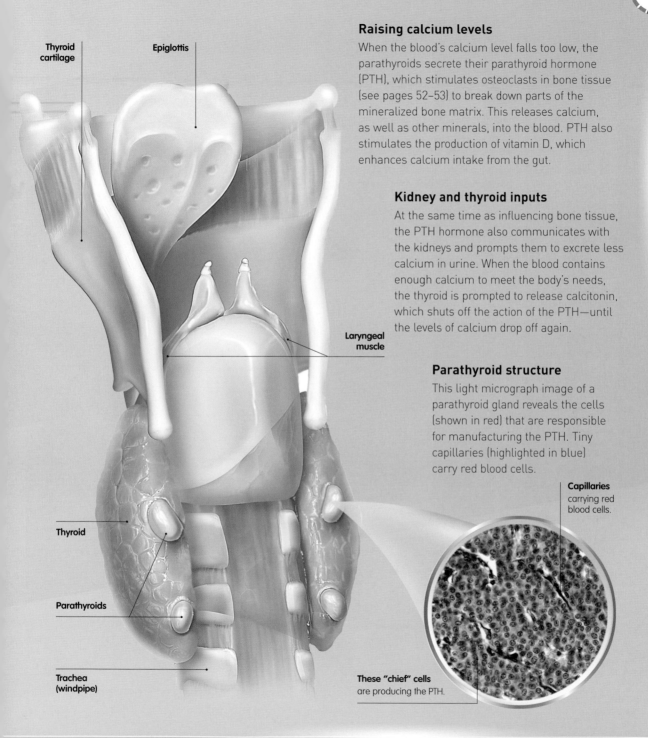

Thyroid cartilage

Epiglottis

Laryngeal muscle

Thyroid

Parathyroids

Trachea (windpipe)

Capillaries carrying red blood cells.

These "chief" cells are producing the PTH.

Raising calcium levels

When the blood's calcium level falls too low, the parathyroids secrete their parathyroid hormone (PTH), which stimulates osteoclasts in bone tissue (see pages 52–53) to break down parts of the mineralized bone matrix. This releases calcium, as well as other minerals, into the blood. PTH also stimulates the production of vitamin D, which enhances calcium intake from the gut.

Kidney and thyroid inputs

At the same time as influencing bone tissue, the PTH hormone also communicates with the kidneys and prompts them to excrete less calcium in urine. When the blood contains enough calcium to meet the body's needs, the thyroid is prompted to release calcitonin, which shuts off the action of the PTH—until the levels of calcium drop off again.

Parathyroid structure

This light micrograph image of a parathyroid gland reveals the cells (shown in red) that are responsible for manufacturing the PTH. Tiny capillaries (highlighted in blue) carry red blood cells.

THE PANCREAS

The pancreas is a large, finger-shaped gland sited behind the stomach. Much of its role is connected with the creation and secretion of enzymes used in food digestion, but it also contains small "islets" of hormone-producing cells. These cells generate three important hormones—insulin, glucagon, and somatostatin—which collectively manage the body's ever-shifting supply of blood sugar. They also produce VIP, gastrin, and ghrelin.

Raising blood sugar

When the levels of glucose (a sugar) in the blood fall below a certain point, alpha cells in pancreatic islets create the hormone glucagon. Glucagon then acts, in the liver and muscles, to make glucose from a storage compound called glycogen.

Lowering blood sugar

When the blood's glucose levels are high, beta cells in the islets secrete insulin, which stimulates body cells to take up more sugar from the bloodstream. A third group of islet cells, called delta cells, secrete the hormone somatostatin. Somatostatin adjusts the activity of the alpha and beta cells, as required.

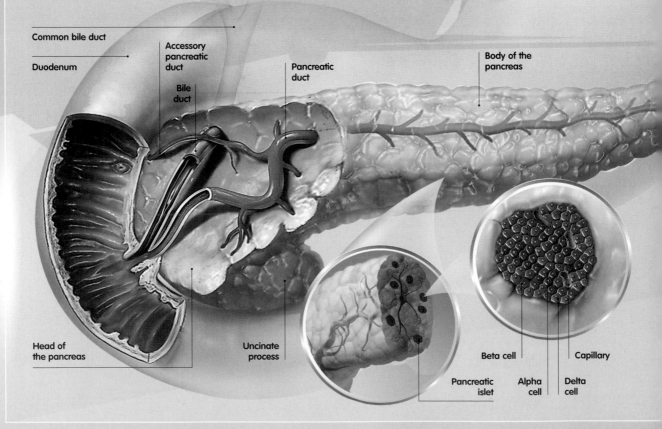

Common bile duct

Duodenum

Accessory pancreatic duct

Bile duct

Pancreatic duct

Body of the pancreas

Head of the pancreas

Uncinate process

Beta cell

Capillary

Pancreatic islet

Alpha cell

Delta cell

SEE THE FULL PROCESS OF URINE FORMATION ON *PAGE 248*.

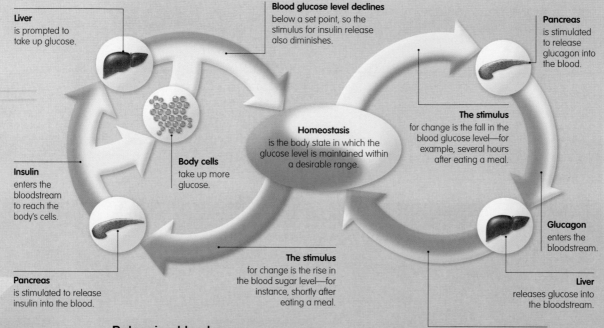

Liver
is prompted to take up glucose.

Blood glucose level declines
below a set point, so the stimulus for insulin release also diminishes.

Pancreas
is stimulated to release glucagon into the blood.

Homeostasis
is the body state in which the glucose level is maintained within a desirable range.

The stimulus
for change is the fall in the blood glucose level—for example, several hours after eating a meal.

Body cells
take up more glucose.

Insulin
enters the bloodstream to reach the body's cells.

Glucagon
enters the bloodstream.

Pancreas
is stimulated to release insulin into the blood.

The stimulus
for change is the rise in the blood sugar level—for instance, shortly after eating a meal.

Liver
releases glucose into the bloodstream.

Blood glucose level rises
above a certain point, so the stimulus for releasing glucose also diminishes.

Tail of the pancreas

Balancing blood sugar

So, insulin lowers blood sugar and glucagon increases it. Together these hormones interact to keep blood glucose levels within a normal range. This balancing act plays a role in weight control and maintaining overall health. It is especially crucial for the brain to have steady access to adequate blood glucose, which is the only fuel that brain cells can use.

Hormone functions (pancreas)
Insulin Promotes the cellular uptake of glucose, which lowers blood sugar levels.
Glucagon Helps to keep the amount of glucose in the blood at a set point by raising blood sugar levels.
Somatostatin Regulates the alpha and beta cells of the pancreatic islets.

INSULIN ACTIVITY

Once they have been created and released, molecules of insulin bind to specific receptor molecules on the cell surface. This triggers the process of transporting the glucose from food across the cell wall, for use as either a source of energy or for storage. Insulin can also be produced artificially and used to treat patients with type 1 diabetes (see pages 172–173).

THE ADRENAL GLANDS

The two adrenal glands, located just above each kidney, also take their orders from the pituitary. They produce several hormones, including steroids that help to maintain blood pressure, adjust the use of fuel molecules in metabolism, and influence the reproductive and sexual functions. Other adrenal hormones prepare the body for coping with stress.

Adrenal gland

Kidney

Structure of the adrenals

Each adrenal gland has an inner medulla and a thick, outer cortex that produces several steroid hormones. Glucocorticoids, including cortisol, regulate the use of proteins and fat in metabolism, help the liver to store excess glucose—as glycogen—and dampen inflammation. Aldosterone, which is a "mineralocorticoid" steroid, helps to regulate blood pressure.

Bladder

THE FIGHT-OR-FLIGHT RESPONSE

When danger looms, the nervous system commands the two adrenal medullas to pump out epinephrine, also known as adrenaline, and norepinephrine. These hormones jointly trigger our "fight-or-flight" reaction—experienced as quicker breathing and an accelerating heartbeat—that primes the body to respond quickly and do whatever the emergency situation demands.

Hormone functions (adrenal)
Aldosterone
RELEASED FROM: Adrenal cortex
FUNCTION: Helps to conserve water for maintaining blood volume and pressure.
Cortisol
RELEASED FROM: Adrenal cortex
FUNCTION: Regulates the use of proteins, fats, carbohydrates, and some minerals.
Epinephrine and norepinephrine
RELEASED FROM: Adrenal medulla
FUNCTION: The hormones elevate heart rate and blood pressure, to help sustain a fight-or-flight response.
Androgens
RELEASED FROM: Adrenal cortex
FUNCTION: Influence sperm production in males and ovulation and menstruation in females.

Medulla
Much smaller than the cortex, the adrenal medulla contains cells that release the fight-or-flight hormones epinephrine and norepinephrine.

Vein

Artery

Adrenal cortex

Secretory cells
in the "zona fasciculata" (inner) region of the adrenal cortex produce hormones such as cortisol.

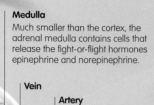

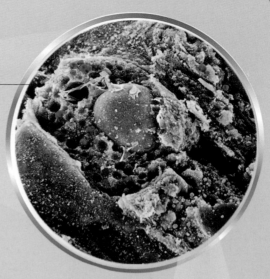

Kidney

Adrenal gland

The adrenal cortex

The cortex releases several hormones, including cortisol and aldosterone. It also secretes the androgens that influence the male testes and female ovaries. The cortex androgen DHEA (dehydroepiandrosterone) is active during the fetal development of the reproductive organs. Later on in life, it is also a building block for estrogen, which is secreted by the ovaries in females, and also contributes to a small amount of the testosterone in men.

Adrenal crisis

A sudden loss of the hormones produced by the adrenal gland, particularly cortisol, can result in dangerously low blood pressure and low blood sugar levels. A cortisol deficiency can hinder the storage of glucose reserves and lead to hypoglycemia, in which the sufferer has abnormally low blood sugar. The image (right) shows a patient suffering from this.

OTHER HORMONE PRODUCERS

In the body, chemical communication is a well-honed tool. In addition to familiar hormone sources—such as the hypothalamus, pituitary, thyroid gland, and reproductive organs—numerous other glands and scattered patches of tissue produce hormones. These pages show some examples of such structures and the roles they play.

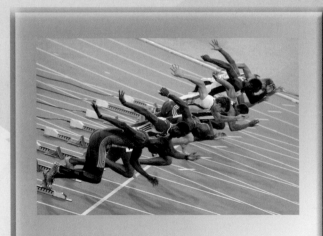

The skin
acts like an endocrine gland when it makes cholecalciferol, a precursor of vitamin D, and then releases it into the bloodstream.

Gut hormones

There are specialized cells in the digestive tract that secrete hormones that stimulate the release of digestive juices, or which have roles in adjusting appetite. Leptin (below) is a protein produced by adipose (fat) tissue. It reports to receptors in the hypothalamus to signal when a person is full. It also assists the brain in regulating appetite and metabolism.

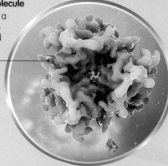

Leptin molecule
shown as a computer-generated artwork.

ERYTHROPOIETIN

The kidneys make the hormone erythropoietin, or EPO, which the bone marrow uses to produce new red blood cells. Some athletes have been known to cheat by "blood doping," which involves withdrawing and storing a quantity of their own blood—and then re-injecting it after their EPO has generated replacement cells. This process increases the amount of oxygen in the bloodstream.

FIND OUT WHICH OTHER SUBSTANCES ARE MANUFACTURED BY THE KIDNEYS ON *PAGE 244*.

The biological clock

Melatonin is sometimes known as the "jet lag" hormone. It is produced by the tiny pineal gland—the organ located between the two hemispheres of the brain—when the environment around us gets darker. The hormone helps to induce the state of sleep, playing a key role in the body's biological clock.

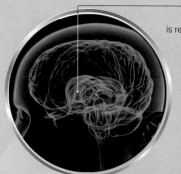

Melatonin
is released by the pineal gland.

A heart hormone

An increase in levels of water (and other substances) in blood plasma can dangerously elevate blood pressure. As the volume of blood rises, the wall of the left atrium stretches. Endocrine cells in the atria respond by secreting atrial natriuretic peptide (ANP). Carried in the blood to the kidneys, ANP promotes the removal of the excess water, which is then excreted in urine.

A molecular model
of atrial natriuretic peptide (ANP).

Pineal gland

Pituitary gland

Hypothalamus

T cell

Thyroid gland

Parathyroids

The renin-angiotensin system

When the flow of blood into the kidney is low, for example if blood pressure is low or there is less fluid in the circulation, specialized cells in the kidney release an enzyme called renin. This starts a process in which angiotensinogen (released by the liver) is changed into the hormone angiotensin I. Another enzyme, from the lungs, converts angiotensin I into angiotensin II, a hormone that causes blood vessels to constrict and increase blood pressure.

left atrium

Right atrium

Heart

Angiotensin II
also triggers the release of the hormone aldosterone from the adrenal cortex. Aldosterone prompts the kidneys to increase the reabsorption of sodium and water into the blood, to increase its volume and pressure.

Pancreas

Adrenal gland

Kidney

HORMONES AND HUNGER

Hunger is a drive to eat in order to replenish the body's declining energy stores. Appetite adds another dimension to this biological basic—it involves a desire to eat because doing so brings pleasure. The nervous system helps to control food intake, just as it assists other life processes. More surprising, perhaps, is that hormones also play a major part in regulating our eating behavior.

Signaling hunger

The bloodstream carries hormones produced in the digestive tract, or by fat cells, to receptors in the hypothalamus. Some of these signals promote intake when blood sugar declines, while others reduce the desire to eat when the person has consumed enough to satisfy their metabolic needs.

Hormones and appetite

Chemical messages from endocrine cells in the stomach, and elsewhere, profoundly influence an appetite-regulating center in the hypothalamus. As these substances bind to receptors in this part of the brain, the hypothalamus sets off nerves impulses designed to trigger sensations of hunger or satiety.

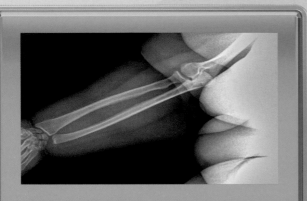

Understanding obesity

Obesity is an unhealthy excess of body fat. Most often the issue is a metabolic imbalance caused by consuming much more food than the body can use for energy. Some, however, struggle with unwanted weight due to genetic or hormonal factors which can leave them more likely to develop obesity than others. The World Health Organization has declared obesity to be a major global health crisis, with links to diabetes, heart disease, and some cancers.

Storing fat

Wrapped in a mesh of connective tissue, these human fat cells (above) are genetically programmed to take up and store excess blood sugar as fat that can be used if other energy supplies run low. Fat cells can expand or shrivel as fat is either added or used.

ACCORDING TO THE WORLD HEALTH ORGANIZATION (WHO), *AT LEAST 2.8 MILLION PEOPLE* DIE EACH YEAR DUE TO BEING OVERWEIGHT OR OBESE.

Hypothalamus

The hypothalamus also exchanges eating-related neural signals with both the limbic system and the cerebral cortex. As a result, neural signals associated with depression or stress also affect the hypothalamus—and may greatly reduce a person's appetite.

Brain

EMOTIONAL EATING

Most people occasionally indulge in "emotional" eating—consuming food to dampen boredom, stress, loneliness, anger, or some other feeling. Eating for comfort, rather than to satisfy hunger, is an impulsive behavior—and often the eater will crave a particular food item. Chocolate, for example, is among the foods that contain chemicals with mood-elevating effects on the brain.

Leptin

This hormone also suppresses the desire to eat. It is produced, over time, by fat cells in the adipose tissue—as they fill with fat.

PYY

An appetite-suppressing hormone that is released from some of the cells in the small intestine while a meal is being digested.

Insulin

Secreted by the pancreas after a meal, insulin acts on the hypothalamus to suppress appetite.

Ghrelin

Even the sight of food triggers a rise in ghrelin, a hormone produced in various sites including the kidney, pituitary, and pancreas.

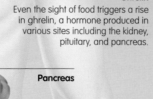

Stomach

Liver

Pancreas

Kidney

Small intestine

Large intestine

Blueberries

Responding to outside stimuli

Certain visual signals can trigger an increase in appetite. Presented with a food-laden buffet, or a bustling social event, people tend to eat more no matter how hungry they are. Other signals can decrease appetite. The color blue is an appetite suppressant. Very few foods are naturally blue—and, as a result, we have no automatic response to blue-colored food.

ENDOCRINE DISORDERS

Endocrine glands produce tiny quantities of hormones in short, intricately timed bursts. Often, several hormones must interact in some way to produce a certain effect. Several key endocrine organs—such as the thyroid, the adrenals, and the reproductive organs—are themselves regulated by the overarching control of hormones from the pituitary and hypothalamus. Usually, these processes keep hormones in balance, preventing too much or too little of any hormone from circulating. If some factor disrupts the controls, the result may affect the workings of tissues and organs, or cause an abnormal change in body form.

Altered body processes

Some of the most common endocrine disorders involve altered body growth or metabolism due to malfunctions of the pituitary or the thyroid. Often, the physical impacts are wide-ranging, because cells in many types of tissues respond to the hormones that these glands release. In some cases, the underlying problem is an autoimmune disorder in which the immune system attacks endocrine cells or otherwise interferes with their functioning.

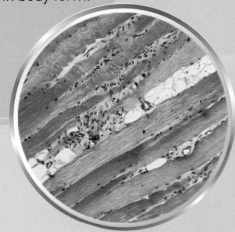

GIGANTISM

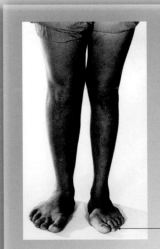

The condition known as pituitary gigantism develops when the long bones grow excessively during childhood, because the anterior pituitary produces too much growth hormone. An affected person may grow as tall as 8ft (2.4m). The condition of acromegaly leads to the excess growth of body tissues over time, and is usually caused by a pituitary adenoma (a benign brain tumor).

Gigantism of the feet

Cushing's disease

This image (above) shows muscle tissue damaged by excess cortisol. This and other symptoms, such as fat deposits in the trunk and face, develop when the adrenal cortex (see page 165) overproduces cortisol. The root cause may be a pituitary tumor that boosts the output of ACTH, a hormone that controls cortisol release.

 CORTISOL, OR HYDROCORTISONE, IS A STEROID HORMONE THAT CAN BE USED TO TREAT INFLAMMATORY SKIN CONDITIONS SUCH AS ECZEMA.

DWARFISM

In pituitary dwarfism, the long bones grow unusually slowly. The maximum height of somebody affected by this disorder is around 4ft (1.2m). As with pituitary gigantism, people with this condition tend to have normal body proportions.

Many endocrine-related conditions
are treatable with replacement hormones or other therapeutic drugs—or by surgery to remove all or part of the diseased gland.

Pituitary gland
Pituitary tumors can lead to conditions such as acromegaly, gigantism, and dwarfism.

Thyroid gland
The thyroid can become overactive (hyperthyroidism) or underactive (hypothyroidism).

Parathyroid gland
Hyperparathyroidism is a rare disorder affecting this gland.

Adrenal gland
Adrenal disorders include Addison's disease, Cushing's disease, and hyperaldosteronism.

Endocrine disorders

DISEASE: Acromegaly (see page 155)

DESCRIPTION: A tumor in the pituitary gland increases growth hormone.

SYMPTOMS INCLUDE: Enlarged body parts, such as hands, feet, jaw, and lips.

DISEASE: Addison's disease

DESCRIPTION: The adrenal glands do not produce enough cortisol. Aldosterone production also fails.

SYMPTOMS INCLUDE: Weight loss, fatigue, muscle weakness, and low blood pressure.

DISEASE: Goiter (see page 159)

DESCRIPTION: The thyroid fails to release the TH hormone in response to a stimulating hormone, TSH, from the pituitary. Iodine deficiency can also interfere with TH production.

SYMPTOMS INCLUDE: An extreme enlargement of the thyroid gland in the neck.

DISEASE: Graves' disease (see page 159)

DESCRIPTION: An autoimmune condition in which antibodies of the immune system prompt the cells of the thyroid to overproduce the TH hormone.

SYMPTOMS INCLUDE: Bulging eyes, brittle hair, and an overactive metabolism.

DISEASE: Hyperaldosteronism

DESCRIPTION: The adrenals overproduce aldosterone. Abnormality of salts in the blood.

SYMPTOMS INCLUDE: Fluid retention, high blood pressure, weakness, and muscle spasms.

DISEASE: Hyperparathyroidism

DESCRIPTION: A rare condition in which the parathyroid glands secrete too much PTH (parathyroid hormone).

SYMPTOMS INCLUDE: Fatigue, bone loss, and osteoporosis.

DISEASE: Hyperthyroidism

DESCRIPTION: A raised level of TH (thyroid hormone), often as a result of Graves' disease.

SYMPTOMS INCLUDE: Restlessness, hand tremors, weight loss (despite increased appetite), heart palpitations, sweating, increased thirst, menstrual changes, tiredness, muscle weakness.

DISEASE: Hypothyroidism

DESCRIPTION: An underactive thyroid gland fails to produce enough TH.

SYMPTOMS INCLUDE: Tiredness, weight gain, fluid retention, constipation, aches, dry skin and hair, depression.

DISEASE: Prolactinoma

DESCRIPTION: Pituitary tumor leads to excess prolactin (see pages 156–157), the hormone that stimulates the production of breast milk in females.

SYMPTOMS INCLUDE: Abnormal lactation, infertility, headaches, and decreased sexual interest.

DIABETES

Diabetes mellitus is one of the most common and serious endocrine disorders. In diabetes, tissues and cells throughout the body cannot correctly process glucose (sugar). If the condition is not controlled, it can lead to acute life-threatening conditions or widespread, long term damage to the body's tissues and organs.

Type 1 diabetes

This form of diabetes causes the immune system to destroy insulin-producing beta cells in the pancreas (see page 162). This autoimmune disorder often develops in adolescence and may be triggered by a viral infection in combination with a genetic susceptibility.

Type 2 diabetes

In type 2 diabetes, the pancreas produces adequate amounts of insulin—but the body cells are not able to respond normally to it, and so do not take up enough sugar from the blood. Often associated with obesity and an elevated risk of heart disease, type 2 diabetes has become a global health crisis.

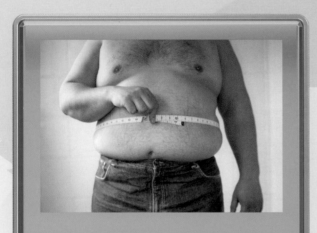

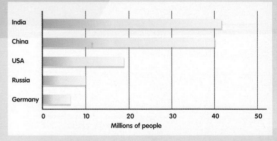

Statistics gathered by WHO show the growing impact of diabetes on every continent, especially in the world's most populous nations.

Metabolic syndrome

Metabolic syndrome is a combination of related risk factors that leave a person at greater risk of cardiovascular disease and stroke. These indicators include a resting blood pressure of 135/85, a low level of HDL (or "good") cholesterol, and elevated levels of blood sugar and triglyceride fats. Type 2 diabetes and a large waist measurement are also risk factors.

A global epidemic

The World Health Organization (WHO) has documented a global increase in reported cases of diabetes—a trend linked to the increase in major health risk factors, such as obesity. Inactive lifestyles and calorie-dense, nutrient-poor convenience foods—and sugary beverages—have contributed to these rising rates of diabetes-related illnesses.

THE *OXFORD HANDBOOK OF ENDOCRINOLOGY AND DIABETES*—EDITED BY JOHN WASS AND KATHARINE OWEN.

Retinal damage

Diabetic retinopathy is the most common diabetic eye disease caused by changes in the blood vessels of the retina. In some people, blood vessels may swell and leak fluid, blurring vision. In others, new fragile, abnormal blood vessels grow on the surface of the retina and can leak blood into the center of the eye. Over time, diabetic retinopathy can get worse and cause vision loss.

Typical complications

Over time, persistently high blood glucose levels damage blood vessels and nerves, so that cells and tissues in the eyes, limbs, kidneys, and elsewhere are starved of blood. As a result, they may start to malfunction or die.

Diabetic retinopathy

All forms of diabetes may cause this damage to blood vessels in the eye.

Kidney failure

Poor diabetic control leads to a gradual decrease in kidney function until the kidneys eventually fail completely.

Heart damage

Damage to the heart's vessels and nerves, caused by diabetes, may lead to heart disease, which may eventually prove fatal.

Blood sugar levels

Correct self-management of diabetes is key to preventing further complications. Various home monitors are available, which allow pepole with diabetes to regularly test a small blood sample, daily—to determine how much glucose it contains. Type 2 diabetes can, in its early stages, be controlled by monitoring it and with lifestyle changes and tablets.

Diabetic neuropathy

For unknown reasons, uncontrolled diabetes damages nerves, often throughout the body.

Damaged blood vessels

Affected blood vessels narrow and stiffen, reducing the flow of blood and raising blood pressure.

Pancreas

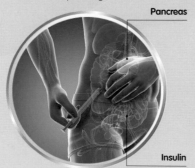

Insulin

Insulin injections

Type 1 diabetes destroys insulin-producing cells in the pancreas. Using a penlike device, which measures the correct dose from a cartridge, a diabetic can self-administer the insulin that his or her body requires—usually either one or two times a day.

Impaired healing

When diabetes is not controlled, persistent sores—such as foot ulcers—are a common problem.

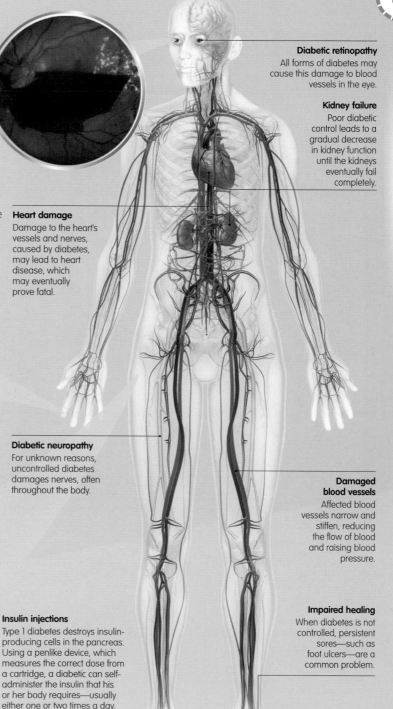

CHAPTER EIGHT

CARDIOVASCULAR
SYSTEM

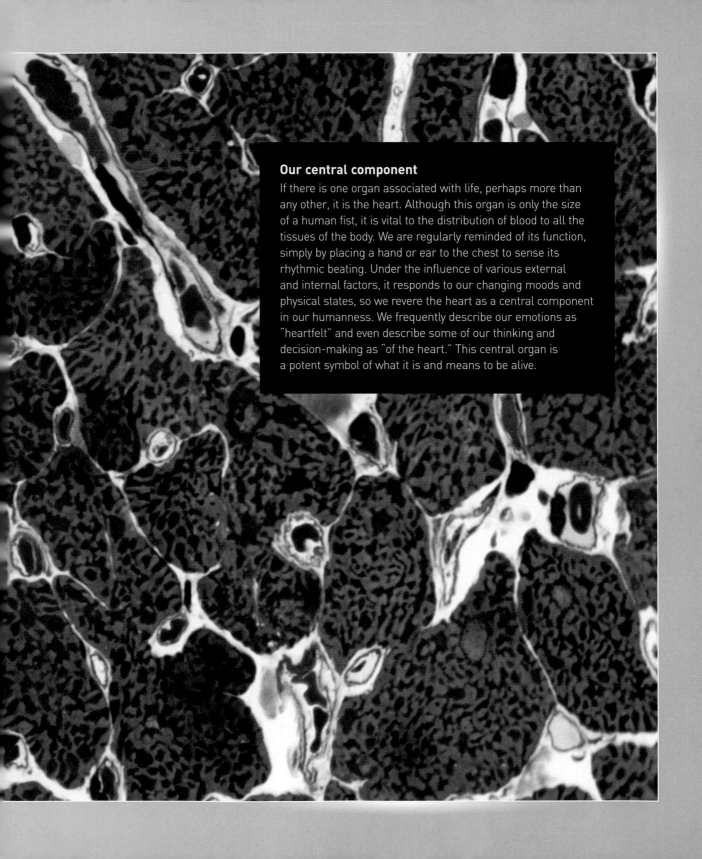

Our central component

If there is one organ associated with life, perhaps more than any other, it is the heart. Although this organ is only the size of a human fist, it is vital to the distribution of blood to all the tissues of the body. We are regularly reminded of its function, simply by placing a hand or ear to the chest to sense its rhythmic beating. Under the influence of various external and internal factors, it responds to our changing moods and physical states, so we revere the heart as a central component in our humanness. We frequently describe our emotions as "heartfelt" and even describe some of our thinking and decision-making as "of the heart." This central organ is a potent symbol of what it is and means to be alive.

BLOOD SYSTEM

Blood is literally the "river of life." Blood carries cargoes of oxygen, nutrients from food, hormones, and other vital substances. The specific role of the cardiovascular system—also known as the circulatory system— is to deliver blood around the body. It must reach to within a short distance of each of the body's trillions of living cells.

Blood vessel pathways

Roughly matching sets of arteries and veins follow the same routes through the body. In general, arteries are large vessels carrying oxygenated blood away from the heart, while veins transport oxygen-depleted blood returning to the heart. In the pulmonary circuit, however, the situation is reversed. Here, arteries return oxygen-poor blood to the lungs, and veins carry oxygenated blood back to the heart— to be pumped outward to body tissues.

Organ or system supply	Approximate % of blood
Digestive tract	21%
Kidneys	20%
Skeletal muscles	15%
Brain	13%
Skin	9%
Liver	6%
Bone	5%
Heart	5%
All other body parts combined	6%

Two circuits of flow

Blood flows in two linked circuits. The pulmonary circuit receives oxygen-poor blood from the right side of the heart and carries it to the lungs, where its load of oxygen is refreshed and waste carbon dioxide is exhaled. In the systemic circuit, the heart's left half receives oxygenated blood from the lungs and pumps it into the aorta—and into the vessels that will carry the blood to tissues.

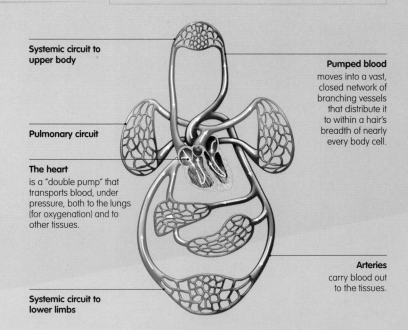

Systemic circuit to upper body

Pulmonary circuit

The heart
is a "double pump" that transports blood, under pressure, both to the lungs (for oxygenation) and to other tissues.

Systemic circuit to lower limbs

Pumped blood
moves into a vast, closed network of branching vessels that distribute it to within a hair's breadth of nearly every body cell.

Arteries
carry blood out to the tissues.

 FIND OUT HOW GAS EXCHANGE TAKES PLACE ON *PAGES 196–197*.

External jugular vein
is one of several viens that return blood from the head and neck to the heart.

Carotid arteries
supply blood to the brain and other tissues of the head.

Aorta
is the largest blood vessel in the body. It takes oxygenated blood as it is pumped from the left side of the heart.

Subclavian artery and vein
are vessels that run deep along the clavicle bone. They handle the blood flow to and from the arms.

Pulmonary trunk
A wide vessel that takes blood pumped from the right side of the heart. It branches into the right and left pulmonary arteries, which carry blood to the lungs.

Superior vena cava
is a vein that returns blood from the arms and head.

Coronary arteries
provide the heart's supply of oxygen-rich blood.

Inferior vena cava
is the body's largest vein. It extends through the entire length of the trunk and returns blood from the lower body to the heart.

Heart
is the body's muscular blood pump.

Celiac trunk
is a large arterial vessel that branches off the aorta in the upper abdomen. It then branches into smaller arteries that service the stomach, pancreas, small intestine, liver, and spleen.

Hepatic artery and hepatic vein
are vessels that service the liver. Blood entering the liver arrives via the hepatic artery and the hepatic portal vein, and then drains into the hepatic vein.

Lumbar arteries and veins
are the pathways for blood traveling to and from the spinal cord.

Renal artery and vein
are vessels that service the two kidneys.

Common iliac artery and vein
are vessels formed by the division of the lower end of the aorta They supply blood to the pelvic organs and lower limbs.

Brachial artery and vein
carry blood through the upper arm to the elbow. At the elbow, the vessels subdivide into the ulnar and radial vessels to service the lower arm.

Radial artery and vein
travel along the radius bone of the forearm. Meanwhile, an ulnar artery and vein lie along the ulna bone.

Ulnar artery and vein

Digital artery and vein
are small vessels that service the fingers. Similar vessels in the foot supply blood to the toes.

Popliteal artery and vein
supply blood to the knee and several muscles of the leg.

Anterior tibial artery and vein

Femoral artery and vein
are large vessels that are continuations of the iliac vessels. They transport blood through the thighs.

Peroneal artery and vein

Posterior tibial artery and vein

Great saphenous vein
is the longest vein in the body. It travels from the arch of the foot all the way to the groin, where it meets the femoral vein.

THE HEART

The heart is about the size of a clenched fist and weighs about 1lb (or 450g). It is located in the pericardial cavity between the two pleural cavities, which each contain a lung. A delicate sac, called the pericardium, wraps around the heart and lines the pericardial cavity. Within the cavity, a film of fluid prevents friction as the heart muscles contract and relax.

Superior vena cava
carries oxygen-poor blood from the upper part of the body.

SA node
signals travel to both atria and the AV node. From the AV node, Purkinje fibers extend down through the thick wall that separates the two ventricles. The fibers then branch upward to distribute the pacemaker's signals throughout the heart.

Pulmonary valve

Right coronary artery

Cardiac plexus

SA node
is located near the top of the right atrium.

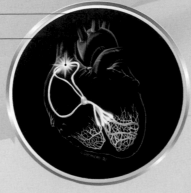

RIGHT SIDE OF THE BODY

Right atrium
pushes deoxygenated (oxygen-poor) blood from the body tissues into the right ventricle.

Atrioventricular (AV) node
is a cluster of cells that transfer the electrical signals that command the heart's rhythmic contractions.

Chordae tendinae
are fibrous chords, also known as the "heart strings," which help control the heart valves.

Purkinje cells
are neurons that make up the branching system of fibers that conduct impulses through the heart.

Right ventricle
pumps blood into the pulmonary arteries and to the lungs.

Inferior vena cava
delivers oxygen-poor blood from the lower part of the body.

The heart's pacemaker

Unlike other muscles, cardiac muscle both contracts and relaxes—causing the heart to "beat"—without commands from the nervous system. This ability comes from the heart's pacemaker, a small cluster of cells called the sinoatrial (SA) node. The cells produce electrical signals 70 to 80 times per minute, or more if the heart needs to beat faster. The node simulates a heartbeat even if all nerves to the heart have been severed. Each signal from the SA is conducted down to the ventricles through the atrio-ventricular (AV) node and along bundles of nerve fibers. Eventually the signal spreads out to the ventricular muscles, and triggers a contraction which forces a pulse of blood out from the heart.

 ON AVERAGE, *OVER 70 YEARS,* A BEATING HEART WILL PUMP APPROXIMATELY *48 MILLION GALLONS (184 MILLION LITERS)* OF BLOOD.

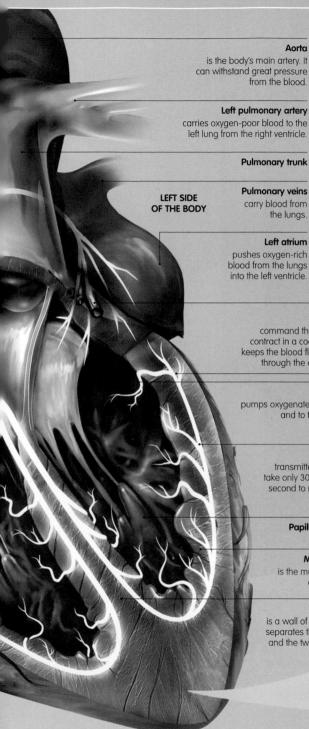

Aorta
is the body's main artery. It can withstand great pressure from the blood.

Left pulmonary artery
carries oxygen-poor blood to the left lung from the right ventricle.

Pulmonary trunk

LEFT SIDE OF THE BODY

Pulmonary veins
carry blood from the lungs.

Left atrium
pushes oxygen-rich blood from the lungs into the left ventricle.

Great cardiac vein

The purkinje cells
command the organ's chambers to contract in a coordinated fashion. This keeps the blood flowing at a steady rate through the cardiovascular system.

Left ventricle
pumps oxygenated blood into the aorta, and to the tissues of the body.

Electrical impulses
transmitted by the Purkinje cells take only 30 one-thousandths of a second to reach all of the muscle fibers in the ventricles.

Papillary muscle

Myocardium
is the muscular wall of the heart.

Septum
is a wall of muscle that separates the two atria and the two ventricles.

Two pumps in one

The heart has two halves, right and left. Each half is divided further into two hollow chambers, an atrium and a ventricle. The two upper chambers—the atria—push blood into the ventricles below. Then, the ventricles each pump blood into vessels with different destinations. While the atria have relatively thin walls, the ventricles have thick, muscular walls to aid the constant circulation of blood.

Cardiac muscle

Muscle fibers in the heart are linked by specialized junctions called intercalated disks, which are visible in this image (below) as dark purple lines. These junctions knit the fibers tightly together, so that nerve impulses can travel more easily from fiber to fiber.

Intercalated disk

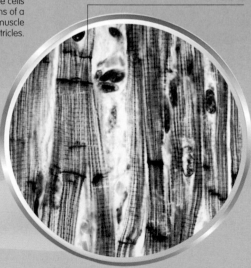

CARDIAC CYCLE

In a day, the heart beats about 100,000 times—and over an average lifetime, it produces 2.6 billion beats or more. Each beat is a rapid sequence of *systole* (contraction) and *diastole* (relaxation), first of the heart's atria, then of its larger ventricles. This sequence, the cardiac cycle, takes less than a second. Electrical signals from the SA node stimulate a contraction, then briefly shut off, then commence again. The valves at work generate the familiar "*lub-dup, lub-dup*" sounds that can be heard through a stethoscope.

Blood from upper body

Pulmonary arteries

Veins from right lung

Right atrium fills up

Veins from left lung

Left atrium fills up

Blood from the lower body

Right ventricle | Left ventricle

Phase one: the heart chambers relax

During this phase, the heart briefly relaxes. Oxygen-rich blood flows from the lungs into the left atrium, and deoxygenated blood from the body's tissues enters the right atrium. As the filling atria expand, some of the blood trickles into the two ventricles below the atria.

HEART VALVES

Valves help to direct blood through the heart. The right atrium empties into the ventricle below it through the tricuspid valve, and the left atrium empties through the mitral valve. The right ventrical then pumps its blood out through the pulmonary valve, while the left ventricle pumps blood via the aortic valve.

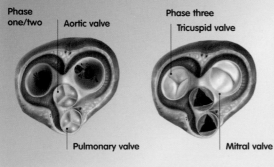

Phase one/two | Aortic valve

Phase three | Tricuspid valve

Pulmonary valve

Mitral valve

Heart rates

Individuals may vary, but a "normal" heart rate is about 70 to 80 beats per minute in adults. Endurance athletes may have a common irregularity, or arrhythmia, known as bradycardia, in which the heart beats fewer than 60 times a minute. Stress, excess thyroid hormone, drugs such as caffeine and nicotine, or other factors may cause tachycardia, a heart rate above 100 beats per minute.

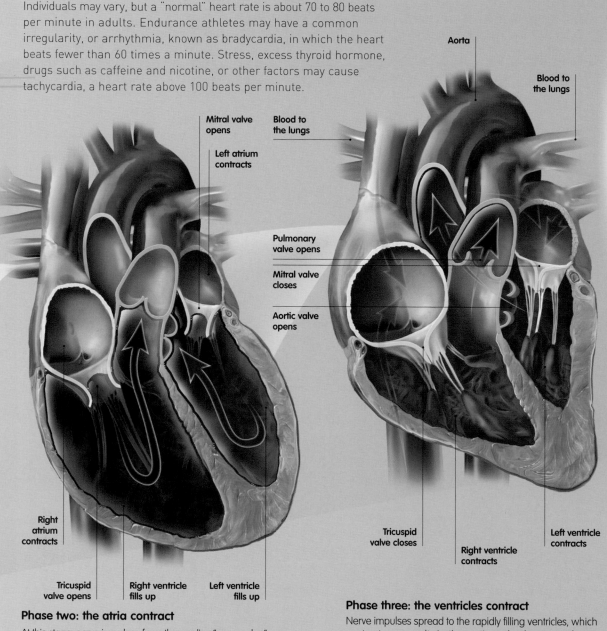

Mitral valve opens

Left atrium contracts

Blood to the lungs

Aorta

Blood to the lungs

Pulmonary valve opens

Mitral valve closes

Aortic valve opens

Right atrium contracts

Tricuspid valve opens

Right ventricle fills up

Left ventricle fills up

Tricuspid valve closes

Right ventricle contracts

Left ventricle contracts

Phase two: the atria contract

At this stage, nerve impulses from the cardiac "pacemaker" (see pages 178–179) stimulate a contraction. The tricuspid and mitral valves then open, allowing blood to pour from the atria into the ventricles. The mounting fluid pressure in the ventricles forces the tricuspid and mitral valves to close.

Phase three: the ventricles contract

Nerve impulses spread to the rapidly filling ventricles, which contract as a result. As the aortic and pulmonary valves open, oxygen-poor blood flows out from the right ventricle to the lungs through the pulmonary artery. Meanwhile, oxygenated blood is forced out from the contracting left ventricle into the aorta, to be carried off to the rest of the body.

HEART HEALTH

The blood circulated by the heart delivers oxygen, hormones, nutrients, and other substances to all the body's organs and tissues. It also functions as a crucial waste carrier, transporting substances such as carbon dioxide and urea from protein digestion to the lungs, kidneys, or other disposal sites. Because these processes are vital to life, an unhealthy or malfunctioning heart is one of the most serious and frightening problems a person can experience.

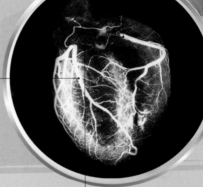

Coronary circulation

Blockages
or narrowing in either of the coronary arteries could lead to a heart attack.

The main coronary arteries
divide into several smaller blood vessels—and these also branch into numerous capillaries.

Oxygen consumption

The heart accounts for about eight percent of the body's total oxygen consumption. The organ does not absorb any oxygen directly from the blood it pumps. Instead, its steady supply of oxygen comes via the right and left coronary arteries, which direct blood from the aorta. Arteriogram X-rays such as this one (right) help to show up conditions such as coronary artery disease, in which the arteries become narrow.

The right atrium
receives only about 60 percent of the oxygen-poor blood returning from the heart tissues via coronary veins and the coronary sinus. The rest of the coronary circulation returns, via tiny veins, directly into the chambers of the heart.

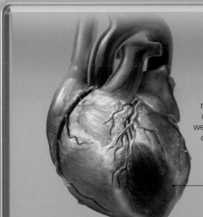

Myocardial infarction
region shows up as a dark, wedge-shaped area of tissue damage.

A heart attack

In a heart attack (a myocardial infarction), a section of the heart muscle dies when its blood and oxygen supply is blocked, due to a blood clot or some other obstruction in an artery. Before a heart attack occurs, episodes of pain and chest tightness (known as *angina pectoris*) may indicate that some portion of the heart muscle is receiving too little blood. Other common symptoms include pain in the left shoulder or arm, and pain between the shoulder blades.

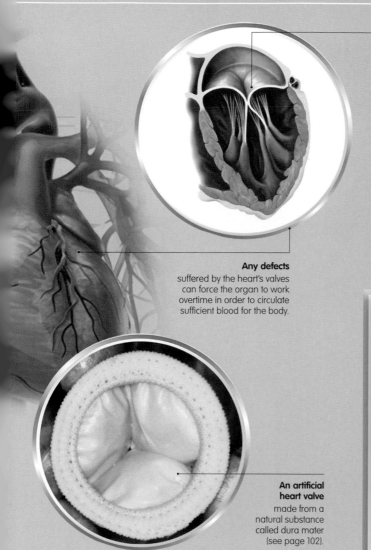

Mitral valve
is also known as the bicuspid
or left atrioventricular valve.

Any defects
suffered by the heart's valves
can force the organ to work
overtime in order to circulate
sufficient blood for the body.

**An artificial
heart valve**
made from a
natural substance
called dura mater
(see page 102).

Tendons and valves

The *chordae tendinae*, or heart strings, are
stabilizing tendons built from collagen. They
hold the valves between the atria and the
ventricles closed while the ventricles contract,
forcing blood out into the circulation. Damage
caused by a heart attack or infection can
prevent the valves from closing fully, so that
blood leaks back into the chamber that pumped
it. Calcium deposits, or other factors, can cause
the valves to become narrow and stiff—this
is called stenosis.

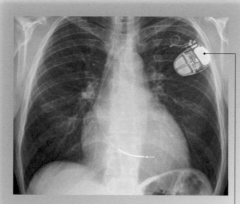

Electronic pacemakers
can be fitted internally or externally. A lead from this
internal pacemaker unit is connected to the heart.

ELECTRONIC PACEMAKERS

The small clusters of cells in the SA node (see
page 178) are the heart's natural pacemaker. If
the SA node malfunctions, or a patient suffers
from an irregular heartbeat, a battery-powered
pacemaker can be surgically implanted to
stimulate or normalize the rate of contractions.
The device, which is about the same size as a
pocket watch, emits electrical signals that
trigger a normal, regular rhythm.

Replacement valves

Defects or disease of the heart valves can force the
entire organ to work overtime in order to circulate
sufficient blood to the body's tissues. Surgery may be
needed to replace the malfunctioning valves with
artificial ones. The most commonly replaced
valves are the mitral, or bicuspid, valve (between
the left atrium and ventricle), and the valve that
leads from the left ventricle to the aorta.

BLOOD VESSELS

Blood vessels come in five types, each one structurally matched to its function. The largest are major arteries, including the aorta. Thick walls allow them to sustain the pressure of freshly pumped blood from the heart. Arteries diverge into narrower arterioles, which have thinner walls and manage the blood flow in the body. From here, blood disperses into slender capillaries, which deliver or pick up oxygen or wastes. Blood moves on into narrow venules, which merge to form veins that transport blood back to the heart.

Type two: arterioles

Arteries diverge into narrower arterioles, which have thinner walls—so they can contract and relax more readily than the arteries can. Arterioles are the major managers of blood flow in the body, increasing or decreasing their internal diameter to adjust the volume of blood entering the body's tissues, as required.

Type three: capillaries

Slender capillaries travel close to every body cell in order to deliver or pick up waste materials or useful substances such as oxygen. They form a delicate network buried in tissues.

Type one: major arteries

These, the largest of all vessels, include the aorta, the brachial arteries in the arms, and the femoral arteries in the thighs. Thick, slightly stretchy walls allow these vessels to expand and contract while they sustain the pressure of blood freshly pumped by the heart.

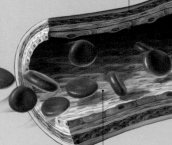

Muscular arteries
have the thickest media, or middle layer, of all the blood vessels. This increases their strength.

Red blood cells
are rich in oxygen.

Large veins
have relatively little smooth muscle or elastin in their media, which keeps their walls thin.

Lumen (space)

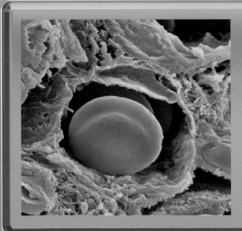

Threadlike vessels

Capillaries are the smallest and most numerous blood vessels in the body. Many substances can move easily across their thin, leaky walls. Their interior space is so narrow that red blood cells often need to pass through them in single file—as shown in this SEM image.

 OVER THE COURSE OF ITS *120-DAY LIFESPAN*, A SINGLE BLOOD CELL MAY TRAVEL MORE THAN *298 MILES (480KM)* THROUGH THE VESSELS OF THE BODY.

Type four: venules

Blood moves from capillaries into the almost equally narrow venules, which merge together to form veins that can transport a large volume of blood back to the heart.

Outer layer

Fatty deposits

These ridges, rising from the lining of an artery, are fatty "cholesterol plaques." They are thought to develop, in part, due to inflammation inside blood vessels. Many heart attacks occur when such plaques restrict the flow of blood in coronary arteries (see page 182).

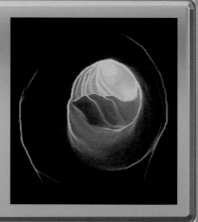

Type five: veins

Blood returns to the heart in veins, which have thinner walls but a larger internal lumen, or space, in which to carry blood. Veins also have valves that close behind the blood as it moves toward the heart, so that it cannot flow backward under the influence of gravity.

Outer elastin

Smooth muscle

Inner elastin

Outer layer

Connective tissue

Inner lining

Lumen

Smooth muscle

Inner elastin

Valve flap

Inner lining

Connective tissue

Understanding blood pressure readings	
Blood pressure	is measured in "millimeters of mercury" (mmHg).
Systolic pressure	is the pressure in the arteries created by the heart's contractions. Normal systolic pressure is 120mmHg and below.
Diastolic pressure	is the pressure in the arteries when the heart is resting between beats. Normal diastolic pressure is 80mmHg or less.
Normal blood pressure	may therefore be measured in the region of "120 over 80" (normally written as simply "120/80").

Shifting pressure

Blood pressure is highest in the aorta and drops as blood flows onward into arterioles and capillaries. When blood enters veins, for its return journey to the heart, its pressure is only a small fraction of the starting value.

Average blood pressure (per vessel type)		
VESSEL	**DIAMETER**	**PRESSURE**
Aorta	25mm	120/80
Large arteries	1–4mm	120/80
Small arteries	0.2–1mm	70/60
Arterioles	0.01–02mm	40/35
Capillaries	0.006–0.010mm	20/16
Venules	0.01–0.2mm	10/8
Small veins	0.2–5mm	5mmHg
Large veins	6–19mm	5mmHg
Vena Cava (superior)	18–22mm	5mmHg
Vena Cava (inferior)	27–36mm	5mmHg

BLOOD AND PLASMA

The average adult contains about 5½ quarts (5-6 liters) of blood, which circulates through the body every minute. Circulating large quantities of blood is vital because blood brings oxygen, nutrients, hormones, and other substances to cells—and carries away the steady stream of metabolic wastes that those cells produce. It also circulates body heat to and from internal organs, helping to maintain a normal core temperature of about 98.6°F (37°C).

The components of blood

By volume, just over half of blood is plasma—a blend of water and a variety of proteins. Blended with the plasma are cells and platelets. Erythrocytes, or red blood cells, carry oxygen throughout the body and make up most of the remainder of blood. Whole blood also contains platelets, which assist in blood clotting, and various types of leukocytes or white blood cells.

Blood plasma

The plasma transports substances to and from cells, so it is the main interface for maintaining the right chemical balance in body fluids. Processes in the kidneys, and elsewhere, continually adjust the types and amounts of substances in the blood.

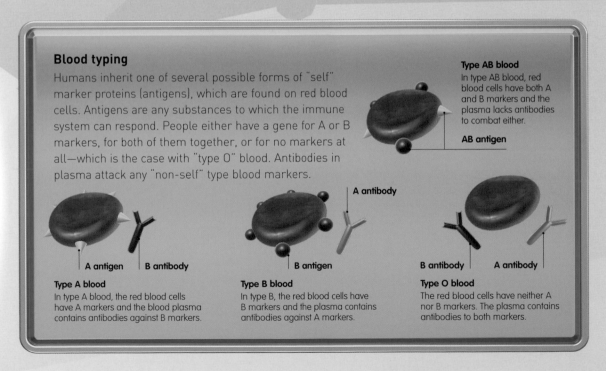

Blood typing

Humans inherit one of several possible forms of "self" marker proteins (antigens), which are found on red blood cells. Antigens are any substances to which the immune system can respond. People either have a gene for A or B markers, for both of them together, or for no markers at all—which is the case with "type O" blood. Antibodies in plasma attack any "non-self" type blood markers.

Type AB blood
In type AB blood, red blood cells have both A and B markers and the plasma lacks antibodies to combat either.

AB antigen

A antibody

A antigen | B antibody

Type A blood
In type A blood, the red blood cells have A markers and the blood plasma contains antibodies against B markers.

B antigen

Type B blood
In type B, the red blood cells have B markers and the plasma contains antibodies against A markers.

B antibody | A antibody

Type O blood
The red blood cells have neither A nor B markers. The plasma contains antibodies to both markers.

 HEMOGLOBIN MAKES UP APPROXIMATELY *33 PERCENT* OF THE OVERALL COMPOSITION OF A RED BLOOD CELL.

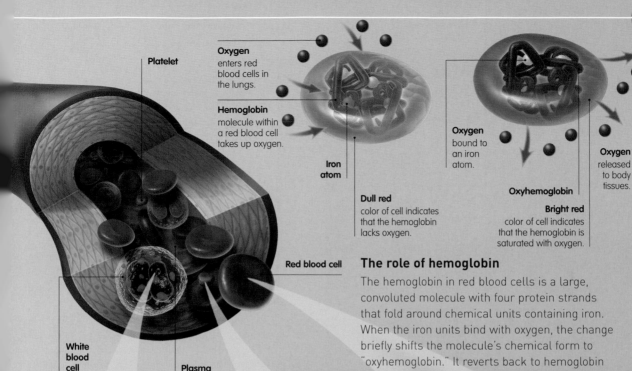

Platelet

Oxygen enters red blood cells in the lungs.

Hemoglobin molecule within a red blood cell takes up oxygen.

Iron atom

Dull red color of cell indicates that the hemoglobin lacks oxygen.

Oxygen bound to an iron atom.

Oxyhemoglobin

Bright red color of cell indicates that the hemoglobin is saturated with oxygen.

Oxygen released to body tissues.

Red blood cell

White blood cell

Plasma

The role of hemoglobin

The hemoglobin in red blood cells is a large, convoluted molecule with four protein strands that fold around chemical units containing iron. When the iron units bind with oxygen, the change briefly shifts the molecule's chemical form to "oxyhemoglobin." It reverts back to hemoglobin as the red blood cells release oxygen while flowing through the body's tissues.

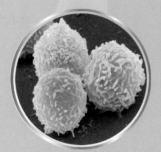

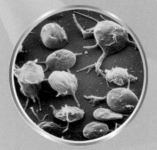

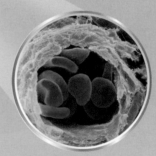

White blood cells

Types of white blood cells make up just one percent of the total volume of blood, but they are a vital part of the body's immune system. Some, such as lymphocytes, combat threats such as bacteria, viruses, and parasites. Others remove debris and foreign material. Certain types die and are replaced after a few days, while others can function for years.

Platelets

These are jagged fragments shed by precursor cells in bone marrow. They plug small tears in blood vessels and promote clotting (see pages 188–189). Platelets only survive for about a week, but they are constantly being replaced. There are always millions of them circulating in the bloodstream.

Red blood cells

Red blood cells resemble crimson disks indented on both sides. Packed with the iron-rich protein hemoglobin, which binds with oxygen, these cells have one main role—to load up with oxygen in the lungs and then deliver it to tissues. These cells live for about four months.

BLOOD CLOTTING

A sudden, massive blood clot is an obvious medical emergency. However, less dramatic—and often completely hidden—breaches of the cardiovascular system occur every day. The body's small blood vessels are incredibly delicate, and cuts, scrapes, blows, and even normal daily activities (such as exercise) can rip or tear them. These seemingly minor injuries are threats as well—for if the body loses more than a small amount of blood, tissues and organs may be damaged or die, and the whole circulatory system could break down.

Hemostasis

Fortunately, several built-in mechanisms—known collectively as hemostasis—act quickly to restrict bleeding from small vessels, whether inside the body or on its surface. Proteins called clotting factors circulate in the blood or are released by injured cells. When a small vessel is torn or punctured, a cascade of clotting factors produces an interaction between an enzyme called thrombin and a blood protein called fibrinogen. This interaction forms a clot.

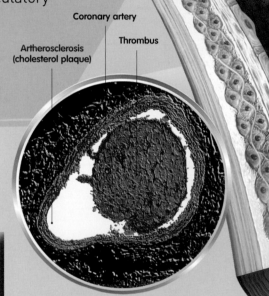

Coronary artery

Thrombus

Artherosclerosis
(cholesterol plaque)

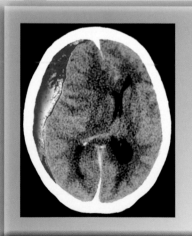

BLEEDING IN THE BRAIN

A broken vessel in the brain may trigger a subdural hemorrhage, between the brain and the skull as shown in the brain's right hemisphere in this CT scan. A hemorrhage or its opposite—an abnormal blood clot in the brain—can both lead to a "brain attack" or stroke (see page 121).

Thrombosis

A clot that forms in an intact blood vessel is called a thrombus. It may cause a dangerous blockage known as a thrombosis. Limited circulation of blood in this region may cause the affected tissue to malfunction or die. A heart attack is usually due to a thrombosis which blocks off a coronary artery serving an area of heart muscle.

 THE WORD *LEUKEMIA* IS BASED ON TWO GREEK WORDS: *LEUKOS* (MEANING "WHITE") AND *HAIMA* (MEANING "BLOOD").

Hemophilia

People with an inherited disorder called hemophilia lack one of the usual blood clotting factors, so their blood does not clot normally. Administering the missing factor by injection can help to avert lethal bleeding.

Leukemia

In leukemias, white blood cells become cancerous (right). The abnormal cells overwhelm healthy ones as they multiply, uncontrolled, in bone marrow. Lacking enough normal white blood cells and platelets, the person is susceptible to infections and internal bleeding.

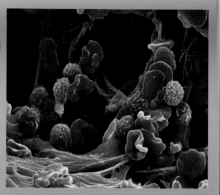

Red blood cell

Platelets

Platelet filaments

Platelet plug forms

Platelet

Vitamin K

is used by liver cells to produce several clotting factors. This is why foods rich in this vitamin are important in our diets. Supplements of vitamin K are recommended for people with rare disorders that inhibit natural blood-clotting.

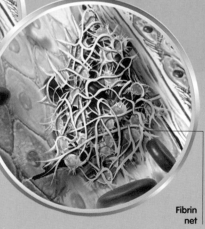

Fibrin net

Phase one: sticky platelets

When a small vessel ruptures, its walls constrict to reduce the the flow of blood. Meanwhile, the platelets in the bloodstream become sticky and change shape, extending long filaments.

Phase two: thrombin acts on fibrinogen

The platelet's filaments attach to the exposed collagen in the vessel wall, and begin to form a plug to prevent further blood loss. Next, prompted by clotting factors, the enzyme thrombin begins to act on the protein fibrinogen.

Phase three: fibrin net

The fibrinogen molecules form a net of fibrin that snares (traps) platelets and blood cells in a thick, sticky clump. The blood clot is now complete.

DAMAGE AND DISORDERS

Ailments that clog or impair the body's blood transport channels prevent the blood from flowing efficiently to tissues and organs. This change to normal circulation is known as cardiovascular disease. It can result in painful symptoms when it deprives the tissues of the blood supply they need for good health and normal functioning.

Atherosclerosis

The most common source of cardiovascular disease is "hardening of the arteries," otherwise known as atherosclerosis. Arteries narrow as fatty plaques full of cholesterol develop on their walls. Over time, these scarlike lesions become calcified, making the walls much less elastic. Plaques may affect vessels in the heart, brain, and elsewhere—and the reduced blood supply starves cells of oxygen.

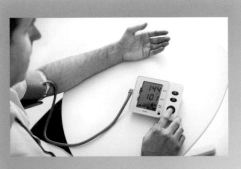

Factors that raise the risk of hypertension
include a family history of the condition, excess weight, stress, and smoking.

HYPERTENSION

Chronic high blood pressure, or hypertension, is a stealthy killer. The vast majority of hypertensive people do not have any symptoms and are unaware of their condition —but over time, the walls of the blood vessels, the kidneys, and the heart muscle may all become damaged. Hypertension also causes hemorrhagic stroke, in which an artery bursts in the brain.

Artery
A healthy artery's thick, multilayered wall is resilient, but becomes much less so as the atherosclerosis advances.

Blood
As inflammation develops at the plaque site, white blood cells arrive via the bloodstream. Ironically, this defensive response causes adverse changes that encourage the growth of the plaque.

Plaque
In an atherosclerotic plaque, deposits of bad cholesterol, or LDL, infiltrate the wall of the artery and create a bulging obstruction. This triggers inflammation which causes the plaque to swell further, narrowing the artery and making blood flow turbulent. The surface of the plaque may crack, triggering a blood clot to form on it, further obstructing flow.

Lumen
The lumen, or space, inside the artery often remains sufficiently open for adequate blood flow until the atherosclerosis reaches an advanced stage.

Sickle-cell anemia

In sickle-cell anemia, the blood's hemoglobin is abnormal. Affected red blood cells take on a sickle shape (right) and die prematurely. People with the full-blown disease have inherited a faulty gene from both parents and may suffer greatly from the pallor and weariness of anemia, and from painful damage to major organs. The symptoms are much milder in those who inherited only one copy of the faulty gene.

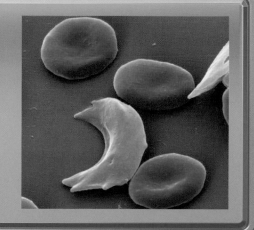

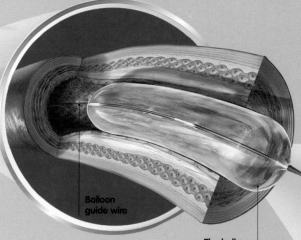

Balloon guide wire

The balloon is inflated via the catheter tube.

A stent

A small, wire cylinder called a stent may be inserted—via an angioplasty procedure—to help to keep a vessel open. "Drug-eluting" stents are coated with a chemical to inhibit the development of scar tissue that might otherwise form a new blockage.

Angioplasty

Operations on the internal walls of an artery are known as angioplasty. Laser angioplasty uses a high-energy light beam to vaporize small plaques. In balloon angioplasty, a small balloon (above) is threaded—through an arterial catheter tube—into a blocked vessel, where it is inflated to flatten the plaque.

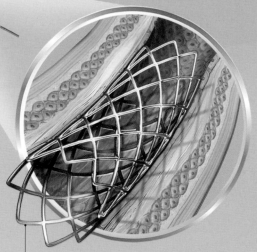

Wire stent

RESPIRATORY SYSTEM

Fingers of filtration

Taking air into the lungs—for the extraction of oxygen and the expulsion of carbon dioxide—is vital to the body's survival, but it's also an act that draws foreign particles and potentially toxic substances deep into the body. Luckily, our airways produce mucus and are lined with these microscopic "carpets" of hairlike structures, called cilia. With every movement of air, in and out of the body, the cilia wave back and forth to sweep up any debris that gets trapped in the mucus. It is an in-built filtration system that helps to reduce the chances of microbial infection.

ANATOMY OF BREATHING

The respiratory system fills our spongy, expandable lungs with air and provides a site where oxygen can move into the bloodstream and carbon dioxide—a major metabolic waste—can be expelled from the body. This function of gas exchange is so crucial that permanent brain damage can occur within minutes if the system stops—and death follows quickly unless breathing resumes.

The system's upper parts

The upper parts of the system include the nasal passages, the pharynx, and the larynx. The main function of these parts is to provide a route for air to reach the trachea, or windpipe.

Hairlike cilia
project from the epithelial cells that line the respiratory system.

Nasal passages
receive inhaled air, which warms and takes on moisture as it moves through the nasal cavity. Toward the front of the nasal passages, just inside the nostrils, mucus-coated hairs may trap some dust and debris.

Oral cavity (mouth interior)
provides an alternative route for taking air in during heavy exertion or when the nasal passages are clogged.

Epiglottis
is a flap of tissue that moves down over the larynx, during swallowing, to stop food entering the airways.

Pharynx
funnels air in towards the trachea, and food toward the esophagus.

Trachea
is the airway that connects the larynx with the two bronchi, the major airways into the lungs. Rings of cartilage help to prop open the trachea.

Larynx (voice box)
is a short passage that contains the vocal cords. It is the site where speech sounds are produced (see page 199).

Cleaning the airways

The respiratory system is exposed to airborne debris and toxic substances, including dust and particles emitted from vehicles or products such as paints, pesticides, and carpets. Its primary defense is the mucus produced by cells or glands in the epithelium lining the airways. Larger particles become trapped in the sticky mucus, which is then swept upward by the hairlike cilia (above) that extend out of the epithelial cells. When the material reaches the throat, it can be expelled through the mouth or swallowed and eliminated via excretion.

 A MAN'S LUNGS HAVE A MAX. VOLUME OF *1.3 GALLONS (6 LITERS)* OF AIR, WHILE A WOMAN'S HAVE A VOLUME OF ABOUT *0.9 GALLONS (4.2 LITERS)*.

The diaphragm

The diaphragm is a dome-shaped skeletal muscle that separates the thoracic and abdominal cavities. Its rhythmic cycle of contraction and relaxation is partly responsible for the normal "in-out" rhythm of quiet breathing. It also plays a part in vomiting: the diaphragm is contracted sharply downward to create negative pressure in the thorax. At the same time, the muscles of the abdominal walls vigorously contract, squeezing the stomach and thus elevating intra-gastric pressure—so that the stomach's contents are directed upward.

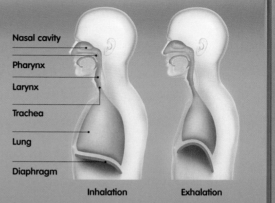

Nasal cavity

Pharynx

Larynx

Trachea

Lung

Diaphragm

Inhalation   Exhalation

The system's lower parts

Held open by tough rings of cartilage, the trachea funnels air to the point where two large branches, the bronchi, diverge. At this fork in the respiratory road, air reaches its destination—the lungs. From this point onward, the so-called "respiratory tree" branches repeatedly into ever-narrower passages leading to clusters of microscopic sacs. In these "alveoli," oxygen crosses into the blood and carbon dioxide exits the blood to be exhaled.

Lung
is a spongy, elastic organ with several lobes. The two lungs jointly contain an estimated 300 million alveoli (see page 196).

Bifurcation of the trachea
is the point where the main airway splits into the two bronchi. This junction is supported by a larger ring of cartilage known as the carina.

Bronchus
carries air into one of the two lungs. Each bronchus branches into ever-smaller air passages. This inverted branching network is often called the respiratory tree.

Bronchioles
are the narrowest passages of the respiratory tree. They end at the alveoli, the microscopic sacs where oxygen moves into the blood and carbon dioxide moves out.

Plural membrane
is a two-layered membrane that surrounds the lungs and lines the pleural cavity. Fluid between the layers prevents friction with the cavity's inner wall as the lungs repeatedly expand and contract.

Diaphragm
is a sheet of skeletal muscle that separates the thoracic cavity above it and the abdominal cavity below it. Its contractions are a fundamental part of the breathing sequence.

Thoracic cavity
is the large cavity inside the chest that is filled with the lungs, heart, and other organs.

Abdominal cavity

GAS EXCHANGE

In one minute of breathing, about 1.6 gallons (7.5 liters) of air flows into the lungs, and a similar quantity rushes out. Every breath is an exercise in gas exchange—oxygen in, carbon dioxide out. The gases move across pressure gradients: a lower pressure of oxygen in the blood in the lungs pulls oxygen in from the air, while a lower pressure of carbon dioxide in the air in the lungs pulls this waste product from the blood.

Pressures within the body
change during breathing, which serves to draw fresh air into the lungs (inhalation) and expel stale air (exhalation).

The lungs at work

Air entering the lungs is about 21 percent oxygen and 0.04 percent carbon dioxide. There is much less oxygen in the blood flowing in the capillaries hugging the alveoli. Oxygen and carbon dioxide move down the pressure gradient to where there is less of them—so the oxygen is pulled into the capillaries, where it binds to hemoglobin in the red blood cells. Meanwhile, the pressure of carbon dioxide is higher in the blood than in the air, so it is drawn the other way, out of the bloodstream and into the internal environment of the lungs, where it forms about four percent of exhaled air.

Lowering the pressure
in the lungs is driven by the movement of the ribs: they lift up and out—like pail handles—to increase the chest volume. This creates a negative pressure in the lungs, drawing air in and causing them to expand.

Cluster of alveoli

Alveolus

The ribs move back down
as the intercostal muscles relax (see page 198). This allows the natural, "elastic recoil" of the lungs to push air—containing carbon dioxide—back out of the body.

A smooth muscle layer
is in the bronchioles' walls. It is very thin, but it can contract or relax to adjust the amount of air flowing through each bronchiole.

Gas exchange terminals

Like tiny bunches of hollow grapes, alveoli are clusters of sacs surrounded by a lacework of thin blood vessels. Carbon dioxide diffuses from arterioles into the sacs, while inhaled oxygen moves inward into the blood capillaries and body.

 LAID SIDE BY SIDE, THE ALVEOLI IN AN ADULT'S LUNG WOULD COVER *THE AREA OF A TENNIS COURT.*

In and out of the capillaries

In the lungs, oxygen passes into the capillaries around the alveoli and then binds on to the hemoglobin in the red blood cells. Simultaneously, carbon dioxide departs from the blood and enters the alveoli. These steps require that each gas dissolves in water, which coats the thin walls of the alveoli. As blood circulates through the body's tissues, the steps are reversed. Carbon dioxide steadily moves into the blood, and the red blood cells gradually release their cargo of oxygen to the cells.

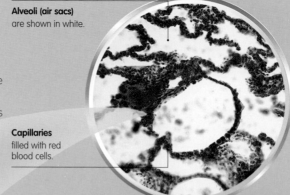

Alveoli (air sacs)
are shown in white.

Capillaries
filled with red blood cells.

Exchange terminals

The moist, gossamer-thin walls of the alveoli are just one cell thick. Nevertheless, the walls of the 300 million or so alveoli make up most of the volume of lung tissue. They are the chief sites of gas exchange.

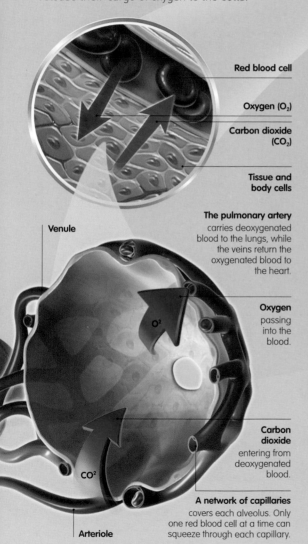

Red blood cell

Oxygen (O$_2$)

Carbon dioxide (CO$_2$)

Tissue and body cells

The pulmonary artery carries deoxygenated blood to the lungs, while the veins return the oxygenated blood to the heart.

Oxygen passing into the blood.

Carbon dioxide entering from deoxygenated blood.

A network of capillaries covers each alveolus. Only one red blood cell at a time can squeeze through each capillary.

Venule

O^2

CO^2

Arteriole

ALTITUDE SICKNESS

At sea level, air is about 21 percent oxygen, but at altitudes greater than 8,000ft (2,500m) above sea level this percentage dips dramatically. At 19,685ft (6,000m), it has dropped by a half. At these oxygen levels, the gradient between breathable gases in the atmosphere and those in the blood is much less, so oxygen cannot pass into the body as readily. Without proper breathing apparatus, climbers risk hypoxia—an oxygen shortage that may cause headaches, vomiting, and dangerous accumulations of fluid in the lungs and brain.

BREATH CONTROL

The constant rhythm of breathing depends on controls that operate in the brain, the lungs, and elsewhere. Generally speaking, people do not have to consciously remember to breathe. Automatic commands from the brain stem regulate inhalation and exhalation. The body also has a way of monitoring internal levels of carbon dioxide, so that more of it can be exhaled as and when necessary.

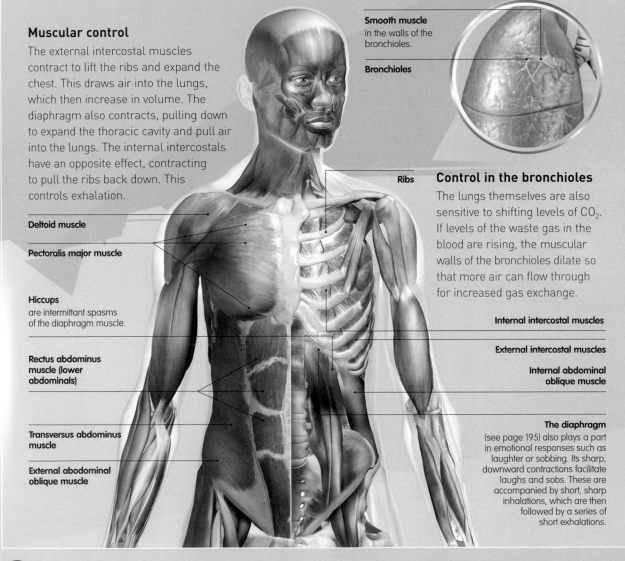

Muscular control

The external intercostal muscles contract to lift the ribs and expand the chest. This draws air into the lungs, which then increase in volume. The diaphragm also contracts, pulling down to expand the thoracic cavity and pull air into the lungs. The internal intercostals have an opposite effect, contracting to pull the ribs back down. This controls exhalation.

Deltoid muscle

Pectoralis major muscle

Hiccups
are intermittant spasms of the diaphragm muscle.

Rectus abdominus muscle (lower abdominals)

Transversus abdominus muscle

External abodominal oblique muscle

Smooth muscle
in the walls of the bronchioles.

Bronchioles

Ribs

Control in the bronchioles

The lungs themselves are also sensitive to shifting levels of CO_2. If levels of the waste gas in the blood are rising, the muscular walls of the bronchioles dilate so that more air can flow through for increased gas exchange.

Internal intercostal muscles

External intercostal muscles

Internal abdominal oblique muscle

The diaphragm
(see page 195) also plays a part in emotional responses such as laughter or sobbing. Its sharp, downward contractions facilitate laughs and sobs. These are accompanied by short, sharp inhalations, which are then followed by a series of short exhalations.

 MOST PEOPLE WILL TAKE ABOUT *HALF A BILLION BREATHS* OF AIR IN THEIR LIFETIME.

Sensory control

Instead of being concerned with falling oxygen levels, the body is actually more focused on monitoring its levels of carbon dioxide. Sensors in the aorta and the carotid arteries in the neck track the amount of carbon dioxide in the blood.

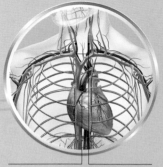

Aorta   Carotid arteries

Control in the vessels

The blood capillaries of the lungs also dilate or constrict to help to match the actual moment-to-moment flow of blood to the amount of oxygen present in the air being inhaled.

Capillaries

Alveolus

Medulla

Pons

Levels of CO_2
in cerebrospinal fluid (see page 102) are also monitored by the brain, which increases the rate and depth of breathing if it is necessary to reduce the levels of CO_2.

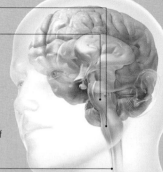

The role of the brain

People who suffer brain stem damage may suffocate without the aid of an artificial respirator. This is because respiratory centers in the medulla and pons manage the mechanics of breathing, sending a steady stream of nerve impulses to the diaphragm and ribcage muscles. The result is the in-and-out flow of air known medically as "ventilation."

Making sounds and speech

Most human speech sounds begin in the larynx at the paired ligaments called vocal cords. The cords generate vibrations as exhaled air, rushing outward from the lungs, passes through an opening between them, called the glottis. Our muscular control of the cords can make them taut and tense, which controls the vibrations and the nature of the resulting sounds.

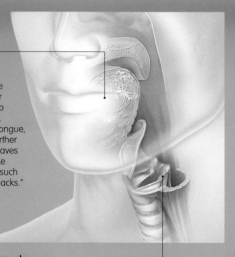

Movements of mouth parts
and changes in the shape of the upper airways combine to alter the flow of air. Parts such as the tongue, lips, and palette further refine the sound waves into words, or make additional sounds such as "clicks" and "smacks."

Glottis

Vocal cords in
closed position

Vocal cords in
open position

Skeletal muscle
contracts or relaxes to control the degree of tension on the vocal cords, and hence the size of the slitlike opening in the glottis.

RESPIRATORY DISORDERS

Under normal circumstances, fresh air is inhaled into the airways—and stale air is exhaled—12 to 15 times every minute. Humans take this natural sequence for granted, until an infection or respiratory disease interferes with it. Here are some common respiratory problems and the effects that they can have on the body.

Upper respiratory infections

Our defensive responses to viruses and bacteria produce the congested, swollen nasal passages of a cold, the irritation of laryngitis, and the coughing and wheezing of bronchitis. Viral infections develop in the upper respiratory tract when virus particles penetrate the mucus covering the surface epithelium and enter the cells there. This process normally takes about two to four days, the "incubation period" of an impending cold virus.

Tonsillitis
The tonsils contain cells that intercept microbes, but which can be overwhelmed and become infected and inflamed.

Pharyngitis (sore throat)
Viruses cause most sore throats, but the bacterium *Streptococcus pyogenes* causes an illness known as "strep throat."

Laryngitis
Inflammation due to the viral or bacterial infection of the larynx (voice box) prevents the vocal cords from vibrating normally.

A typical rhinovirus

Cellular receptor

The common cold virus

The mild respiratory infection *coryza* may be caused by any of hundreds of different viral pathogens. Roughly half of all colds are caused by "rhinoviruses," "coronaviruses," and their relatives. Other unidentified viruses are probably responsible for many more. Most colds last about seven days, producing symptoms such as congestion, a sore throat, and headaches. Colds are highly contagious, moving easily from person to person via sneezes, coughs, and contaminated objects such as tissues.

CYSTIC FIBROSIS (CF)

CF is an inherited disorder most common among people of European descent. Among other effects, cells that produce mucus malfunction, resulting in thick, dry mucus clogging the airways. Severe lung infections develop when bacteria colonize the mucus. CF is incurable, but medicines—such as enzymes to thin the mucus or antibiotics to control the infections—can help to keep a person healthy. Massaging the back and chest (above) can also loosen the mucus so that it can be expelled orally.

COPD, OR CHRONIC OBSTRUCTIVE PULMONARY DISEASE, IS THE COLLECTIVE NAME FOR LUNG DISEASES SUCH AS CHRONIC BRONCHITIS AND EMPHYSEMA.

Lower respiratory disorders

Infections and disorders of the lower respiratory system can lead to more serious problems. In cigarette smokers, for example, bronchial inflammation can become chronic, causing a near-constant cough and breathing problems. Among adults, lung diseases of this kind are significant killers. Asthma is an allergic response to air pollutants or stress that can bring a lifetime of small crises and occasional emergencies in which the sufferer is in danger of suffocation.

Specialized drugs
administered by simple aerosol inhalers can either reduce the symptoms of asthma or make them less likely to occur.

Swelling of the airways
in bronchitis.

Bronchitis

In bronchitis, the bronchi and bronchioles connecting the trachea to the lungs can become inflamed due to an infection or a smoking-related illness. The infected airways also produce a thick mucus, which in turn triggers coughing spasms. Antibiotics can help to prevent these bacterial infections from spreading more deeply into the lungs.

Mucus
produced by the infected airways.

Asthma

Like some other airway disorders, asthma disrupts the functioning of the whole of the respiratory tree with inflammation and remodeling of the airways, which leads to airflow obstruction and symptoms that include wheezing, chest tightness, coughing, and shortness of breath.

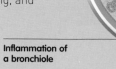

Inflammation of a bronchiole

Aerosol inhalers

Asthmatics can use a variety of inhalers to treat their condition. "Reliever" inhalers contain "bronchodilator" drugs to ease symptoms if a sufferer becomes wheezy, tight-chested, and short of breath. "Preventer" inhalers usually contain a steroid drug that reduces inflammation in the airways. This minimizes the chances of the airways becoming narrow enough to trigger the usual breathing difficulties.

LUNGS UNDER THREAT

Approximately 17,000 times a day, outside air fills tens of millions of alveoli, the tiny air sacs in the lungs. In addition to oxygen, nitrogen, and the other gases in air, each inhaled breath may contain an array of bacteria, viruses, fungal pathogens, industrial pollutants, toxins from cigarette smoke, and the like. All of these inhaled irritants have the potential to drastically reduce the number of healthy alveoli.

Damaging the delicate tissues

Lung diseases and disorders range from curable pneumonias and tuberculosis to COPD—which includes crippling bronchitis and emphysema—and potentially deadly cancers such as mesothelioma, which is linked to exposure to asbestos. The damage that these conditions cause to the lungs' tissues can severely limit their capacity to take oxygen into the bloodstream and expel carbon dioxide from the body.

Damage to the alveolar-capillary barrier
can be seen in various direct lung injuries (from pneumonia, toxic inhalation, or drowning, for example) and indirect lung injuries (from conditions such as sepsis, acute pancreatitis, and anaphylactic shock). This damage sometimes leads to pulmonary edema, or lung congestion, in which fluid is leaked from the capillaries and into the alveoli.

Partially thickened walls
of a diseased alveolus, which is characteristic of diseases collectively known as "diffuse interstitial fibrosis." This thickening impairs the process of gas exchange.

 CARCINOGENS ARE SUBSTANCES OR AGENTS THAT COULD POTENTIALLY CAUSE CANCER IN LIVING TISSUE.

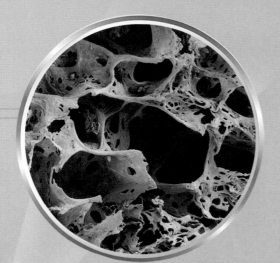

Smoking-related disorders

Cigarette smoke contains a blend of carcinogens and toxins. It is a major cause of, or contributor to, emphysema and chronic bronchitis (known collectively as chronic obstructive pulmonary disease, or COPD), lung cancer, heart disease, and several other malignancies. Inhaled smoke also impairs immunity and slows normal healing processes. This image (left) shows diseased lung tissue. In emphysema, the alveoli are damaged and enlarged. The walls surrounding them deteriorate, so that gas exchange cannot work as efficiently. Sufferers become increasingly short of breath as the condition advances.

Fingerlike projections
of the cancer cell membrane, called microvilli, increase the surface area of the cell. An increased number of microvilli may be linked to the cell's ability to move through the tissues—but their exact significance is not yet clear.

Mycobacterium tuberculosis
is a rod-shaped bacterium. The bacteria are shown up in red in this SEM image.

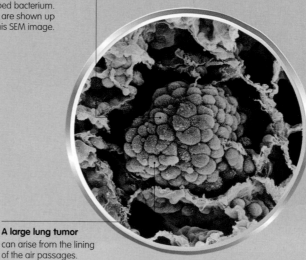

A large lung tumor
can arise from the lining of the air passages.

Tuberculosis

Tuberculosis (TB) is a communicable disease caused by a bacterium called *Mycobacterium tuberculosis*. It is characterized by the growth of nodules, or tubercles, in the tissues, mainly in the lungs. Symptoms include coughing up blood as the lungs deteriorate. Antibiotics once used to treat TB can no longer kill certain highly virulent strains. This means the disease is re-emerging as a major, global health threat.

Lung cancers

Metastasis (division and spreading) is very aggressive in lung cancers, so only a minority of patients survive for more than two or three years after diagnosis. The disease usually begins in the bronchial tubes and may spread to elsewhere in the lung tissues, lymph nodes, bones, and other sites. There is plenty of room for a tumor to expand in the soft, squashy lungs—without initially causing problems—so the early symptoms are often mistaken for other respiratory disorders.

CHAPTER TEN

LYMPHATIC
SYSTEM

Trained guard on duty

Scanning electron microscope images can plunge us into an eerie, almost science fiction-like world in which we can view the activities of specialized cells that defend the human body from attack. Our internal army includes different ranks of white blood cells, which are groomed for their specific tasks by the chemical functioning of the lymphatic system. This macrophage (shown in white) is just one example of a phagocyte, a cell that has been adapted to destroy and ingest invading pathogens or bits of potentially harmful debris. The system learns how to recognize different pathogens, bacteria, and other foreign bodies, so that our immune responses can target a specific type of threat.

DEFENSE SYSTEM

A far-flung network of lymphatic vessels threads through tissues everywhere in the body—except the central nervous system, which has its own system of lymph drainage. But the lymphatic system is not merely a passive network designed to drain and channel fluid. It is, in fact, an active system capable of collecting antigens (such as invading organisms) and presenting them to defensive cells in organs such as the lymph nodes, bone marrow, and the spleen.

Thymus
In this gland, T cells mature and acquire the capacity to mount the type of immune response known as cell-mediated immunity.

Thoracic duct
All but a few lymphatic trunks empty into this duct.

Peyer's patches
Clusters of lymphoid tissue in the lower small intestine, these patches house defensive cells that respond to pathogens in the gastrointestinal tract.

Cervical nerves
These lymph nodes receive lymph from tissues of the head and neck.

Right lymphatic duct
This duct collects lymph from the right arm and the right-hand side of the chest, neck, and head.

Tonsils
Humans have four tonsils located in the throat and tongue. They are positioned in these sites to intercept microbes that are either inhaled or consumed in food.

Left jugular trunk
Lymph draining from the left side of the head and neck enters this trunk.

Left subclavian trunk
Lymph from the left arm and shoulder flows into this trunk.

Auxiliary nodes
Lymph from tissues in the arms and breast filters through this system of 20 to 30 large lymph nodes around the armpits.

Spleen
This is the largest lymphatic organ. It removes defunct blood cells, bacteria, and debris from the blood. It is also where B cells develop the capacity to manufacture antibodies.

Red bone marrow

Lacteals
These lymphatic capillaries in the small intestine absorb digested dietary fats and shunt them into the bloodstream.

LYMPH IS A COLORLESS TISSUE FLUID THAT CIRCULATES THROUGH THE LYMPHATIC SYSTEM.

Hip bone marrow cavity

Bone marrow

In red bone marrow, stem cells give rise to blood cells, including B and T lymphocytes (see pages 212–215).

Popliteal nodes

There are six or seven of these nodes located in the fatty tissue behind each knee. They help to balance out the whole system by draining the surrounding areas of extra fluid to prevent a build-up.

Lymphatic vessel

Many miles of lymphatic vessels collect lymph from lymph capillaries and channel it onward.

Function one: hosting the immune system

The primary function of the lymphatic system's vessels, tissues, and organs is to serve as a bodywide staging area for defense. On its way to the larger veins near the heart, lymph fluid trickles through lymph nodes and other lymphoid tissues. At these sites, white blood vessels—including macrophages and lymphocytes—may intercept microbes, and other threats, and launch the immune system's defensive counterattacks. The thymus gland is slightly different, in that it only serves its defensive function until the end of puberty. After this stage, it slowly shrinks and is replaced by fat.

Function two: the cycle of lymph fluid

Tiny lymph capillaries take up leaked fluid—containing vital cells and proteins—from the spaces between cells in a tissue. The clear lymph fluid then passes into larger vessels and is filtered inside a succession of lymph nodes. Vessels that receive the cleansed lymph converge into lymph "trunks" that deliver their fluid cargo into ducts that return the lymph to large veins near the heart. In this way, the useful contents of the lymph is returned to the bloodstream.

NODES AND VESSELS

Lymph glands, or nodes, can basically be described as small, pea-sized lumps of tissue that contain white blood cells. Their network of locations along the lymph vessels is strategic. It allows the filtration of lymph fluid to be spread efficiently throughout the body, as well as ensuring that the whole of the anatomy is well served by the defensive cells housed in the nodes—a bit like siting a fire station at the edge of every neighborhood.

The filtering tissues

All lymphatic tissues, including GALT—gut associated lymphatic tissue, such as Peyer's patches—and the spleen, contain macrophages that collect (or "filter out") bacteria and other antigens, so that they can "present" them to the specialized cells of the immune system.

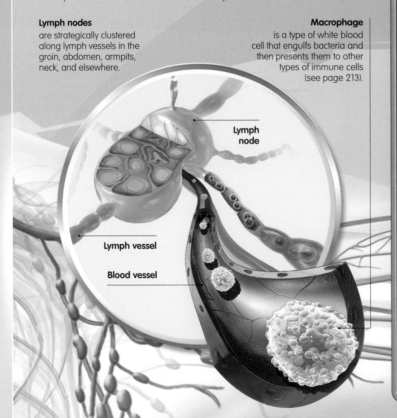

Lymph nodes
are strategically clustered along lymph vessels in the groin, abdomen, armpits, neck, and elsewhere.

Macrophage
is a type of white blood cell that engulfs bacteria and then presents them to other types of immune cells (see page 213).

Lymph node

Lymph vessel

Blood vessel

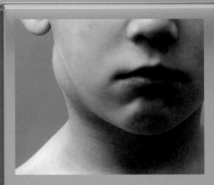

Swollen lymph glands

During an infection, lymph nodes servicing the affected area may swell up with general debris, which includes dead bacteria consumed by macrophages and T and B cells recruited to the node. Many different types of illness can cause swollen glands, including viral infections such as glandular fever or the common cold. Many cancers spread to the lymph glands, too, filling them with cancerous cells. Swollen glands may also be a sign of inflammation caused by an immune system disorder such as rheumatoid arthritis (see page 221).

 THE MOST COMMON CAUSE OF *SECONDARY LYMPHEDEMA* IS A PARASITIC WORM INFESTATION KNOWN AS FILARIAL DISEASE.

Blocked lymph vessels

Lymphedema is an accumulation of lymph fluid in the tissues that can cause severe swelling in areas such as the legs and ankles, leading to pain and loss of mobility. Less commonly, it can also affect the chest, head, and genitals. There are several types of primary lymphedema, caused by the abnormal development of the lymphatic system in the womb—although it is not always clear which genes are at fault. In some types, the swelling of the limbs does not develop until puberty. Secondary lymphedema is triggered by damage to the lymphatic system as a result of an infection, disease, injury, surgery, or cancer. It can also develop as a side effect of cancer treatments such as radiotherapy.

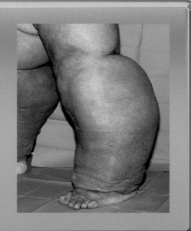

The paths of lymph vessels

Lymphatic capillaries are positioned close to the blood capillaries and venules in the body's tissues. The blind-ended capillaries converge to form the lymphatic vessels, in which valves prevent the lymph from flowing backward. As a result of this structure—and unlike the blood of the circulatory system—lymph flows in one direction only, toward the heart. Lymphatic vessels close to the skin generally follow veins, while those deeper in the body typically follow the paths of arteries.

Lymph capillary

Arteriole

Blind (closed) end of a lymph capillary

Venule

INFLAMMATORY RESPONSE

The body has a system of inborn or innate immunity—general but fast-acting responses that are deployed as soon as tissues are damaged, regardless of the source of the damage. Leading the list of these responses is inflammation, which mobilizes blood-borne substances and white blood cells to mount an immediate counterattack to injury.

Painful progress

Aspects of the process do produce discomfort, but an acute or sudden inflammatory response to tissue damage is essential to healing. Without it, wounds would not heal and even the most minor infections would advance unchecked.

Phase one: releasing cytokines

A breach of our outer covering, such as an open wound, exposes the body's inner tissues to invading bacteria. Tissue damage stimulates macrophages (see page 213) and healthy cells near the injury site to release chemicals called cytokines. Cytokines are "cell movers" that circulate in the blood and trigger the cascade of inflammation responses that follow.

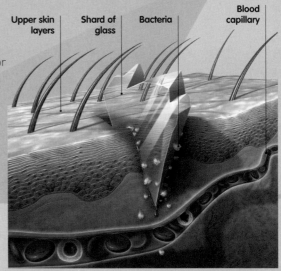

Upper skin layers | Shard of glass | Bacteria | Blood capillary

Uncontrolled inflammation

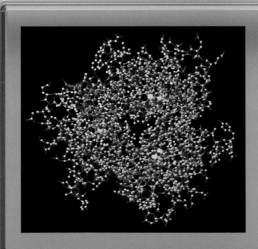

The internal mechanisms that regulate inflammation, and bring it to a close, are crucial to the body's health. A protein called tumor necrosis factor (left), or TNF, is a "messenger" molecule that communicates with immune cells and tissues in the onset of the healing process. However, TNF can also initiate "necrotic cell death," which leads to unwanted inflammatory responses and is also involved in autoimmune diseases. Uncontrolled, chronic inflammation can encourage the development of disease or the spread of tumors. It is a major factor in cancer, coronary heart disease, and arthritis—and is also related to the aging process.

Phase two: increasing blood flow

Once the cytokines have launched the inflammation process, the resulting flood of defensive chemicals—especially histamine—dilates small blood vessels and loosens connections between the cells in their walls. This makes the vessels "leaky."

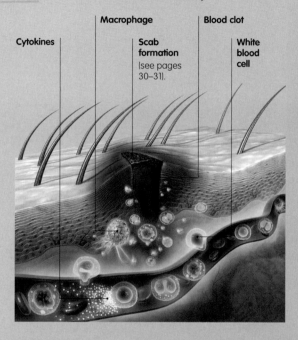

Cytokines

Macrophage

Scab formation (see pages 30–31).

Blood clot

White blood cell

Mast cells

Mast cells are a category of white blood cells that congregate near blood vessels in connective tissue. They release histamine, which dilates blood vessels during inflammation and allergic responses. During an infection, mast cells also function as cell-eating phagocytes, attaching themselves to invading bacteria in order to ingest and destroy them.

Phase three: delivery of white blood cells

As more blood flows to the affected area, various types of white blood cells squeeze out of the leaky vessels and into damaged tissues. These defensive cells—including neutrophils and macrophages—detect, bind on to, and destroy bacteria, and then consume the debris.

Elevated core temperatures

An infection of the body may result in a fever, an abnormally elevated core temperature rising above 98.6°F (37°C). Fever develops when macrophages and other white blood cells release pyrogens, chemicals that stimulate the hypothalamus to shift the activity of brain centers that regulate body temperature. The good news is that mild to moderate fevers speed up the process of tissue repair.

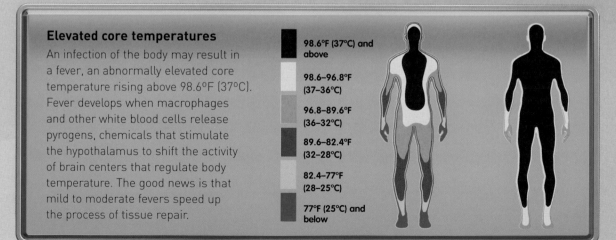

98.6°F (37°C) and above

98.6–96.8°F (37–36°C)

96.8–89.6°F (36–32°C)

89.6–82.4°F (32–28°C)

82.4–77°F (28–25°C)

77°F (25°C) and below

IMMUNE RESPONSES

The defensive strategies known as adaptive or acquired immunity use lymphocytes. These are the specialized white blood cells that develop in parts of the lymphatic system, including red bone marrow and the thymus. Among these cells are T and B lymphocytes, located within lymph nodes and other lymphatic tissues.

T cell production

Once stem cells in red bone marrow have given rise to lymphocytes, a subset of those freshly-formed defenders travels in the blood to the thymus, where they are exposed to thymic hormones for several days. During that time, a "teaching and selection" process makes changes to these lymphocytes, producing "T cells" that can recognize invaders and mount a counterattack. The key part of this system is the creation of an "immune memory," so that subsequent responses to the same pathogen are rapid and enhanced.

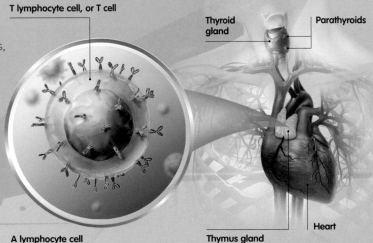

T lymphocyte cell, or T cell

Thyroid gland

Parathyroids

Heart

A lymphocyte cell
T and B cells play the major role in adaptive immune responses, which target specific invaders of the body's tissues and cells.

Thymus gland
is large and active in childhood, but it shrinks steadily after puberty—to be replaced by fatty tissue.

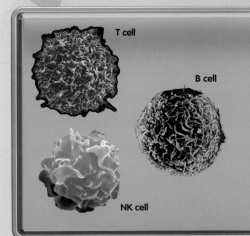

T cell

B cell

NK cell

Lymphocytes

T cells are the catalysts of cellular immunity. They launch and support the activities of other cells that can detect or destroy infected or abnormal body cells. B cells, by contrast, produce antibodies—defensive proteins that counteract threats that have yet to enter body cells. These threats include bacteria, viruses, protozoa, and toxins circulating in tissues or body fluids such as blood. "Natural killer" (NK) cells are a third type of lymphocyte. They are mainly active in inborn responses that destroy body cells that are either cancerous or infected by a virus.

Adaptive immunity

The actions of B and T cells are known as adaptive immunity. This refers to their ability to tailor their response to a specific pathogen or abnormal cell. They develop a "memory" of the different pathogens they encounter.

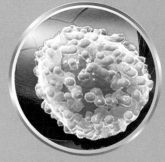

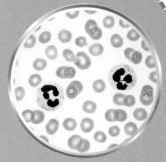

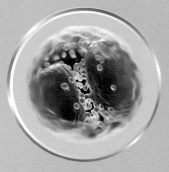

Macrophages

Macrophages are antigen-presenting cells (APCs). The main job of APCs is to capture and display antigens to lymphocytes. Most APCs operate in the periphery, where they survey tissues for antigens. They have receptors that recognize broad classes of microbial antigens. When stimulated, these receptors cause the stimulating antigen to be "endocytosed" (swallowed up).

Neutrophils

Neutrophils (purple) are the most abundant white blood cells. Like macrophages, they are phagocytes ("cell eaters") that chemically "clean up" as part of an immune response. They converge on inflamed, infected, or damaged tissues by following chemical trails released by injured cells.

Basophils

Normally, up to one percent of white blood cells are basophils, which release histamine to promote inflammation. They circulate in the bloodstream but perform their function in connective tissue. In their cytoplasm, they have granules (shown in light blue, above) containing histamine and other chemicals.

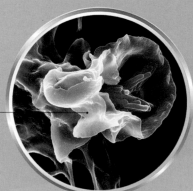

This macrophage is engulfing TB bacteria (shown in pink). The process is known as phagocytosis.

Inside a lymph node

A lymph node consists of clusters of white blood cells, including lymphocytes and macrophages. As lymph passes through small lymph vessels, these defenders attack and kill bacteria or other antigen-bearing material they detect in it.

Recognizing foreign bodies

The body needs to be able to recognize cells and substances that belong and those that are foreign. Lymphocytes and macrophages can detect gene-coded chemical features on the surface of a cell that signify "self" and "non-self." Self markers, called MHC proteins, are normally ignored. Non-self markers, known as antigens, normally trigger an immune response. Autoimmune disorders can develop when the immune system mistakes normal body cells for foreign material—and starts attacking them.

DEFENSE CELLS IN ACTION

When T and B lymphocytes have reached full maturity, they move into lymph nodes, the spleen, and other lymphatic tissues. In these places, they monitor lymph for bacteria, viruses, defective, or cancerous body cells—or anything else chemically recognizable as foreign, or "non-self." If invading bacteria are not destroyed by the inflammatory response, T cells, B cells—or both—will activate and begin to mobilize.

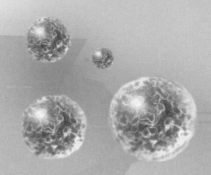

Parasites

White blood cells called eosinophils can attach to and chemically destroy parasitic worms in the body. Like other defensive cells, they respond to surface antigens that indicate a foreign cell, substance, or parasite. This image shows the *Schistosoma* worm, which causes a parasitic disease called schistosomiasis, also known as snail fever.

Recognizing pathogens

The huge ranks of T cells and B cells, shown in this illustration (right), also include "memory cells" that remain in the bloodstream after the invasion of foreign material has been dealt with. This means that they are available to mount a more rapid and efficient counterattack if the exact same pathogen enters the body again.

T cell activity

There are several types of T cell. "Helper" T cells release cytokines (see page 210) that stimulate cytotoxic T cells and NK (natural killer) cells to multiply, forming armies of defenders primed to destroy infected body cells.

B cell activity

Clones of B cells develop, each one creating a flood of antibodies (defensive proteins) that are attuned to a different potential threat. The antibodies attach themselves to their targets and "label" them for destruction by other defensive components of the immune system.

 DENDRITIC CELLS PROCESS ANTIGEN MATERIAL AND THEN PRESENT IT TO T CELLS.

Viral attacks

When a virus infects a cell, it introduces its foreign DNA, then quickly multiplies and destroys its host. Immune defenders called dendritic cells display the remains of the dead cell to T cells in the lymph nodes or spleen. This interaction stimulates the multiplication of cytotoxic, "cell-killing" T cells, which then enter the bloodstream and kill any body cells infected with the same virus.

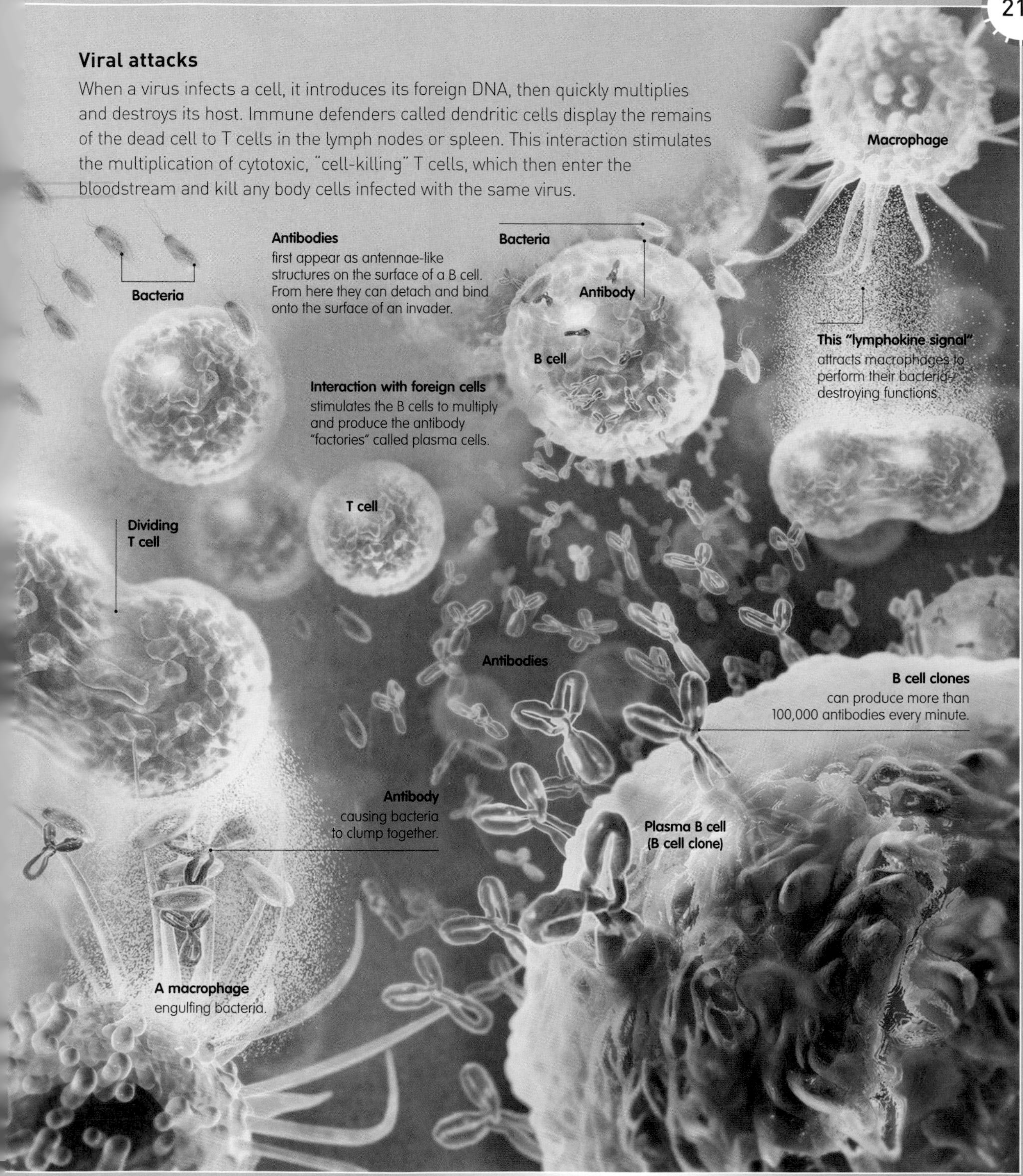

Macrophage

Bacteria

Antibodies
first appear as antennae-like structures on the surface of a B cell. From here they can detach and bind onto the surface of an invader.

Bacteria

Antibody

This "lymphokine signal"
attracts macrophages to perform their bacteria-destroying functions.

B cell

Interaction with foreign cells
stimulates the B cells to multiply and produce the antibody "factories" called plasma cells.

T cell

Dividing T cell

Antibodies

B cell clones
can produce more than 100,000 antibodies every minute.

Antibody
causing bacteria to clump together.

Plasma B cell (B cell clone)

A macrophage
engulfing bacteria.

BOOSTING IMMUNITY

Active immunity develops the first time a pathogen challenges the immune system, stimulating B cells to produce both antibodies and memory cells to act against it. This "primary response" often involves a bout of illness. Immunization gives the body an "acquired" immunity by introducing it to a dead or weakened pathogen that provokes a mild—or even unnoticeable—response, which also triggers the formation of memory cells.

Harnessing the immune system

The components of natural immunity are making major contributions to clinical advances and even consumer products. Monoclonal antibodies (MABs) are used to diagnose allergies, rabies, and hepatitis—and to screen for prostate cancer and other malignancies. MABs can also identify drug residues in a person's bloodstream and are used in pregnancy tests.

Creating monoclonal antibodies

One method for making monoclonal antibodies is by injecting a mouse, rat, or rabbit with an antigen (toxin) to trigger the formation of B cells, the producers of natural antibodies. The B cells are then fused with modified cancer cells, yielding hybrid cells that produce antibodies and multiply rapidly.

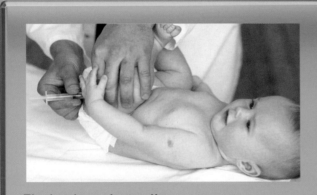

The battle against polio

Poliomyelitis, or polio, was a much-feared disease for centuries. Poliovirus causes nerve damage that results in varying degrees of paralysis, often in the legs. In one type (bulbar polio) acute respiratory paralysis can be fatal. The first polio vaccines began to be administered worldwide in the 1950s and '60s. Although polio is now rare, it is on the increase in war-torn areas, and in other regions that have poor access to healthcare.

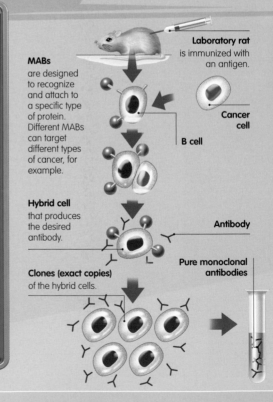

Laboratory rat is immunized with an antigen.

MABs are designed to recognize and attach to a specific type of protein. Different MABs can target different types of cancer, for example.

Cancer cell

B cell

Hybrid cell that produces the desired antibody.

Antibody

Pure monoclonal antibodies

Clones (exact copies) of the hybrid cells.

 MONOCLONAL ANTIBODIES (MABs) ARE LAB-CREATED COPIES OF ONE SPECIFIC TYPE OF ANTIBODY.

Macrophages on the attack

Many vaccines contain "attenuated" (weakened) bacteria or viruses. This artwork shows a macrophage (left) engulfing weakened bacteria (shown in pink). The macrophage later "presents" fragments of the bacteria to B cells—the first step toward generating antibodies and memory cells for dealing with the same bacteria in the future.

This chest X-ray shows a lung cancer tumor being treated with a genetically-engineered drug called interleukin-2 (IL-2).

An implant chamber delivers the artificial drug to where it is needed.

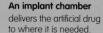

Immunotherapy

Monoclonal antibodies have been developed for use against common malignancies such as colorectal cancer and breast cancer. Therapeutic "immunotoxins" join toxic proteins with MABs to deliver a chemical poison to the cancerous cells. Other forms of biological therapy employ cytokines (see page 210), including interferons and interleukins, to boost a patient's immune responses.

ROUTINE IMMUNIZATION

Although immunization is not risk-free, today it protects hundreds of millions of people from once-common childhood ills, such as measles, polio, tetanus, diphtheria, and whooping cough. Travelers are routinely vaccinated against infectious diseases such as typhoid fever and yellow fever. Medical immunotherapies also utilize the various natural components in our immune system to treat cancer and other diseases.

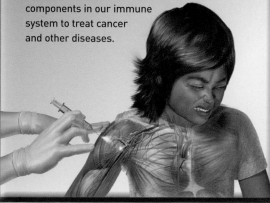

ADDITIONAL BARRIERS

The body's surface contains many extra barriers to infection. We have an intact covering of skin, as well as mucous membranes that line the body cavities that open to the outside—the entire digestive tract, the respiratory airways, and the urogenital openings such as the vagina and urethra. Urine, vaginal secretions, tears, and saliva also contain protective substances, while the thousands of types of harmless bacteria in human tissues may prevent potential pathogens from gaining a foothold.

Hair follicles
Sebum produced in hair follicles contains acids that inhibit the growth of certain bacteria and fungi.

Eyes
Tears contain lysozyme, an enzyme that chemically attacks and helps to destroy many microbes.

Mouth and throat
Like tears, saliva contains antimicrobial chemicals. Coughing also helps to expel foreign particles trapped in mucus lining the airways (see page 200).

Respiratory tract
Mucus-coated cilia line the airways and trap foreign particles. The rhythmic beating of the cilia helps to sweep the trapped material up toward the throat for ejection.

The complement system

There are around 20 proteins in the body that form a "complement system," which enhances the other natural defenses. The proteins circulate in the bloodstream and respond to chemical cues given off by bacteria, some types of viruses and various parasites. At first, contact with a pathogen may activate only a few of the proteins, but the response rapidly expands until large numbers of defensive proteins are working to kill off the foreign cells in the bloodstream.

"Jekyll and Hyde" bacteria

Some beneficial bacteria can become harmful when they spread outside of their normal location. For example, these E. coli bacteria (above) usually inhabit the gut, where they produce vitamin K—a vital factor in blood clotting (see page 189). However, if the same E. coli bacteria get into the urinary system, they can cause disease.

Genitourinary tract
Intact mucous membranes in these passages physically block any foreign microbes. The mucus they secrete is another effective deterrent.

 URINE HAS A PH VALUE OF 4.6 TO 8.0, SO IT IS NOT NEARLY AS ACIDIC AS GASTRIC FLUID (PH 1 TO 2).

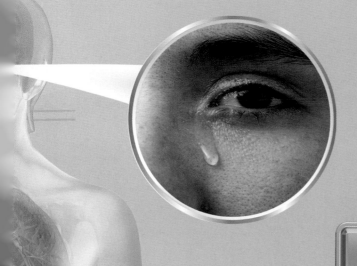

Flushing out the problem

Tears contain antimicrobial substances, such as lysozyme, that act to protect the exposed surface of the eyeball. Urine is normally acidic and therefore inhospitable to most micro-organisms. Urination also physically flushes microbes out of the urinary tract. Diarrhea is equally beneficial for removing intestinal microbes. Doctors recommend allowing moderate diarrhea to take its course, rather than taking drugs to try and prevent it.

Unbroken skin
Most micro-organisms cannot get past the skin's tough, keratinized, acidic upper layer unless it is broken by a cut or scratch.

Stomach
Acid and enzymes in gastric fluid (see page 230) can kill off many bacteria.

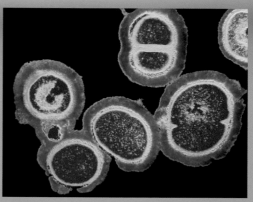

MRSA *Staphylococcus* **bacteria** are resistant to many commonly prescribed antibiotics.

Intestines
The normal, resident bacteria of the gut produce substances that help to destroy foreign bacteria. Mucus in this region also traps micro-organisms.

Using antibiotics

Antibiotic drugs cannot kill viruses, but they have saved millions of lives by augmenting the natural defenses that counteract harmful bacteria, fungi, and parasites. They only work effectively, however, if a patient takes the full course prescribed—otherwise, the pathogen may develop a way of resisting the drug. Our current dependence on antibiotics has become a modern-day medical crisis. There is an increasing and highly urgent need to find ways to deal with antibiotic-resistant disease.

Protein attack strategies

Complement proteins may also form pore-like structures in the offending cells, causing them to burst. In other cases, they add a chemical coating to the invader. This makes the pathogen more easily detectable by white blood cells, which follow the chemical trail to any sites where damage has occurred.

ALLERGIES AND DISEASES

Our immune defenses are based on constant surveillance of blood and tissue fluids for signs of potentially dangerous infection. Hypersensitivities, or allergies, can sometimes confuse these defense mechanisms. Allergic reactions are immune responses launched against normally harmless substances, often particles or chemicals in the air or in food.

Common allergens

Allergies are targeted at foreign proteins. Almost all allergens are proteins, and a range of everyday items can trigger an allergic response. Dander, or material shed by animals, contains dead skin, hair, or feathers and is a common allergen. Pollen from trees, grasses, and other plants is the source of seasonal allergies. Many people are also allergic to foods such as eggs, milk, nuts, strawberries, and shellfish.

Pollen grains
from a ragweed flower, *Ambrosia psilostachya,* one of the allergens that can cause hay fever in those who are susceptible.

Magnified SEM image
of dust mites colonizing household fabric.

Hay fever

In allergic rhinitis, or hay fever, plant pollen or some other substance triggers allergic symptoms in the nasal passages and eyes. Once a person becomes sensitized to a given allergen, B cells produce IgE antibodies to work against it. When the allergen challenges the immune system, these antibodies stimulate mast cells (see page 211), which in turn stimulate the common hay fever symptoms—sneezing, congestion, tearing, or itching in the eyes, and the secretion of copious mucus in the nasal passages.

Dust mites

The secreted wastes of microscopic dust mites can bring on allergy attacks inside the home.

AN *ALLERGEN* IS A SUBSTANCE THAT STIMULATES AN IMMUNE SYSTEM RESPONSE.

Infection, cancer, and malfunctions of lymphatic defenses underlie a wide array of difficult and disabling health challenges. Autoimmune diseases, for example, unleash body defenses against normal, healthy tissues. Medications that suppress the immune system, such as steroids, can help to relieve symptoms of autoimmune disorders, although they also increase a patient's risk of infection.

Autoimmune disorders

In autoimmune diseases, inflammation, misguided T cells, or antibodies from B cells—or a combination of these factors—injure or destroy healthy tissues. In rheumatoid arthritis, for example, the membrane lining the joints in the hands, limbs, and spine becomes inflamed.

Hodgkin lymphoma

In this disease, B cells become cancerous. The cancer often spreads before it has been detected. However, swollen lymph glands sometimes indicate that something is wrong.

Non-Hodgkin lymphoma (NHL)

This type of cancer is much more common than Hodgkin lymphoma. It may develop in either B cells or T cells. Early symptoms mimic those of Hodgkin lymphoma or a severe bout of flu. Treatments include chemotherapy, radiation therapy, and—increasingly—biological therapies that employ monoclonal antibodies (see pages 216–217).

Lupus

Abnormal inflammation also occurs in "systemic lupus erythematosus" (SLE). This autoimmune disease is normally known, more simply, as lupus. The inflammation develops in the blood vessels and causes body-wide damage, which is most severe in the kidneys, heart, lungs, and skin. Patients also experience fatigue and may develop heart and kidney disease.

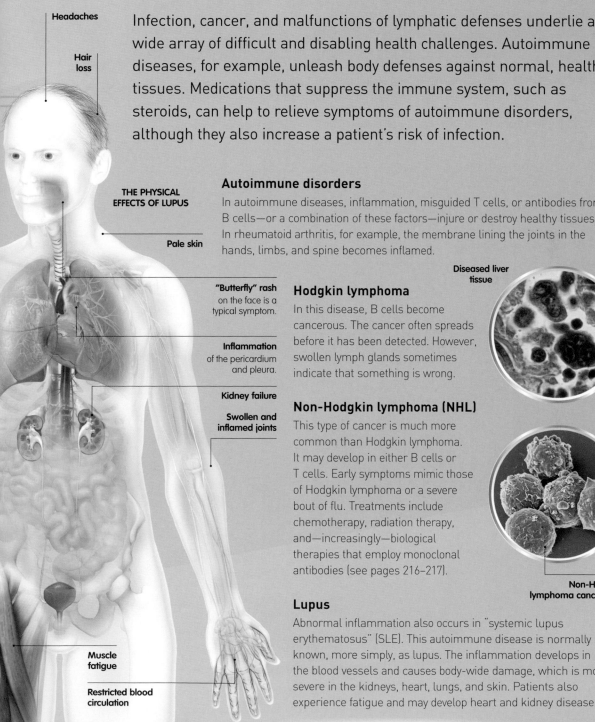

THE PHYSICAL EFFECTS OF LUPUS

Headaches

Hair loss

Pale skin

"Butterfly" rash on the face is a typical symptom.

Inflammation of the pericardium and pleura.

Kidney failure

Swollen and inflamed joints

Muscle fatigue

Restricted blood circulation

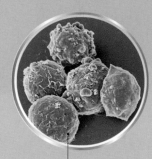

Diseased liver tissue

Non-Hodgkin lymphoma cancer cells

IMMUNE DEFICIENCY DISEASES

Immune deficiency is an inborn or acquired disorder in which the immune system becomes weakened or disabled—providing little or no defense against harmful organisms or abnormal body cells. Congenital immunodeficiency disorders may result from defects in B lymphocytes, T lymphocytes—or both—and can also occur in the innate immune system.

AIDS and the spread of HIV

Acquired immunodeficiency syndrome (AIDS) is caused through infection by the human immunodeficiency virus (HIV). HIV is usually transmitted by contaminated body fluids, such as during unsafe sexual contact or when needles are shared for intravenous drug use. The epidemic has spurred intensive educational efforts and an ongoing search for an effective vaccine. Patients who receive advanced drug treatments can now live with HIV, in relatively good health, for many years.

An infected T cell

In this SEM image, the HIV particles appear as red specks on the surface of a human T lymphocyte cell. The virus particles are budding from the infected cell, entering lymph nodes or the bloodstream in order to renew the cycle of infection.

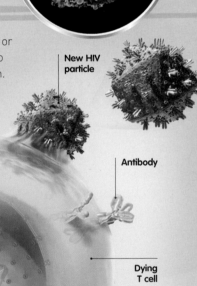

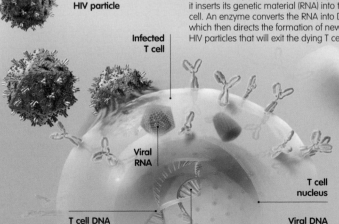

New HIV particle

HIV particle

Infected T cell

How HIV replicates
When an HIV particle infects a T lymphocyte, it inserts its genetic material (RNA) into the cell. An enzyme converts the RNA into DNA, which then directs the formation of new HIV particles that will exit the dying T cell.

Antibody

Dying T cell

Viral RNA

T cell nucleus

T cell DNA

Viral DNA

 CONGENITAL (INBORN) IMMUNODEFICIENCIES ARE ALSO KNOWN AS *PRIMARY IMMUNODEFICIENCIES*.

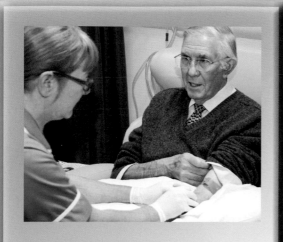

CHEMOTHERAPY

Chemotherapy is used to treat cancer and some non-cancerous conditions. It introduces potent substances, such as cytotoxic drugs, into the bloodstream so that they can reach cancer cells and damage them. Unfortunately, this aggressive form of therapy often seriously disables the immune system. It kills other naturally dividing cells, including the stem cells in bone marrow that produce lymphocytes, vital components of the immune system.

Transplants and immune response

When transplants are rejected, T cells, macrophages, and B cells respond to the foreign "self" proteins (our MHC markers, see page 213) on donor cells as antigens. As a result, they launch a swift attack to rid the tissue from the body. Most transplants are "allografts," which are grafts of tissue donated from one human to another. Allografts are screened to ensure that the donors share the patient's blood type and a majority of the same MHC markers. This is why close relatives are usually the best source for donated organs.

Organ transplants

For patients with severely impaired organs, a transplant may be the only hope for survival. Similarly, where disease or injury has damaged certain tissues, replacements can dramatically improve the quality of life. The most commonly transplanted organs and tissues are shown here. Tissue transplants—such as skin transplants—have a fairly high success rate because they rarely trigger rejection.

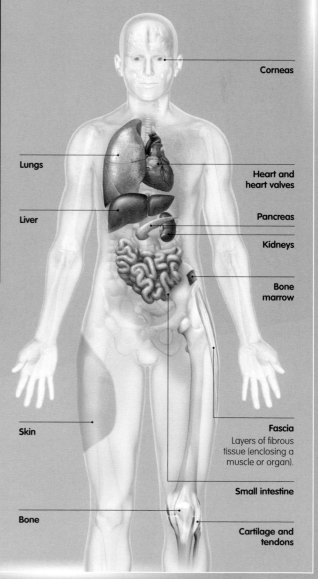

Corneas

Lungs

Heart and heart valves

Liver

Pancreas

Kidneys

Bone marrow

Skin

Fascia
Layers of fibrous tissue (enclosing a muscle or organ).

Small intestine

Bone

Cartilage and tendons

DIGESTIVE SYSTEM

Mucus-making cells

The process of digesting food and bringing its nutritional units into the body is a steady, gradual, and continuous one, which is both mechanical and chemical in nature. The stomach is a perfect example of this dual mechanism. Physically, it's a muscular, churning machine, but it wouldn't be able to perform its function without the acerbic secretions emanating from its lining, called the mucosa (shown here). Our gastric juices have to be acidic and aggressive enough to break down the useful materials in food, so that they can be absorbed. At the same time, the stomach needs to protect itself from its own chemistry—so, cells in its lining release a mucus that prevents the organ from eating away at itself.

DIGESTIVE TRACT

All food must go through the complex process of being broken down into nutrients that cells can use to build and operate their parts. This is the task of the digestive system. Although it appears to have many separate, individual steps, it is important to understand that the system is a single, continuous process. The contents of the gut are constantly changing, and some elements of it transform into materials that are able to pass into blood vessels—for the nourishment of trillions of cells.

Parts of an integrated process

Digestion is an integrated mechanical and chemical process. Each bite of food must first be reduced, by the teeth, into smaller pieces that can be further broken down by enzymes in saliva—and other body chemicals—to yield the simple sugars of proteins, the simple sugars of carbohydrates, the acids that make up fats and oils, and the nucleic acids that make up DNA.

Salivary glands
Three main pairs—and numerous minor sets—of these glands release saliva. Saliva is a mixture of water, mucus, digestive enzymes, and other substances.

Pharynx
This area receives food that is ready to be swallowed. It moves it on to the esophagus.

Epiglottis
During swallowing, this movable flap of tissue closes over the larynx to prevent food from entering the respiratory airways.

Oral cavity (mouth)
The system begins at the mouth, or oral cavity, where food is moistened by saliva, chewed by teeth, and then swallowed. The digestion of carbohydrates also starts here.

Teeth
Human teeth are specialized for tearing and chewing a wide variety of foodstuffs.

Upper esophageal sphincter
This muscular ring regulates the movement of swallowed food into the esophagus itself.

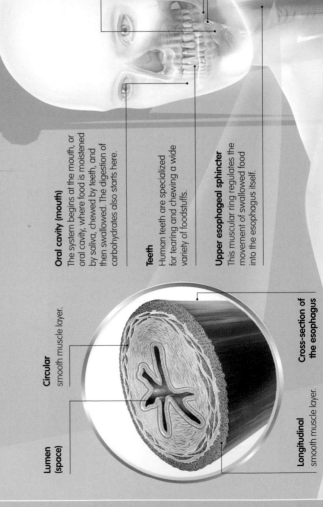

Lumen (space)

Circular
smooth muscle layer.

Longitudinal
smooth muscle layer.

Cross-section of the esophagus

The internal structure

The primary digestive organs, such as the esophagus, stomach, and intestines, share the same basic structure. Lined with epithelium, they are hollow and able to swell, with a wall built from smooth muscle layers oriented in different directions. Contractions of the layered muscle keep ingested food moving through the system.

Stomach

Muscular and stretchable, this organ receives and stores swallowed food and mechanically mixes it with enzymes that begin the digestion of proteins and complete the digestion of carbohydrates. Food usually remains in this organ for three to three-and-a-half hours.

Liver

The liver is the most massive body organ. One of its digestive roles is the secretion of bile, which aids the digestion of fats.

Esophagus

Contractions of smooth muscle in this tubular organ shift food on toward the stomach. Food moves from the esophagus to the stomach in about ten seconds.

Lower esophageal sphincter

This sphincter normally relaxes when food is swallowed, allowing it to pass smoothly into the stomach.

Pancreas

Most of the pancreas provides digestive enzymes that empty into the small intestine, while small islets of endocrine cells produce hormones, such as insulin, which regulate blood sugar.

Small intestine

Most of the chemical digestion and absorption of food occurs here, in a series of regions called the duodenum, jejunum, and ileum. Food spends between four and eight hours here.

Large intestine (or colon)

This includes the cecum, the ascending, transverse, descending, and sigmoid colons, and the rectum. Its primary functions are to absorb water and electrolytes and to eliminate solid wastes. Material spends between 12 and 36 hours in this part of the gut.

Descending colon

Transverse colon

Gallbladder

Ascending colon

Cecum

Appendix

Sigmoid colon

Rectum

This receives and expels feces.

Anus

Feces pass to the outside through this terminal opening of the digestive tract. The waste form of food emerges here up to two days after the food was originally ingested.

Villi

are the tiny, fingerlike projections that reach out from the lining of the small intestine (see pages 232–233).

The digestive tube

The digestive system, or gastrointestinal tract, is essentially an elaborate tube that begins at the mouth and ends at the anus. Biologically speaking, food passing through this tube is still "outside" the body. In fact, only the nutrients from digested food enter the body when they cross the intestinal lining into the bloodstream.

FOOD PROCESSING

The digestive system obtains nutrients from food by dismantling ingested material mechanically and chemically. These processes begin in the mouth, where food is manipulated to produce a "bolus" of chewed material. A series of voluntary and involuntary muscle contractions then combine to move the food into the esophagus, so that it can be conveyed to the stomach for further chemical and mechanical processing.

Biting and chewing

For solid foods, biting and chewing are the initial stages of food processing. Pointed incisors and conical canine (cuspid) teeth spear and tear food, while broader premolars and molars mash and grind it. Sequential muscle contractions then push a bolus into the pharynx, raise the larynx, and direct food into the esophagus.

Food on the move

Muscles in the esophagus begin to contract and relax as food passes into the tube (see page 231). This mechanism forces the bolus downward. A sphincter at the base of the esophagus allows small amounts of food into the stomach, where the muscles of the stomach wall grind it further.

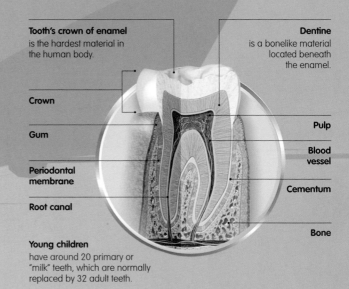

Tooth's crown of enamel is the hardest material in the human body.

Crown

Gum

Periodontal membrane

Root canal

Dentine is a bonelike material located beneath the enamel.

Pulp

Blood vessel

Cementum

Bone

Young children have around 20 primary or "milk" teeth, which are normally replaced by 32 adult teeth.

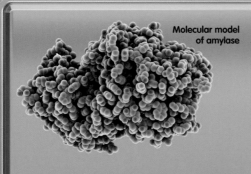

Molecular model of amylase

Digesting carbohydrate

The digestion of simple carbohydrates begins as soon as a bite of starchy food—such as bread, cereals, or dried fruit—enters the mouth. Foods high in carbohydrates begin to dissolve in the mouth as salivary amylase breaks the chemical bonds that hold the starch molecules together. This enzyme is, in fact, the first of many that act on various types of substances in food, including proteins and fats, as it travels through the system.

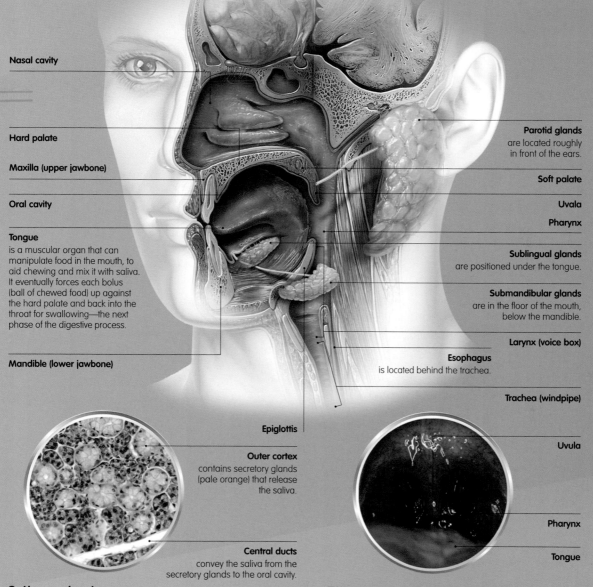

Nasal cavity

Hard palate

Maxilla (upper jawbone)

Oral cavity

Tongue
is a muscular organ that can manipulate food in the mouth, to aid chewing and mix it with saliva. It eventually forces each bolus (ball of chewed food) up against the hard palate and back into the throat for swallowing—the next phase of the digestive process.

Mandible (lower jawbone)

Parotid glands
are located roughly in front of the ears.

Soft palate

Uvala

Pharynx

Sublingual glands
are positioned under the tongue.

Submandibular glands
are in the floor of the mouth, below the mandible.

Larynx (voice box)

Esophagus
is located behind the trachea.

Trachea (windpipe)

Epiglottis

Outer cortex
contains secretory glands (pale orange) that release the saliva.

Central ducts
convey the saliva from the secretory glands to the oral cavity.

Uvula

Pharynx

Tongue

Salivary glands

The action of chewing also moistens and mixes food with saliva that enters from the salivary glands. This mix of substances contains water, sticky proteins called mucins—which help to bind bits of chewed food into a ball or bolus—and salivary amylase, which begins the breakdown of starchy carbohydrates.

The muscular action of swallowing

The tip of the tongue first pushes the bolus toward the throat. The uvula and larynx then move upward, forcing the bolus down. Muscles in the pharynx contract to close off the larynx and trachea. The bolus then slides into the esophagus and continues on its journey toward the stomach.

THE STOMACH

The human stomach is a hollow, J-shaped, expandable, muscular organ about 10in (25cm) in diameter. It briefly stores food, mixes it with enzymes—and other secretions—and regulates the food's transmission into the small intestine. The sheets of smooth muscle in its walls (right) contract in waves. This mechanism churns up the food boluses to continue the mechanical process of digestion.

Gastric secretions

Secretions of gastric juices—which include hydrochloric acid, water, and the building blocks of enzymes, called pepsins—accompany the waves of peristalsis (see page 231) that keep the material shifting steadily through the system. The acid kills off many food-borne microbes and helps to transform ingested food into the milky substance called chyme. Meanwhile, pepsins begin to chemically break down any large proteins in the chyme.

Serosa (outer covering)

Longitudinal layer of smooth muscle.

Circular layer of smooth muscle.

Oblique layer of smooth muscle.

Stomach folds
are known as *rugae*. The stomach wall contracts and folds into these *rugae* when the organ is empty. As food enters, the *rugae* smooth out.

Peristalsis (see panel, right)
operates continually to advance the digesting food all the way through the system. This gradual, steady movement of partially digested food material allows the small intestine to process it without being overburdened.

Small intestine begins here.

Pyloric sphincter (or pylorus)
is a muscular valve located at the base of the stomach. It closes the stomach when its muscles contract. When the pylorus relaxes, the sphincter opens—and this allows the gastric muscles to squeeze out the stomach's contents (as chyme) into the upper small intestine. Only a few teaspoonlike quantities move through it at a time. It can take up to four hours, or sometimes longer, for a completely full stomach to empty via the pyloric sphincter.

Duodenum

Not just a mashing machine

The stomach is not simply a device for mixing up masses of food. It is also an integral part of the self-regulating "feedback circuit" of the gastrointestinal system. The stomach produces hormones—such as gastrin, ghrelin, and leptin—that control other aspects of nutrient intake. Gastrin stimulates the secretion of gastric fluid. Ghrelin (the "hunger hormone") stimulates appetite, while leptin suppresses food intake and regulates fat storage.

Stomach capacity
is normally about a quart (liter) of food and drink. However, this capacity can swell to as much as 1.1 gallons (4.2 liters), or about 20 times its volume when empty.

GASTRIC MUCUS LUBRICATES FOOD MASSES AND PREVENTS THE MUCOSA FROM BEING DAMAGED BY ITS OWN (ACIDIC) GASTRIC FLUID.

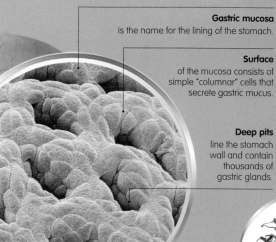

Gastric mucosa
is the name for the lining of the stomach.

Surface
of the mucosa consists of simple "columnar" cells that secrete gastric mucus.

Deep pits
line the stomach wall and contain thousands of gastric glands.

Nutrients and substances
that cannot be absorbed into the bloodstream here are absorbed via the small and large intestines.

The stomach's inner surface

Although enzymes begin to chemically digest carbohydrates, proteins, and fats in the stomach, only a few substances are actually absorbed into the bloodstream here. This is because the cells of the stomach lining cannot absorb most nutrients. The lining's mucus-secreting cells, however, can absorb some water, alcohol, a few drugs (such as aspirin), some mineral ions, and fragments from dismantled fat molecules.

Lipase molecule

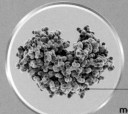

Pepsin molecule

Stomach enzymes

Two major enzymes (above) form part of the gastric juices. Pepsin begins the digestion of proteins, while gastric lipase breaks down fat molecules into smaller fragments.

Peristalsis

The muscle layers that form the wall of the digestive tube "criss-cross" each other (see page 226) and contract in sequence. This "squeeze-relax-repeat" sequence, known as peristalsis, accomplishes two important functions. Firstly, it mixes material in the tube with digestive enzymes that chemically dismantle large molecules in food, such as proteins and fat. In addition, the wall movements move the food through the gastrointestinal tract at a steady, gradual, controlled rate—so that nutrients can be extracted along the way.

THE SMALL INTESTINE

The long, folded tubes of intestines are divided into two major sections: the small intestine, where most food digestion occurs, and the large intestine (or colon), where the processing concludes, water is absorbed and food residues are stored—prior to being eliminated from the body.

Most nutrients
contained in the chyme entering the small intestine are absorbed in the jejunum and ileum.

Duodenum

Jejunum
is approximately 3ft (1m) long.

Spiraling folds
of the duodenum's inner lining.

Ileum
is roughly 12ft (3.6m) long and the last part of it, the terminal ileum, empties into the large bowel at the cecum (or the ileocecal junction).

Cecum
of the large intestine (colon).

Appendix

The duodenum

The first section of the small intestine is the duodenum. It is only about 10in (25cm) long. This is the entry point for chyme, pancreatic enzymes, and bile. The spiraling folds visible here produce a churning action that helps to mix up these ingredients. This structure also maximizes opportunities for nutrients in the chyme to be absorbed.

A long, coiled tube

The small intestine is approximately 20ft (6m) long and consists of three sections—the duodenum, jejunum, and ileum. This coiled tube contains roughly 2,700 square feet (300 square meters) of surface area for absorbing nutrients into the bloodstream.

 DUODENUM COMES FROM A MEDIEVAL LATIN WORD, *DUODENI*, MEANING "IN TWELVES"—AS ITS LENGTH IS ROUGHLY THE BREADTH OF 12 FINGERS.

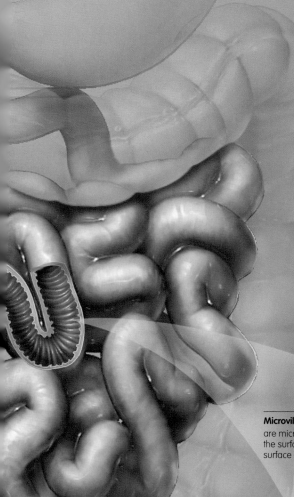

Liver
is where bile is
manufactured.

Gallbladder
stores the bile.

Common bile duct
carries bile into the
small intestine.

Pancreas

Absorbing fats

Fats are never absorbed directly into the
bloodstream. Firstly, intestinal peristalsis breaks
apart the larger fat molecules (called triglycerides),
which pancreatic enzymes then digest into smaller
bits. Bile formed in the liver keeps the fragments
from separating out of the watery chyme. The
fragments eventually enter the villi of the intestinal
lining. They recombine into large globules and
are channeled into lymphatic vessels that finally
deliver them to the general circulation.

Microvilli
are microscopic projections on
the surface of each cell on the
surface of the villi.

**Lymph
vessel**

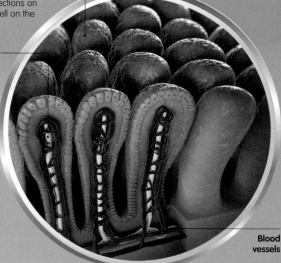

**Blood
vessels**

Intestinal villi

The interior lining of the small intestine is covered
in millions and millions of intestinal villi. Each one of
these tiny, absorptive, fingerlike structures contains
blood vessels and a lymph vessel—and is also covered
in minute "microvilli." The microvilli are what give the
larger villi their velvety appearance. Simple sugar
molecules and most amino acids pass into the blood
vessels, and some fats enter the lymph vessel.

THE LARGE INTESTINE

The large intestine, or colon, functions as a container where water and electrolytes can be reabsorbed into the bloodstream, and where undigested material is stored as feces. About 30 percent of the weight of feces consists of bacteria that normally inhabit the gastrointestinal tract, living on food residues and manufacturing vitamin K and some other useful substances.

An "inverted U"

The large intestine begins on the right side of the abdomen with a pouch-like area called the cecum. From there the ascending colon travels upward to become the transverse colon. The descending colon merges with the S-shaped sigmoid colon, which leads on to the rectum.

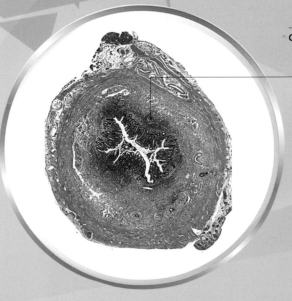

Ascending colon

Folds of the large intestine are gathered in a parallel formation, creating segmental pouches called *haustra*. These are different to the spiraling folds of the small intestine.

Terminal ileum

Ileocecal valve

Cecum

Blue-stained areas in this LM image show up the lymphoid follicles in the wall of the appendix. These lymphatic tissues may help to defend against intestinal infection.

Appendix

The appendix

Because the appendix can be removed with no ill effects, it was long considered to be a "vestigial" organ with no apparent function. In more recent times, however, populations of beneficial bacteria have been found in the tissues of the appendix. This suggests that the fingerlike structure may help to restock the intestines with "good" bacteria—for example, when they have been flushed out by a bout of severe diarrhea.

 THE NAMES OF THE COLON'S PARTS DESCRIBE THE DIRECTION OF THE GUT'S CONTENTS: *ASCENDING* (UP); *TRANSVERSE* (ACROSS); *DESCENDING* (DOWN).

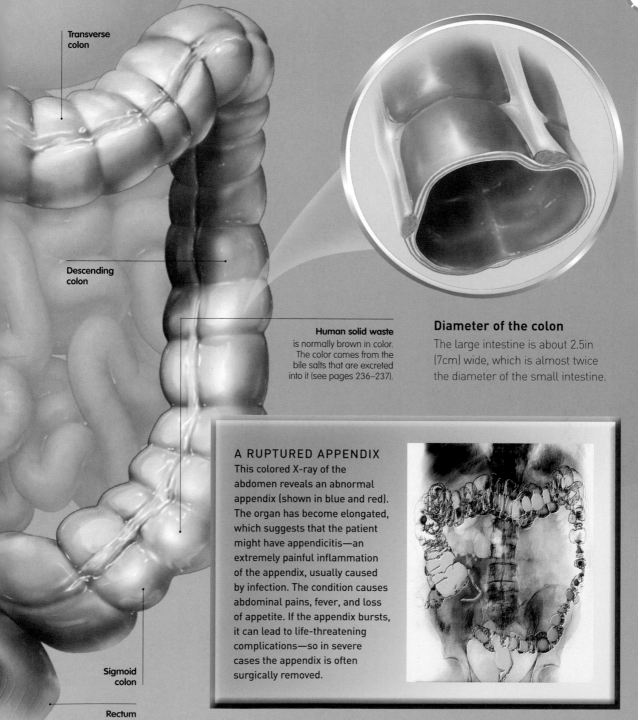

Transverse colon

Descending colon

Human solid waste is normally brown in color. The color comes from the bile salts that are excreted into it (see pages 236–237).

Diameter of the colon

The large intestine is about 2.5in (7cm) wide, which is almost twice the diameter of the small intestine.

A RUPTURED APPENDIX

This colored X-ray of the abdomen reveals an abnormal appendix (shown in blue and red). The organ has become elongated, which suggests that the patient might have appendicitis—an extremely painful inflammation of the appendix, usually caused by infection. The condition causes abdominal pains, fever, and loss of appetite. If the appendix bursts, it can lead to life-threatening complications—so in severe cases the appendix is often surgically removed.

Sigmoid colon

Rectum

THE PANCREAS AND LIVER

Several organs provide support for food processing and nutrition. The pancreas is a hormone- and enzyme-producing organ that plays a major role in regulating blood sugar and breaking down molecules in food. The liver secretes bile, which aids the digestion of fats and the removal of excess cholesterol from the blood. Meanwhile, the gallbladder stores the bile and feeds it into the small intestine.

Bile production

The liver's bile is a greenish substance that contains chemical salts derived from cholesterol. So, as well as assisting in fat digestion, the organ's production of bile salts is a means of removing excess cholesterol from the blood.

Blood processing

The hepatic portal vein (right) carries blood from the small intestine into and through the liver. There, cells remove and store excess sugar and process other nutrient molecules into substances such as blood plasma proteins. The organ also cleanses the blood of hormones and residues of alcohol and other drugs—and converts ammonia from the breakdown of proteins into a less toxic "urea" that is excreted in urine.

Liver disorders

Hepatitis, or inflammation of the liver, may be caused by a number of different viruses, as well as toxic chemicals such as alcohol. Hepatitis A is a virus usually spread by the fecal-oral route, by eating contaminated food. It leads to an acute illness lasting several weeks. Hepatitis B and C are picked up through contact with contaminated body fluids, especially blood. The initial symptoms (often flulike) may go unnoticed until complications set in years later. These may include chronic inflammation—which causes scar tissue and fatty deposits to replace much of the liver's healthy tissue—and liver cancer. Symptoms of liver failure include jaundice, nausea, bruising, and bleeding, and the build-up of fluid (edema) in the lower half of the body.

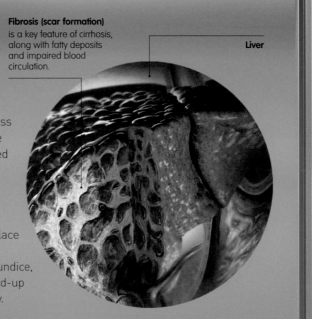

Fibrosis (scar formation) is a key feature of cirrhosis, along with fatty deposits and impaired blood circulation.

Liver

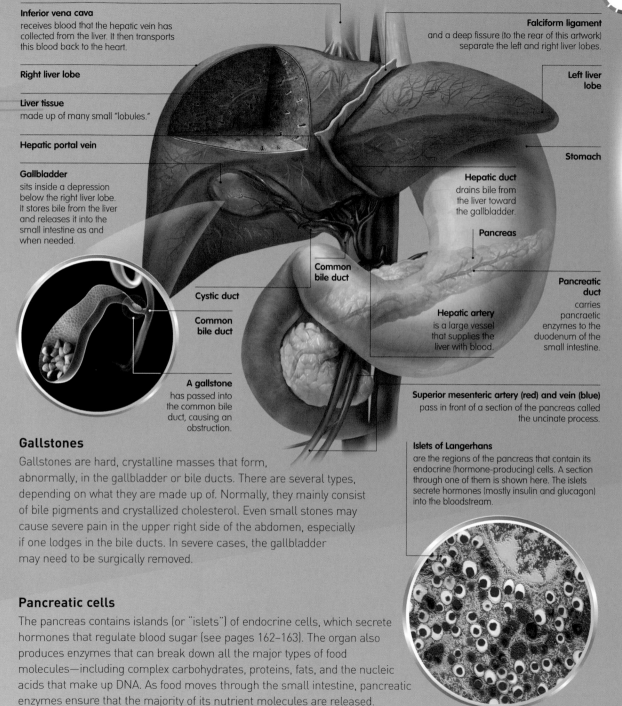

Inferior vena cava
receives blood that the hepatic vein has collected from the liver. It then transports this blood back to the heart.

Right liver lobe

Liver tissue
made up of many small "lobules."

Hepatic portal vein

Gallbladder
sits inside a depression below the right liver lobe. It stores bile from the liver and releases it into the small intestine as and when needed.

Cystic duct

Common bile duct

A gallstone
has passed into the common bile duct, causing an obstruction.

Common bile duct

Falciform ligament
and a deep fissure (to the rear of this artwork) separate the left and right liver lobes.

Left liver lobe

Stomach

Hepatic duct
drains bile from the liver toward the gallbladder.

Pancreas

Pancreatic duct
carries pancreatic enzymes to the duodenum of the small intestine.

Hepatic artery
is a large vessel that supplies the liver with blood.

Superior mesenteric artery (red) and vein (blue)
pass in front of a section of the pancreas called the uncinate process.

Islets of Langerhans
are the regions of the pancreas that contain its endocrine (hormone-producing) cells. A section through one of them is shown here. The islets secrete hormones (mostly insulin and glucagon) into the bloodstream.

Gallstones

Gallstones are hard, crystalline masses that form, abnormally, in the gallbladder or bile ducts. There are several types, depending on what they are made up of. Normally, they mainly consist of bile pigments and crystallized cholesterol. Even small stones may cause severe pain in the upper right side of the abdomen, especially if one lodges in the bile ducts. In severe cases, the gallbladder may need to be surgically removed.

Pancreatic cells

The pancreas contains islands (or "islets") of endocrine cells, which secrete hormones that regulate blood sugar (see pages 162–163). The organ also produces enzymes that can break down all the major types of food molecules—including complex carbohydrates, proteins, fats, and the nucleic acids that make up DNA. As food moves through the small intestine, pancreatic enzymes ensure that the majority of its nutrient molecules are released.

ORAL HEALTH

Common mouth disorders include dental plaque—a pale film of cells, food particles, and colonizing bacteria that thrive in the mouth. Plaque that is not removed by daily brushing and flossing of the teeth can lead to areas of decay, where bacteria break down the enamel and dentine. If plaque hardens into tartar, or calculus, a mild infection called gingivitis may make gums tender and prone to bleeding. Some oral infections are more serious.

Periodontal disease

Worldwide, nine out of ten people over the age of 40 have some form of periodontal disease, a more serious infection that develops when bacteria move deeper and break down the bony tooth sockets. This is the most common cause of adult tooth loss and may contribute to, or aggravate, some forms of heart disease, due to bacteria entering the bloodstream and triggering inflammation and clot formation in diseased coronary arteries.

Oral hygiene

Although a child's deciduous teeth, or "milk" teeth, have natural replacements, good oral hygiene is encouraged from an early age. Dentists recommend brushing the teeth twice a day with a fluoride toothpaste, limiting the intake of sugary food and drink during the day, and drinking only milk or water in the evenings. In adulthood, flossing between the teeth helps to remove food and plaque not reached by brushing, which also maintains healthy gums.

Bacteria (magnified view)

Plaque

Gingivitis is an inflammation of the gums, due to bacteria not being removed through proper brushing and flossing. The bacterial infection of the gum tissue can lead to periodontal disease, which affects the tooth sockets.

Pockets

Epithelium

Tartar (dental calculus)

Reduced bone mass in the tooth socket.

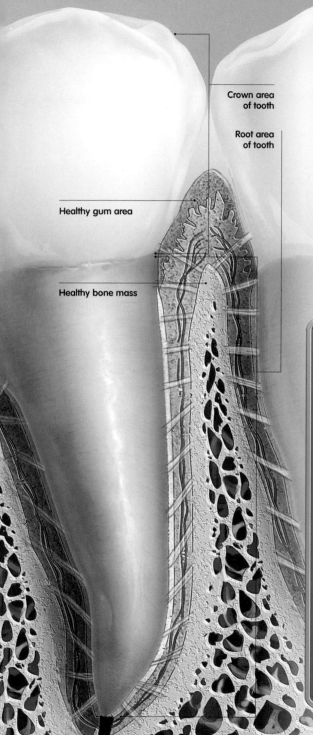

Crown area
of tooth

Root area
of tooth

Healthy gum area

Healthy bone mass

Enamel
is the hard, protective
coating of the tooth.

Dental caries

Dentine
is the dense, bony
tissue that forms the
bulk of each tooth.

Dental caries

Tooth decay, or dental caries, develops as bacteria—those
that metabolize food residues—produce acids that eat away
tooth enamel, as well as the dentine and pulp (the living
tissue inside the tooth). Untreated, the resulting cavity may
deepen until the infection destroys the pulp, crown, or root.

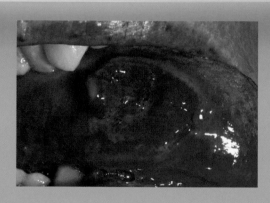

Oral cancers

Oral cancers may require disfiguring surgery
and can potentially spread elsewhere in the
body. Cancerous tongue tumors are the most
common type. Most develop in patients who use
tobacco or chew material, such as betel nuts,
which irritate tongue tissue. Treatment options
include radiation therapy and the surgical
removal of the infected area.

DIGESTIVE DISORDERS

The gastrointestinal tract is a complex organ system, which is prone to damage through a range of disorders. Common malfunctions include acid reflux, oral diseases, peptic ulceration, and functional bowel conditions such as irritable bowel syndrome (IBS) and constipation. More serious and long-term conditions include inflammatory bowel diseases (such as Crohn's disease and ulcerative colitis), malabsorption conditions (such as coeliac disease), and gastrointestinal cancers.

GERD

Gastro-esophageal reflux disease, or GERD, is a condition in which the sphincter between the esophagus and stomach malfunctions and allows stomach contents—saturated with hydrochloric acid—to back up into the esophagus. Medications can slow the release of the acid, and sufferers are advised to limit their intake of foods (such as tomatoes and coffee) that boost acid production.

Peptic ulcers
are painful, bleeding sores that form in the lining of the stomach or upper small intestine. About 90 percent of them are caused by the bacterium *Helicobacter pylori*, which can also cause inflammation in the duodenum. Excess stomach acid or the over-use of non-steroidal, anti-inflammatory drugs (NSAIDs) may also trigger the damage.

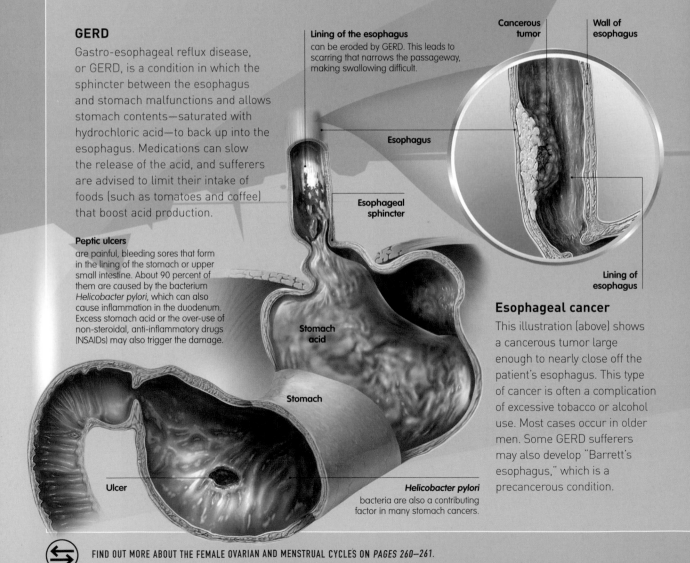

Lining of the esophagus
can be eroded by GERD. This leads to scarring that narrows the passageway, making swallowing difficult.

Cancerous tumor

Wall of esophagus

Esophagus

Esophageal sphincter

Lining of esophagus

Stomach acid

Stomach

Ulcer

Helicobacter pylori
bacteria are also a contributing factor in many stomach cancers.

Esophageal cancer

This illustration (above) shows a cancerous tumor large enough to nearly close off the patient's esophagus. This type of cancer is often a complication of excessive tobacco or alcohol use. Most cases occur in older men. Some GERD sufferers may also develop "Barrett's esophagus," which is a precancerous condition.

FIND OUT MORE ABOUT THE FEMALE OVARIAN AND MENSTRUAL CYCLES ON *PAGES 260–261*.

Eating disorders

By contrast, eating disorders are a combination of psychiatric problems and the malnutrition to which they lead. In some otherwise healthy people, particularly adolescent girls and young women, mental factors can result in drastic measures being employed to reduce the body's supply of energy in order to lose or avoid gaining weight.

Bulimia

Bulimia is a binge-purge syndrome in which the individual drastically overeats several times a week, then uses vomiting, extreme exercise, laxatives—or other strategies—to purge food from the digestive tract. This condition is typically associated with depression, stress, or an intense fear of being perceived as overweight.

THE PHYSICAL EFFECTS OF EATING DISORDERS

Hair
Hair follicles malfunction, causing the hair to fall out.

Heart
Heart muscle weakens, the heartbeat slows or becomes erratic, and blood pressure falls abnormally. An estimated 10–20 percent of people dying from *anorexia nervosa* do so through heart failure.

Blood
Anemia develops because the body's iron intake is too low.

Kidneys
Dehydration and malnutrition greatly increase the risk of kidney failure.

Hormones
In women, the menstrual cycle ceases as the ovaries stop making their reproductive hormones.

Brain
A lack of electrolytes impairs the nervous system, so that thinking and natural reflexes slow down.

Skin and nails
Dehydration and malnutrition cause the skin to become dry and the nails to become brittle.

Intestines
Motility (the shifting of food material) slows, so the intestines are unable to properly absorb nutrients.

Muscles, joints, and bones
Skeletal muscles atrophy (waste away); the bones and joints become increasingly fragile.

Anorexia nervosa

An anorexic person is fixated on consuming as little food as possible, regardless of hunger. This process of self-starvation deprives the body of energy, which severely upsets the balance of fluid and electrolytes required for nerve impulses and muscle contraction. The lack of nutrients and the breakdown of muscle tissue eventually triggers lethal heart failure.

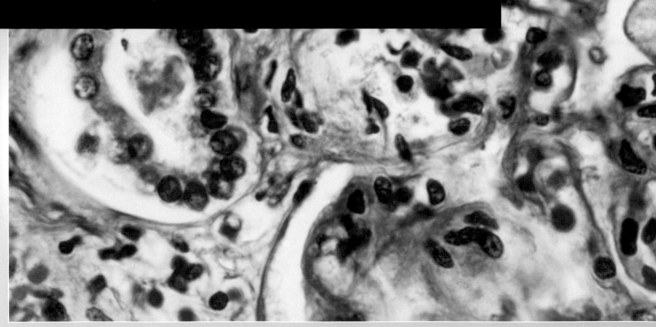

CHAPTER TWELVE

URINARY
SYSTEM

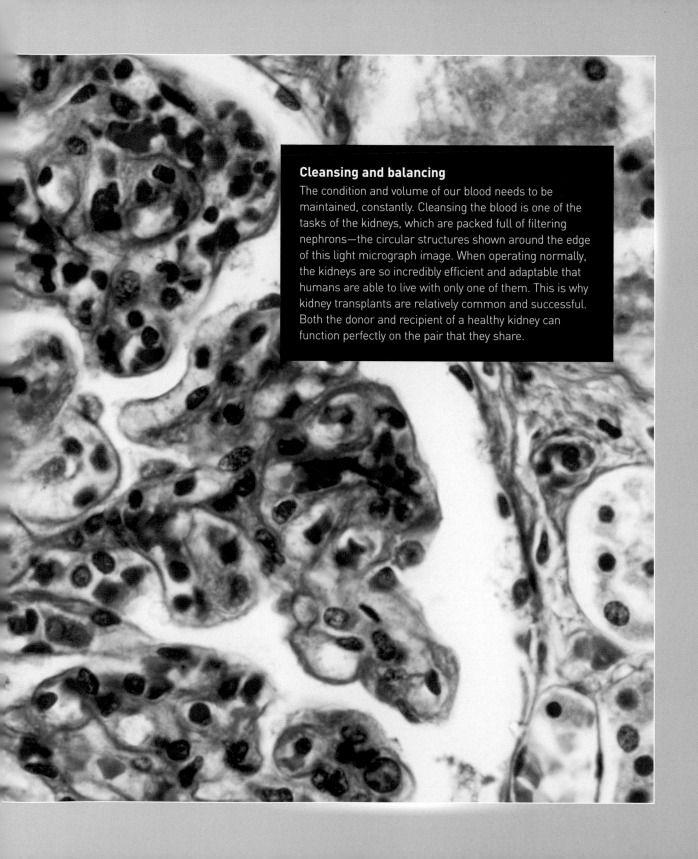

Cleansing and balancing

The condition and volume of our blood needs to be maintained, constantly. Cleansing the blood is one of the tasks of the kidneys, which are packed full of filtering nephrons—the circular structures shown around the edge of this light micrograph image. When operating normally, the kidneys are so incredibly efficient and adaptable that humans are able to live with only one of them. This is why kidney transplants are relatively common and successful. Both the donor and recipient of a healthy kidney can function perfectly on the pair that they share.

FILTRATION SYSTEM

Like some other organ systems, the urinary system is multipurpose: it functions as a combination blood cleanser and chemical-balancing apparatus, and its hormones stimulate enzyme and red blood cell production. Around the clock, millions of microscopic structures—in the system's two, bean-shaped kidneys—filter the blood of water, impurities, metabolic by-products, and other substances.

Filtering substances

The fluid that is initially removed from the blood vessels is called filtrate, which then passes through the tubes of nephrons—the operational units of the kidneys (see pages 246–248). Nephrons act as filters to remove excess salt, acid from cell metabolism, and other potential toxins, as well as unnecessary substances such as drug residues.

Balancing water levels

While the filtering process is being carried out, the nephrons retrieve useful materials from the filtrate. In addition, the nephrons remove water from the filtrate, taking it back into the blood vessels in a carefully controlled system that helps to keep blood pressure steady—by maintaining the volume of blood in the circulation.

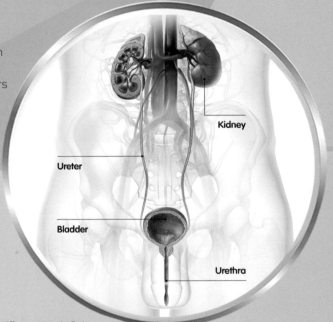

Kidney

Ureter

Bladder

Urethra

The urethra
is the only part of the system that differs, anatomically, in males and females. In males, this channel is about 9in (23cm) long, while in females it is roughly 2in (5cm) long.

Kidney enzymes and hormones	
Substance	Function of substance
Renin	An enzyme that helps to regulate blood pressure; triggers reactions that produce angiotensin II (see page 167) when the body needs to retain water.
Angiotensin II	A protein that stimulates the adrenal cortex to secrete the hormone aldosterone (ADH, see page 164), which signals to the kidney nephrons to excrete less water (and salt).
Erythropoietin	A hormone that stimulates the production of red blood cells in bone marrow.

EXCESS ACID CAN ONLY BE PERMANENTLY REMOVED BY THE URINARY SYSTEM. WITHOUT THIS PROCESS. THE LEVELS OF ACID COULD BECOME LETHAL.

The male and female systems

Males and females have identical urinary systems except for the length of the urethra (below, left). This difference means that females are more likely to get bladder infections (see pages 250–251)—because bacteria from the urogenital area have a much shorter distance to travel to reach the protected environment of the bladder.

Adrenal gland

Renal artery
Paired renal arteries deliver blood to the kidneys, subdividing within the organ to supply a steady stream of blood to each of the kidneys' filtering units (see pages 246–247).

Renal vein
Paired renal veins transport cleansed blood back into the general circulation.

Renal pyramid

Kidney
The two bean-shaped kidneys filter wastes from the blood and regulate the amount of water and salt it contains. They are situated at the back of the abdominal cavity, slightly above waist level.

Urine
is the end result of all the chemical adjustments carried out in the kidneys. In both males and females it is eliminated from the body through urination.

Ureter
Urine formed in a kidney passes through this long tube to the urinary bladder.

Urinary bladder
This hollow, muscular, stretchable organ stores urine until it is voided to the outside.

External urethral sphincter
This sphincter, around the outer opening of the urethra, consists of skeletal muscle. It facilitates the voluntary control of urination.

Urethra
This channel carries urine out of the body during urination, or micturition.

Controlling blood pressure

The kidneys exert their control over blood pressure in various ways. They produce hormones—such as renin—that regulate the levels of salt and water retained by the body, and how well the blood vessels can expand and contract. By retaining water, blood pressure can increase, while losing water lowers the pressure. Renin helps to control the narrowing of the arteries, which also increases blood pressure. Failing kidneys often make too much renin, which leads to hypertension (abnormally high blood pressure).

THE KIDNEYS

The two kidneys are the body's main blood filters. Each one is only about 4in (10cm) long and 2in (5.5cm) thick, but is packed with roughly one million microscopic filtering units called nephrons. This huge supply of filters reflects the main function of the kidneys—to remove metabolic wastes from the blood and adjust the balance of water, salt, and other substances.

Renal artery

Renal vein

Anatomy of a nephron

Each nephron is a long, thin tube that is closed off at one end. It has two "twisted" regions and a long "hairpin" loop section, known as the loop of Henle (see page 248). It ends in a long, straight portion and the entire structure is surrounded by capillaries.

Urine
flows via the calyx to the renal pelvis, then onward into the ureter.

Ureter
conveys urine down to the urinary bladder.

This LM image
shows a cross-section through the renal cortex.

Glomerulus

Nephron tubules

The cortex and the medulla

The cortex of each lobe contains much of the blood-filtering parts of the nephron—in particular the glomeruli, where filtrate is initially removed from the blood. Most of the nephron's tubules are also to be found in the cortex, but some reach down into the medulla. The medulla contains some of the longer filtering tubules—the loops of Henle—which dip down and back from some of the nephrons. It also houses the collecting ducts that carry urine out of the nephrons and into the renal pelvis (see page 247).

Bowman's capsule

Productive organs

The hormone erythropoietin, which stimulates the production of red blood cells, is produced by the kidneys. The two organs convert vitamin D into a form required for the absorption of dietary calcium. They also make an enzyme called renin, which helps to regulate blood pressure (see page 167).

A male's kidneys
filter and process about 100 gallons (378 liters) of fluid, from the incoming blood, every 24 hours.

A female's kidneys
process about 83 gallons (314 liters) of filtrate (fluid filtered from the blood) every 24 hours.

A DEVELOPING EMBRYO HAS A PAIR OF TINY KIDNEYS, IN ITS PELVIC AREA, BY THE TIME IT IS EIGHT WEEKS OLD (*SEE PAGES 268–269*).

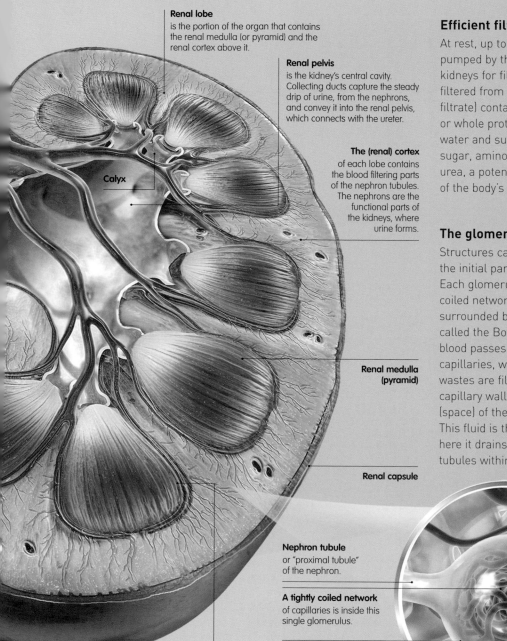

Renal lobe
is the portion of the organ that contains the renal medulla (or pyramid) and the renal cortex above it.

Renal pelvis
is the kidney's central cavity. Collecting ducts capture the steady drip of urine, from the nephrons, and convey it into the renal pelvis, which connects with the ureter.

Calyx

The (renal) cortex
of each lobe contains the blood filtering parts of the nephron tubules. The nephrons are the functional parts of the kidneys, where urine forms.

Renal medulla (pyramid)

Renal capsule

Nephron tubule
or "proximal tubule" of the nephron.

A tightly coiled network
of capillaries is inside this single glomerulus.

Bowman's capsule
surrounds the capillaries to collect filtered fluid and pass it on to the nephron tubules—where most of the reabsorption of the filtrate takes place—to retrieve (into the blood) the water and materials that are needed.

The medulla
is the inner region of the lobe, below the cortex. This area contains the "lower loop" where needed water is reabsorbed into the blood.

Efficient filters

At rest, up to 25 percent of blood pumped by the heart enters the kidneys for filtration. The fluid filtered from this blood (the filtrate) contains no red blood cells or whole proteins. It consists of water and substances such as sugar, amino acids, sodium, and urea, a potentially toxic by-product of the body's protein use.

The glomeruli

Structures called glomeruli form the initial part of each nephron. Each glomerulus contains a tightly coiled network of capillaries, surrounded by a cuplike structure called the Bowman's capsule. As blood passes through the glomerular capillaries, water and metabolic wastes are filtered through the capillary walls—into the lumen (space) of the Bowman's capsule. This fluid is the filtrate, and from here it drains into a series of tubules within the nephron.

URINE FORMATION

The urine production process reveals the essential work that the kidneys do to cleanse the body of wastes, toxins, and foreign substances such as medicines—for example, antibiotics—while retaining much-needed water and salts. The flow diagram shown below illustrates the phased process of keeping what the body requires while integrating what is not wanted into the urine.

A phased process

The flow diagram below illustrates the work of a single nephron, showing how fluids and salts are moved in different directions—through the arterioles (white arrows), through the tubules of the nephron (orange arrows), and between the arterioles and tubules (blue arrows). This phased process recycles what the body requires while expelling what is not wanted into the urine.

Phase one: filtering processes

Urine formation begins when kidney nephrons filter out water and dissolved materials from the blood—in other words, the activity that takes place in the nephron's glomerulus to create filtrate. The "cleaned" blood is now ready to return to the general circulation.

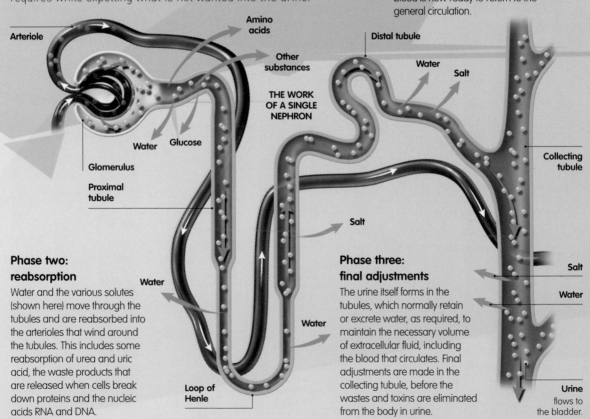

Arteriole

Amino acids

Other substances

Distal tubule

Water

Salt

THE WORK OF A SINGLE NEPHRON

Water   Glucose

Glomerulus

Proximal tubule

Collecting tubule

Salt

Phase two: reabsorption

Water and the various solutes (shown here) move through the tubules and are reabsorbed into the arterioles that wind around the tubules. This includes some reabsorption of urea and uric acid, the waste products that are released when cells break down proteins and the nucleic acids RNA and DNA.

Water

Water

Water

Loop of Henle

Phase three: final adjustments

The urine itself forms in the tubules, which normally retain or excrete water, as required, to maintain the necessary volume of extracellular fluid, including the blood that circulates. Final adjustments are made in the collecting tubule, before the wastes and toxins are eliminated from the body in urine.

Salt

Water

Urine
flows to the bladder.

URINE GETS ITS NAME FROM THE NITROGEN-CONTAINING BY-PRODUCTS OF THE SYSTEM, WHICH INCLUDE UREA AND URIC ACID.

Water consumption and content

By weight, an average baby is about 80 percent water, while an average adult is 65–70 percent water. As people get older, this figure goes down to roughly 55–60 percent. All body cells require water for the chemical reactions that sustain life. In a temperate climate of 64.4–68°F (18–20°C), a sedentary adult needs to consume at least 4 pints (2.5 liters) of water each day to replace the water being lost through biological processes.

Urinalysis

Studies of urine can inform us about our health. The presence of white blood cells suggests there may be an infection in the urinary tract. Red blood cells may also be found in a urine infection, but may also be due to trauma or stones in the bladder or kidney. Urine's yellow color comes from excreted bile salts. High levels of these compounds may indicate liver or gallbladder disease.

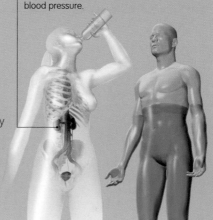

Drinking
a large quantity of water, in a short space of time, spurs the kidney filters to act quickly to remove the excess as diluted urine. Otherwise, if it remains in the bloodstream, it could raise blood pressure.

Common urine tests		
Testing for	**Normal range**	**Reason for testing**
Color	Pale to dark yellow	Indicates how much water is in urine. Certain foods, vitamins and medicines —as well as high levels of the bile pigment bilirubin—can change the color.
Clarity	Clear	Cloudy urine may contain bacteria, mucous, or other substances.
Odor	Slightly "nutty" odor to fresh urine	Some food or medicines may alter the odor; bad-smelling urine may indicate infection; diabetes or starvation can make it smell "fruity."
pH balance	4.6–8.0 (slightly acidic)	Indicates how acid or basic (alkaline) the urine is. The pH may be affected by certain foods, medications, or disorders.
Protein content	None present	Protein in the urine may be a sign of kidney disorders, severe hypertension, or some other circulatory disease. However, it can also occur as a result of fever, pregnancy, or strenuous exercise.
Glucose content	None present	The most common cause of glucose, or sugar, in urine is diabetes. It may also be caused by kidney disease.
Ketones content	None usually present	Ketones are formed when the body breaks down fat for energy. Their presence in urine may be caused by starvation, a low-carbohydrate diet, diabetic acidosis—and sometimes by alcohol toxicity.
Blood cell content	None present	Red or white blood cells in urine may be a sign of urinary tract infection (UTI) or injury.
Bacterial content	None present	Bacteria in the urine may indicate infection. Bacteria may also show up as nitrates in the urine.

URINARY TRACT DISORDERS

The urinary system is often a cause of health troubles, especially later in life. It is particularly vulnerable to infection by microbes, including bacteria and viruses spread by sexual contact. Symptoms of urinary infection typically include fever, frequent urination and pain on passing urine, or pain higher in the loins. Other common problems include kidney or bladder stones, cancers, and obstructions of the flow of urine (known as urinary retention) caused by an enlarged prostate gland.

Mobile infections

Harmful micro-organisms usually enter the urinary system at the lower end of the urethra, having been swept there from the skin around the anus (as most of these bacteria originate in the intestines). They may cause an infection of the urethra (urethritis) but tend to move swiftly up into the bladder to cause cystitis. They may travel further up the system through the ureters to the kidneys to cause pyelonephritis. All these infections are types of urinary tracts infections, or UTIs.

This X-ray urogram shows urine (red) traveling upward via the ureter.

Ureter

Bladder

Urinary reflux
Urine normally flows in one direction, down from the kidneys. The point at which the ureter enters the bladder acts as a valve to prevent back-flow. But, in some children, there is poor valve function and urine can easily "reflux" back up the ureters to cause chronic scarring of the kidneys.

CRANBERRY CURES: FACT OR MYTH?
For patients who suffer repeated UTIs, doctors sometimes recommend drinking cranberry juice. Some researchers believe that the cranberries contain certain antioxidants that alter the bacteria so that they do not attach to the walls of the urinary tract and thrive there. Others suggest that the berries produce a substance that coats the cells lining the urinary system, so that bacteria cannot bind on or spread into the bladder.

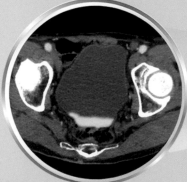

Bladder cancer
This CT scan (of a person lying horizontally) shows a cancerous bladder tumor on the back wall of the bladder (shown in yellow). Cancer of the bladder's epithelial tissue is fairly common, especially among smokers. Early symptoms include blood in the urine and the sensation of pressure as the malignant mass enlarges. Treatment ranges from chemotherapy to the surgical removal of the tumor.

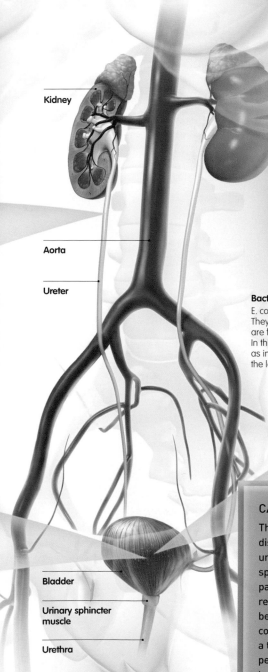

Kidney

Aorta

Ureter

Bladder

Urinary sphincter muscle

Urethra

UTIs in females and males

Because the female urethra is only about 2in (5cm) long, UTIs are far more common in women. As well as frequent, burning, or painful urination, patients may also develop lower back pain and distressing, minor incontinence. Males can also develop UTIs, and untreated infections may spread to the prostate gland (see page 259).

Blood in the urine

Blood in the urine (hematuria) may be a sign of a UTI, but needs careful investigation—as it can also be a sign of bladder cancer. Usually readily treatable in its early stages, bladder cancer is most common in men and is associated with exposure to carcinogens in tobacco smoke and certain industrial chemicals.

Bacterial infections
E. coli bacteria are highlighted here in yellow. They originate in the gastrointestinal tract but are frequently a cause of infection in the bladder. In this case, the infection has caused bleeding, as indicated by the red blood cells visible to the left-hand side of this SEM image.

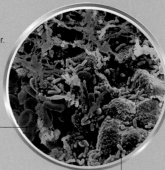

Red blood cells

E. coli bacteria

CATHETERIZATION

The flow of urine is often disrupted by disease. Incontinence (lack of control over urination) can be due to weakened bladder sphincter control, complications of surgery, paralysis, or other conditions. Urinary retention (where the flow is blocked) may be caused by an enlarged prostate or simply constipation. To remedy these problems, a tube called a catheter is temporarily or permanently placed through the urethra to reach the bladder. Urine can then be drained into an external bag.

KIDNEY DISORDERS

Because the kidneys play a vital role in removing toxins, damage by disease may be life-threatening. Fortunately, most chronic kidney conditions progress slowly and the kidneys have a very large reserve, so many people can survive with a degree of chronic kidney failure. However, some acute conditions, such as septicemia, can rapidly overwhelm the kidneys, leading to disruption of salt and water balance that needs urgent treatment.

Renal artery

Renal vein

Stone

Ureter

Kidney stones

Kidney stones are hard, often jagged deposits that form in the organ's interior cavity. There are several types of stone, depending on the chemical contents, which may include calcium salts, uric acid, and other substances that collect in the renal pelvis—and, in rare cases, in the renal tubules. Small stones may pass out in urine with little or no trouble, but larger ones can cause excruciating pain when they enter or block a ureter, the bladder, or the urethra. A treatment called lithotripsy uses high-energy sound waves to break up the stones.

Kidney

Light brown patches show damage from inflammation, or nephritis.

Pseudopodia ("false feet") of the cancer cell.

Cysts have replaced most of the tissue.

Unaffected tissue is dark red.

Polycystic kidney disease

As many as half of all people over 50 have cysts in their kidneys. But some people inherit a genetic disorder called polycystic kidney disease, which progressively destroys kidney function. Fluid-filled cysts form and gradually enlarge, replacing normal kidney tissue. Ultimately, this causes the organs to fail.

Nephritis

Inflammation of the kidneys may be triggered by an infection or a toxin (including medications), or as a result of an autoimmune disease. Most patients recover once the cause is treated—by stopping the offending medication, for example, or with drugs known as immunosuppressants.

Kidney cancer

These cancer cells, taken from a kidney tumor, have extended their slender pseudopodia, which enable them to break away from the parent tumor —the first step in metastasis, the migration of cancer to a different part of the body.

 SUFFERERS OF *POLYCYSTIC KIDNEY DISEASE* ARE EXTREMELY VULNERABLE TO URINARY TRACT INFECTIONS.

Long-term solutions

If the kidneys' functions have been damaged by bacterial infection, disease, diabetes, or an autoimmune disorder, hemodialysis or transplant may be the only long-term solutions.

Renal lobe

Renal pelvis

Stone

Kidney stones
forming in the interior cavity of the kidney—the renal pelvis.

Renal capsule
of the kidney.

Kidneys from living donors give the greatest chance of long-term success, although cadaver organs also save lives.

KIDNEY TRANSPLANTS

When a donor and an otherwise-healthy recipient have comparable blood and tissue types, kidney transplants have a high success rate. Recipients typically have advanced disease that has rendered both kidneys nearly or totally non-functional. After surgery, the lone healthy kidney remaining in the donor—as well as the one transplanted into the recipient—gradually enlarges so that the filtering capacity equals about 80 percent of the capacity of the two kidneys combined.

Hemodialysis normally occurs several times a week, for three to five hours each time. It is often used as a temporary measure until the disorder improves, or until the patient is able to undergo a transplant.

KIDNEY DIALYSIS

Two different methods can be used to artificially clean the blood. In hemodialysis, blood is diverted out of the body and through a dialysis machine via an arteriovenous graft, or fistula, which is made by connecting an artery to a vein. This by-passes capillaries and tissues to create a large and easily accessible blood vessel. Blood is then sent through tubes made of a permeable, membrane-like material. Water around the tubes contains a solution that draws impurities across the membrane and out of the blood, which then flows back into the patient's bloodstream. In peritoneal dialysis, special fluid is poured into the peritoneal cavity—in the abdomen—where it collects toxins before being drained out again.

CHAPTER THIRTEEN

REPRODUCTIVE
SYSTEMS

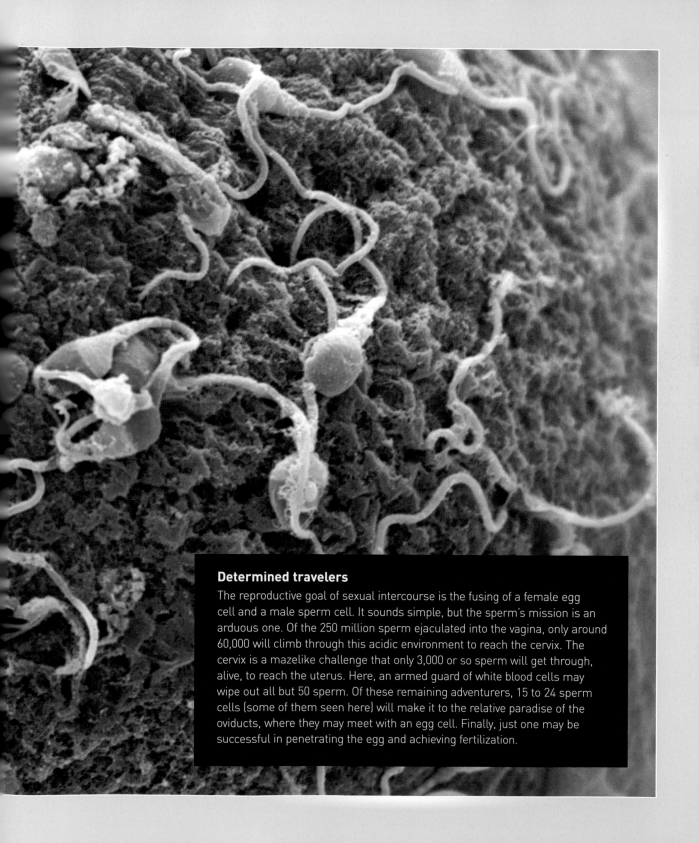

Determined travelers

The reproductive goal of sexual intercourse is the fusing of a female egg cell and a male sperm cell. It sounds simple, but the sperm's mission is an arduous one. Of the 250 million sperm ejaculated into the vagina, only around 60,000 will climb through this acidic environment to reach the cervix. The cervix is a mazelike challenge that only 3,000 or so sperm will get through, alive, to reach the uterus. Here, an armed guard of white blood cells may wipe out all but 50 sperm. Of these remaining adventurers, 15 to 24 sperm cells (some of them seen here) will make it to the relative paradise of the oviducts, where they may meet with an egg cell. Finally, just one may be successful in penetrating the egg and achieving fertilization.

THE FEMALE SYSTEM

The female reproductive system provides the biological means to produce a new generation. The system consists of ovaries, oviducts, the uterus, cervix, and vagina. The ovaries are the primary reproductive organs, and they may perform their function for 40 years or more. Anatomically, the female body develops in ways that facilitate the processes of reproduction and child-bearing.

Physical differences

Many of the anatomical differences between men and women exist to facilitate sexual intercourse and to allow genetic material to be passed reliably from a man to a woman, via the connection of sperm with an egg (see pages 264–265). The broader structure of a woman's pelvis also facilitates the birth of a child.

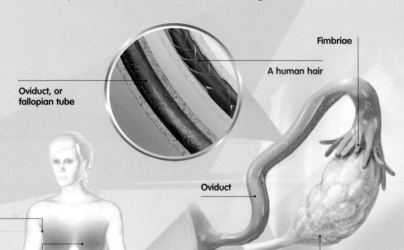

Oviduct, or fallopian tube

Fimbriae

A human hair

Oviduct

Ovary

Underarm (axillary) hair

Breasts, or mammary glands

Pubic hair

Fatty deposits
in areas such as the hips and abdomen.

Anatomical development

As a female enters puberty, typically between the ages of 11 and 16, her ovaries increase their production of estrogen, the female sex hormone that influences the development of secondary sexual traits such as breasts and more pronounced buttocks. The hormones initiate the deposition of fatty tissue, resulting in a more curved body shape, as well as the growth of hair in the armpits and pubic area.

The oviducts

The structure of the oviduct, or fallopian tube, supports the egg following ovulation (release from the ovary) in its journey to meet the sperm and start a new life in the uterus. The two oviducts are not physically attached to the ovaries, so eggs must cross a narrow gap to enter the tubes. The fimbriae help to guide the ova (eggs) into the oviducts—slender channels that are only about the width of a hair. Even so, some eggs are lost into the abdominal cavity. Within the tubes, some of the lining cells have beating cilia that help to move the egg toward the uterus.

 FERTILIZATION USUALLY TAKES PLACE DURING THE JOURNEY OF AN OVUM (EGG) THROUGH THE OVIDUCT, WHERE IT MAY ENCOUNTER MALE SPERM.

SEM image
of the fimbriae at the entrance to a fallopian tube.

Myometrium
tissue is made up of layers of smooth muscle. Contractions of these layers cause menstrual cramps and help to expel a baby during labor.

Oviduct
is about 4in (10cm) long. Each oviduct, or fallopian tube, is positioned to receive ovulated eggs—from an ovary—and channel them toward the uterus.

Fimbriae
are fingerlike extensions of folded tissue, which help to direct ovulated eggs into the oviduct.

Uterus
is a hollow, thick-walled organ. If a fertilized egg implants here, an embryo may develop.

Ovary
is one of a pair of structures that produce ova (eggs) and reproductive hormones, including estrogen and progesterone.

SEM image
of the endometrium.

Bladder
is beneath and slightly in front of the uterus. During pregnancy, pressure from the enlarging uterus can trigger frequent urination.

Cervix
is a narrow passage containing mucus-secreting glands. The mucus forms a barrier to microbes and (except during the midcycle period) male sperm.

Urethra
conveys urine from the bladder to the outside of the body.

Endometrium
is the inner lining of the uterus, where an early embryo will implant if the conditions are right. This lining also gives rise to most of the placenta (see page 266). The endometrium undergoes cyclical changes—under the influence of hormones secreted by the ovaries—in order to create an environment that is suitable for implantation.

Hormones
prevent the uterine lining from sloughing away during the fertile part of a woman's cycle. This is so that the tissues remain thick enough for a newly-formed embryo to implant itself and grow in the uterus. They serve to maintain the lining and placental development after implantation, too.

Vagina
is an expandable passageway that performs a triple role: it is the female organ of sexual intercourse, the channel for menstrual flow, and the canal for childbirth.

A muscular structure

This cutaway view of the organs reveals the muscle layers and linings of the female reproductive system, including the muscular walls of the uterus and the folds of the vaginal wall. In a female who has never been pregnant, the uterus is about 3in (7.5cm) long and only about 2in (5cm) thick. It enlarges after pregnancy and—in later life—shrinks at the onset of the menopause (see page 261).

The lining of the uterus

The major tissues of the uterus are its endometrial lining and the myometrial layer beneath it. The endometrium is basically a highly folded mucous membrane (shown above) covered in epithelial cells, which in turn are covered in cilia. It has two layers: the more permanent, basal layer and a more superficial, inner layer that is built up and then shed with each menstruation (see page 261). Abundant blood vessels supply the raw materials for this cyclical process.

THE MALE SYSTEM

The primary male reproductive organs are the penis, the testes, and the internal, semen-making structres (the prostate and the seminal vesicles). Like a female's ovaries, the testes are a particularly crucial component in producing human offspring. They produce sex hormones and sex cells—sperm—that can unite with an egg and give rise to a new generation.

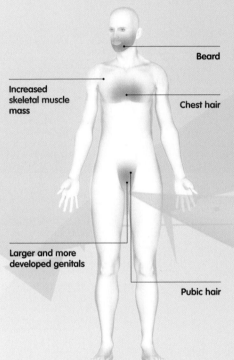

Beard

Increased skeletal muscle mass

Chest hair

Larger and more developed genitals

Pubic hair

The sperm factories

Suspended in the scrotum, each testis (right) is subdivided into 200 or more lobes in which coiled, hair-thin tubules contain sperm cells at different stages of their development, or spermatogenesis. Each day, approximately 120 million sperm are created in the testes of a sexually mature male. The male system also includes the penis and a variety of glands that produce semen, a substance that protects and nourishes the developing sperm.

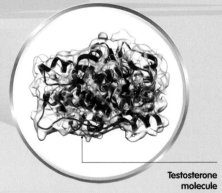

Testosterone molecule

Testosterone

Testosterone is the main human androgen, a type of steroid hormone. Although it is present in both sexes, it is the predominant sex hormone in males. In an embryo that inherits a Y chromosome (see page 21), testosterone secreted by the embryonic testes guides the development of other male reproductive organs. Later in life, it dictates adult male mating behavior and sexual characteristics, including the formation of sperm and the enlargement of skeletal muscles.

Male sexual traits

In puberty, normally between the ages of 12 and 17, the hormone testosterone promotes the development of masculine secondary sexual characteristics. These include the development of the genitals, a deepening voice and the growth of a beard, hair in the armpits, pubic area, and elsewhere. Just as women have a broader pelvis, males tend to have broader shoulders to support their bulkier muscle mass, which is another effect of testosterone in puberty.

 THE AVERAGE SPERM COUNT IN MALE SEMEN IS *40–200 MILLION* PER 0.002 OF A PINT (1 MILLILITER).

Bladder

Prostate gland
encircles the urethra. It secretes sperm-activating substances that form part of semen.

Urethra
serves as a channel for urine—and also for the ejaculation of sperm (in males).

Penis
is the male organ of copulation. It is designed to penetrate deep inside the female vagina, when erect, so that sperm can be delivered into close proximity with an ovulated egg cell.

Erectile tissue
contains many vascular spaces. During sexual arousal, they fill with blood to make the penis erect.

Glans penis
is the very tip of the penis, covered with a loosely folding prepuce (foreskin).

Corpus spongiosum
encloses the urethra.

Ejaculatory duct
is one of a pair of channels. During ejaculation, the two tubes carry sperm from each vas deferens to the urethra.

Seminal vesicle
is one of a pair of structures that secrete several substances, including prostaglandins, that make up a part of semen.

Bulbourethral glands
secrete a lubricating mucus into the male urethra during sexual arousal, to ease the transmission of semen.

Vas deferens
is one of two thick-walled tubes that lead to the ejaculatory ducts. Sperm from the epididymis passes through these channels.

Epididymis
is a folded duct system that receives and stores sperm prior to ejaculation. Stretched out, the epididymis would be about 20ft (6m) long.

Testis
is one of two essential structures that produce sperm. The testes are the primary male reproductive organs.

Lobes
containing seminiferous tubules (see page 263) make up most of the tissue in the two testes. The tubules connect with the epididymis, where the maturing sperm are stored.

The two sections
of the corpora cavernosa.

Scrotum
is an external sac, at the base of the penis, that encloses and physically supports the testes.

Urethra
remains open, which is essential for ejaculation to occur.

The corpora cavernosa

The two large, circular sections of the penis (left) are the corpora cavernosa. Each one encloses an artery in the penis. During sexual arousal, brain signals activate nerves in the penis that relax the arterial smooth muscle. The arteries dilate and the corpora cavernosa fills with blood, resulting in an erection. The corpus spongiosum also fills with blood, but it remains flexible—so that the urethra is not pinched shut.

THE OVARIAN CYCLE

During a woman's reproductive years, her menstrual cycle is driven by a cycle in the ovaries, which produces oocytes (immature ova, or eggs). As part of the ovarian cycle, estrogen and other hormones guide a sequence of stages in which the egg cell grows larger and readies itself to be released from the ovary. A tiny, developing egg is the first step toward pregnancy, since it contains the chromosomes that determine the mother's genetic contribution to her offspring.

Hormones in control

In the female body, estrogen and progesterone (in addition to other hormones from the ovaries and brain) ebb and flow, typically in a 28-day cycle. During this cycle, one or more eggs develop and are released (ovulated). LH and FHS hormones, from the pituitary gland, stimulate the development of a number of microscopic, fluid-filled sacs in the ovaries. These sacs are called follicles, and each one contains a develping oocyte. After ovulation has taken place, progesterone and estrogen from the follicle prepare the endometrium for a possible pregnancy.

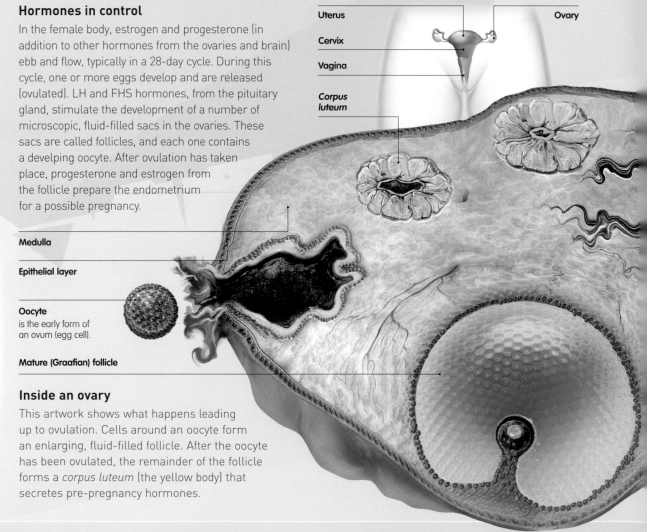

Uterus

Ovary

Cervix

Vagina

Corpus luteum

Medulla

Epithelial layer

Oocyte
is the early form of an ovum (egg cell).

Mature (Graafian) follicle

Inside an ovary

This artwork shows what happens leading up to ovulation. Cells around an oocyte form an enlarging, fluid-filled follicle. After the oocyte has been ovulated, the remainder of the follicle forms a *corpus luteum* (the yellow body) that secretes pre-pregnancy hormones.

! AT BIRTH, A FEMALE HAS ABOUT *1,000,000* FOLLICLES. BY PUBERTY, ROUGHLY *300,000* REMAIN. OF THESE, *300–400* WILL BE OVULATED AS OVA.

Two coordinated cycles

The cycles in the ovaries and uterus each last about 28 days. As pituitary hormones stimulate the growth of an ovarian follicle and the maturation of an egg, the ovary releases estrogen and progesterone to stimulate the thickening of the endometrium. A combination of hormonal signals triggers ovulation in the ovary and maintains the endometrium for about two weeks. If no pregnancy occurs, the production of ovarian hormones falls and part of the endometrium disintegrates, forming the monthly menstrual flow.

FSH (follicle stimulating hormone).

The egg enlarges and cells around it thicken.

The follicle grows larger and fills with fluid.

Oocyte

Fluid

Immature follicle begins to develop.

Follicular cells

FSH and LH spur the growth of the egg and follicle.

Estrogen

Menstruation occurs.

LH (luteinizing hormone).

Progesterone

Estrogen

Ovarian suspensary ligament

The corpus luteum now develops.

The egg erupts from the follicle.

Blood vessels

Primordial follicle

Primary follicle

Oocyte

Ovary

The moment of ovulation

A surge of LH hormone triggers ovulation, when the swollen follicle bursts and releases the oocyte. This SEM image (left) captures the moment when an oocyte emerges from an ovary and begins its journey through the fallopian tube, or oviduct, where fertilization is most likely to occur.

Fluid-filled antrum

Oocyte

From menarche to menopause

Menarche, a female's first menstruation, usually occurs between the ages of 10 and 14. In a woman's early to mid-40s, she enters the phase of perimenopause, in which her body's production of reproductive hormones slows and her ovarian and menstrual cycles become increasingly unsettled and irregular. The cycles gradually stop altogether when the full menopause arrives, normally in a woman's early to mid-50s.

SPERM PRODUCTION

Spermatozoa, or sperm, are the gametes that carry a male's genes. Over a period of nine to ten weeks, sperm become swimming cells propelled by a whiplike tail called a flagellum. Like oocytes, sperm develop in a process guided by hormones—including testosterone and some of the same hormones that operate during a female's ovarian cycle, such as the follicle-stimulating hormone (FSH).

How sperm cells mature

Beginning at puberty, a series of genetically determined steps continually transform cells called spermatogonia—firstly into spermatocytes, and then into spermatids. The spermatids grow a slender tail and finally become young sperm. During this time, chemical signals from nearby support cells nourish the maturing sperm, which ultimately enter the long, coiled epididymis.

Leydig cells

Sperm

Egg cell

Sperm cells

begin their development toward the outer edge of each tubule, gradually moving inward as they mature.

The seminiferous tubules

This colored SEM image (above) shows a cross-section of seminiferous tubules, the site of sperm development in the testes. Sperm cells are visible inside each tubule. Surrounding the tubules is tissue containing Leydig cells, which produce the hormone testosterone.

Whipping tails

Propelled by its lashing tail, a sperm cell can move toward a possible encounter with an egg—only by swimming. As the thick, viscous semen is ejaculated, chemical changes make the fluid more watery, so that the sperm can swim more easily.

Flagellum

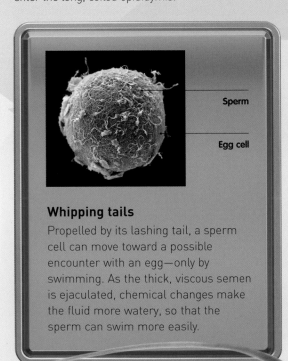

A *GAMETE* IS A MATURE REPRODUCTIVE CELL, OR "GERM" CELL, THAT IS ABLE TO UNITE WITH A GAMETE PRODUCED BY THE OPPOSITE SEX.

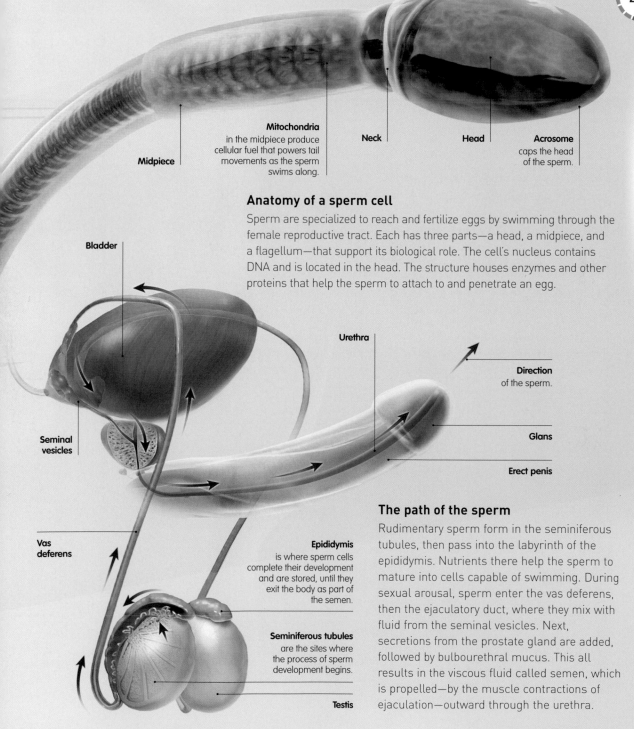

Midpiece

Mitochondria in the midpiece produce cellular fuel that powers tail movements as the sperm swims along.

Neck

Head

Acrosome caps the head of the sperm.

Anatomy of a sperm cell

Sperm are specialized to reach and fertilize eggs by swimming through the female reproductive tract. Each has three parts—a head, a midpiece, and a flagellum—that support its biological role. The cell's nucleus contains DNA and is located in the head. The structure houses enzymes and other proteins that help the sperm to attach to and penetrate an egg.

Bladder

Urethra

Direction of the sperm.

Seminal vesicles

Glans

Erect penis

Vas deferens

Epididymis is where sperm cells complete their development and are stored, until they exit the body as part of the semen.

The path of the sperm

Rudimentary sperm form in the seminiferous tubules, then pass into the labyrinth of the epididymis. Nutrients there help the sperm to mature into cells capable of swimming. During sexual arousal, sperm enter the vas deferens, then the ejaculatory duct, where they mix with fluid from the seminal vesicles. Next, secretions from the prostate gland are added, followed by bulbourethral mucus. This all results in the viscous fluid called semen, which is propelled—by the muscle contractions of ejaculation—outward through the urethra.

Seminiferous tubules are the sites where the process of sperm development begins.

Testis

FERTILIZATION

Fertilization is never guaranteed. Of the millions of sperm a male ejaculates, fewer than a thousand may reach an oviduct. Acidic fluid in the vagina will kill many, and mucus in the cervix can block survivors from the uterus. In the uterus, defensive cells may even attack sperm—perceiving them to be "foreign" to the female's body. How, then, can the sperm reach their goal?

Uterus

Sperm

Cervix

Preparation of the sperm

The ejaculated sperms need to be capacitated, or "made able," by chemical changes that weaken the acrosome covering the sperm's head (see page 263). This change requires six to eight hours and is necessary for fertilization to occur.

An individual sperm's journey

It takes a sperm several hours to swim from the cervix to the uterus, through to an oviduct and—eventually—to an ovulated egg. Mitochondria in a sperm's midpiece (see page 263) provide the chemical reserves needed to support this long and arduous journey.

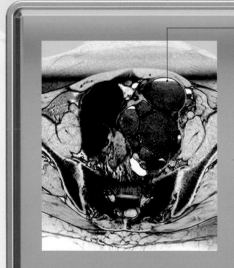

Large cysts (shown in blue) have formed in the abdominal cavity as a result of this condition. Cells from the endometrium grow under the influence of monthly hormonal cycles, but they cannot be shed during menstruation, so they build up.

Endometriosis

This condition affects as many as one in ten women, most often during early adulthood. It involves the movement or back-flow of cells—such as blood and menstrual material—into and through the oviducts. When endometrial tissue begins to grow outside the uterus, it responds to the usual hormone fluxes of a woman's cycle, building up and then disintegrating. The accumulating material causes symptoms including pelvic pain, especially during menstrual periods and sexual intercourse, and can lead to infertility.

FERTILIZATION TAKES A MINIMUM OF *4–6 HOURS* AND A MAXIMUM OF *48–72 HOURS*. SPERM DON'T SURVIVE FOR MUCH LONGER IN A WOMAN'S BODY.

A successful sperm

Chemical barriers around a human egg allow only one single sperm to penetrate it. Soon after the sperm cell has fertilized the egg cell, chemical changes thicken the outer layer (the *zona pellucida*) of the egg. The head of the sperm cell then releases its genetic material, which mixes with the egg cell's genetic material. This results in a "zygote" containing a full set of genes for the development of a new human being.

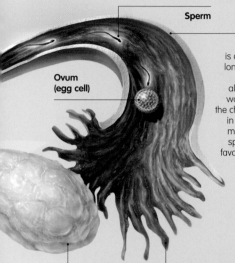

Sperm

Ovum (egg cell)

Oviduct
is only about 4in (10cm) long, but it takes sperm many hours to swim along it. The journey is worthwhile, though, as the chemical environment in the oviducts is much more hospitable to the sperm—and therefore favorable for fertilization.

Zona pellucida
is a thick coat that surrounds the fully-developed oocyte (young egg).

Ovary

Fimbriae

Sperm cell
penetrates the outer layer of the egg cell.

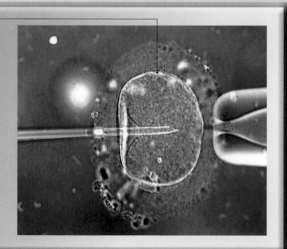

Egg
being injected with the DNA (genetic material) from a male sperm.

IVF

In vitro ("in glass") fertilization, or IVF, is often recommended in cases where either a male or female partner is infertile, or where the female's fallopian tubes are blocked. The process involves removing eggs from the woman's ovaries and fertilizing them with sperm in a laboratory. Once an egg has been fertilized, the embryo is placed into the woman's womb, so that it can develop and be born naturally.

IMPLANTATION

The fertilization of the egg by a sperm—combining the genetic material of the two cells—is the beginning of pregnancy, the 39-week gestation process that culminates in the birth of a baby. One of the first stages of gestation is implantation, whereby the early embryo (the fertilized egg cell) attaches itself to the lining of uterus, the central site of embryonic development.

The "extra-embryonic" membranes

The developing embryo is supported by four membranes and the placenta. A yolk sac produces early blood cells, among other functions. The amnion forms the fluid-filled sac that surrounds the embryo. The allantois generates blood vessels linking the embryo to the placenta via the umbilical cord. The chorion surrounds all of these structures. It secretes hCG (human chorionic gonadotropin), a hormone that prevents the endometrium from eroding until the placenta has formed.

Endometrium is the lining of the uterus, or womb.

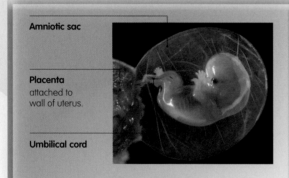

Amniotic sac

Placenta attached to wall of uterus.

Umbilical cord

FUNCTIONS OF THE PLACENTA

The placenta is a flattened, circular organ that develops in the uterus of a pregnant female. It nourishes and maintains the growing fetus through a cordlike structure called the umbilical cord. As well as providing nutrients, this connection with the mother's blood supply enables the fetus to get rid of waste products—including carbon dioxide, via gas exchange. The organ also provides cells that assist in fighting internal infection and producing hormones to support the pregnancy.

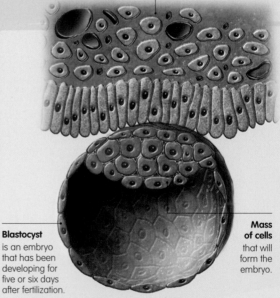

Blastocyst is an embryo that has been developing for five or six days after fertilization.

Mass of cells that will form the embryo.

Phase one: implantation begins

Implantation occurs in three main phases. Firstly, cells on the blastocyst's surface begin to infiltrate the endometrium. As this takes place, the mass of cells from which the embryo will develop is nearest to the endometrium.

Miscarriage

An estimated 20 percent or more of conceptions result in "miscarriage," the spontaneous expulsion of an embryo or fetus. About 50 percent of miscarriages are thought to occur when a genetic disorder or a fault with the development of the embryo in the uterus prevents the pregnancy from progressing. Miscarriage can also be triggered by an imbalance in pregnancy-related hormones, structural problems in the uterus or cervix, and by maternal disorders or diseases such as diabetes. The risk is also greater if the mother is carrying more than one fetus.

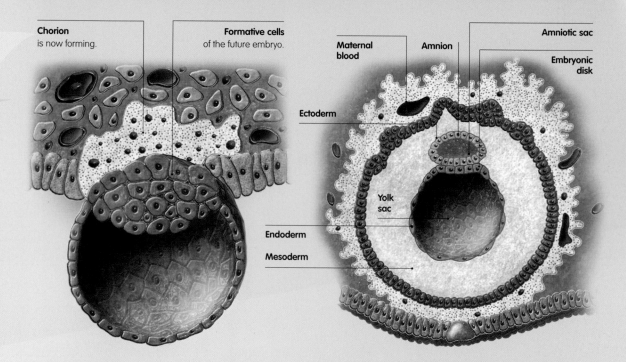

Chorion is now forming.

Formative cells of the future embryo.

Maternal blood

Amnion

Amniotic sac

Embryonic disk

Ectoderm

Yolk sac

Endoderm

Mesoderm

Phase two: implantation deepens

Over the next few days, the blastocyst sinks deeper into the endometrium, which eventually closes over it. Meanwhile, the embryo itself has begun to develop, as have the extra-embryonic membranes. By the third week, the chorion and amniotic cavity have both formed.

Phase three: the primary layers form

The third phase occurs during the second and third weeks of pregnancy. At this time, the embryonic disk divides into three circular sheets, or layers, of tissue—the ectoderm, the endoderm, and the mesoderm. These three layers will eventually develop into all body tissues and organs.

EMBRYONIC PERIOD

From the moment a blastocyst forms, human development progresses rapidly. The first eight weeks in the womb—the embryonic period—are a time of tremendous growth, during which the embryo is transformed from a disk of cells into a tiny but recognizably human figure. These pages give an overview of the main developmental stages between weeks two and eight.

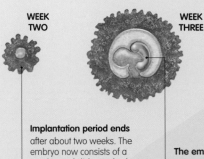

WEEK TWO

WEEK THREE

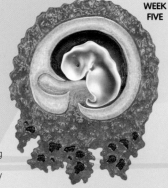

WEEK FOUR

WEEK FIVE

Implantation period ends
after about two weeks. The embryo now consists of a two-layered disk attached to a yolk sac.

The embryo lengthens
during week three, and a neural tube—the early incarnation of the brain and spinal cord—begins to form (see page 96).

Heart starts beating
by week four, sending blood through the embryo's rudimentary blood vessels.

Weeks one to four

During the first four weeks, the placenta and umbilical cord are established and the embryo grows to 500 times its original size. Although it is still only about 0.2in (0.5cm) long—and clearly has a "tail" of sorts—its heart, brain, eyes, limbs, and muscles are all beginning to form.

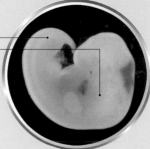

Embryonic tail

Pharyngeal arches

MATERNAL HEALTH AND NUTRITION

A mother's meals and any dietary supplements need to provide the nutrients required by her growing offspring. Supplements typically include vitamins, iron, and folic acid (folate). Folic acid helps to prevent *spina bifida*, in which the embryo's neural tube fails to close off totally, so that part of the spinal cord remains exposed. An unborn child can be harmed by a poor diet, alcohol, and tobacco use, and even through the use of some therapeutic drugs.

At four weeks old

A four-week-old embryo has two typical vertebrate features—a tail and "pharyngeal arches" in the neck region. In humans, the tail becomes the coccyx (see page 55) and the pharyngeal arches develop into parts of the face, neck, and nasal cavities.

 FOLIC ACID IS ALSO KNOWN AS VITAMIN B9. FOODS SUCH AS LEAFY GREEN VEGETABLES, LIVER, AND KIDNEY ARE RICH IN FOLIC ACID.

The embryo in the seventh week

In the seventh week of development, paddlelike, webbed hands and feet are present at the ends of the embryo's tiny limbs. Over the following days, a process of genetically programmed cell death normally removes the excess tissue between the digits. This produces five distinct fingers or toes at the ends of each hand and foot. Within each one is cartilage that will gradually be replaced with bone during the weeks to follow.

WEEK SEVEN

Basic form of the eyes and ears.

Fingers

Ribs

Toes

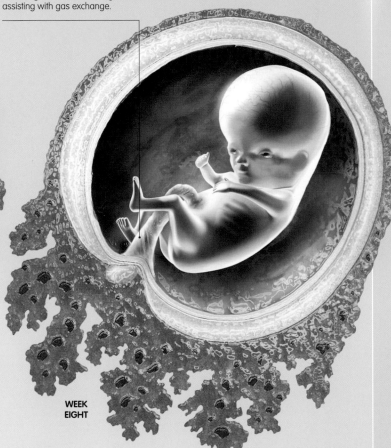

Elongation
of the embryo continues during week five. Its head grows rapidly and paddlelike plates develop—the early forms of the hands and feet. The body has doubled in length by the sixth week. The basic forms of the eyes and ears are also now in place.

All major organs
are in development by the time the embryo reaches eight weeks old. By this stage, the umbilical cord is also fully functional, linking the embryo to its mother's bloodstream—delivering nutrients, removing wastes, and assisting with gas exchange.

WEEK SIX

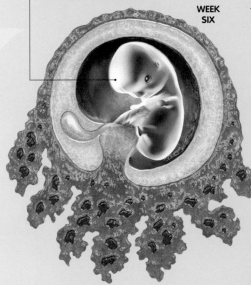

WEEK EIGHT

Weeks five to eight

In this period of gestation, the embryo's head enlarges as the brain expands, its tail disappears and the limbs, genitals, and internal organs all take shape. Over the next few weeks, toward the end of the first trimester (weeks four to 12) the health and status of the fetus is normally checked by an ultrasound scan. At this point, the fetal monitor will be able to detect its heartbeat.

FETAL DEVELOPMENT

After eight weeks of development, a growing human is known as a fetus. By the end of the first trimester (weeks four to 12) of pregnancy, the fetus is around 2.4–3.2in (6–8cm) long—from crown to rump—and its organ systems have formed. Here are the major stages of the second trimester (weeks 13 through 28) and third trimester (weeks 29 through 40).

The fetal nervous system

The nervous system is becoming established during the second trimester of pregnancy, when it has connections to the developing muscles. As a result, the mother can start to feel the movements of her infant's arms and legs during the second trimester, usually after about 16 weeks. Although the fetus is nourished via the mother's bloodstream, its mouth makes sucking movements and other facial movements crinkle its face into frowns and squints.

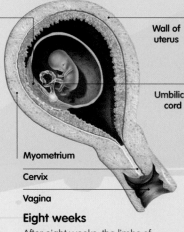

Placenta

Wall of uterus

Umbilical cord

Myometrium

Remains of the yolk sac

Cervix

Vagina

Eight weeks
After eight weeks, the limbs of the fetus are well formed and soon its genitals will develop.

Twelve weeks
By 12 weeks old the fetus has grown to approximately 2.4–3.2in (6–8cm) in length, which is roughly the size of a lemon. A greasy substance, called the *vernix caseosa*, protects its delicate skin.

Fetal circulation

A fetus's lungs and liver develop more slowly than some other internal organs because the mother's body manages their functions via the placenta. The lungs receive a small quantity of blood from the heart, but most of the blood bypasses the lungs by moving either through a small hole in the heart (between the right and left atria) called the *foramen ovale*, or through a second fetal channel—the *ductus arteriosus*—that diverts blood from the pulmonary artery directly into the aorta. Meanwhile, a blood vessel called the *ductus venosus* bypasses the liver. All these detours normally close down as normal blood circulation is established in the first weeks after birth.

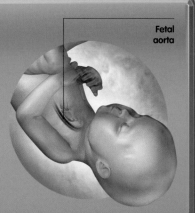

Fetal aorta

UNTIL IT IS 20 WEEKS OLD, THE LENGTH OF A FETUS IS NORMALLY MEASURED *FROM THE CROWN OF ITS HEAD TO ITS RUMP*.

Maturing body systems

During the second trimester, the fetus will open its eyes (normally in the seventh month), drink amniotic fluid, and urinate as its body systems mature and while it grows toward its birth size. In the final weeks before birth, its lungs and respiratory system become capable of functioning in air. By the ninth month of pregnancy, the development of all the body systems is virtually complete.

Lanugo hairs

Eyelashes

Twenty weeks

A 19-week-old fetus is normally about 5.9in (15cm) long. At 20 weeks, its body is covered with soft, delicate hairs known as lanugo. Eyebrows and eyelashes will soon appear, too.

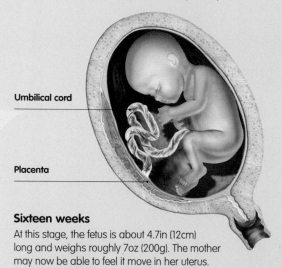

Umbilical cord

Placenta

Head is now pointing downward, in preparation for birth.

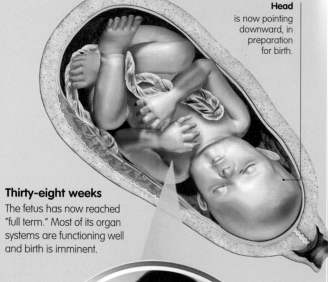

Sixteen weeks

At this stage, the fetus is about 4.7in (12cm) long and weighs roughly 7oz (200g). The mother may now be able to feel it move in her uterus.

Multiple fetuses

Due to the limited capacity of the uterus, multiple fetuses are often born before full term. Twins, for instance, are normally delivered after about 37 weeks.

Thirty-eight weeks

The fetus has now reached "full term." Most of its organ systems are functioning well and birth is imminent.

The evolving skeleton

The skeleton of the fetus develops slowly throughout the term of gestation. Cartilage and other embryonic connective tissues provide a structural model for each bone. Later, bone cells replace the soft model with mineralized bone tissue. The skull begins to develop during the fourth week, followed by the spinal vertebrae, ribs, and the pectoral and pelvic girdles. By week six, a cartilage skeleton has begun to form in the limbs.

BIRTH

Birth, or "parturition," is an infant's entry into the world. Normally, a mother experiences three stages of labor. These are the pre-birth stage of physical changes, which are a prelude to the birth itself; the baby's transit out of the uterus and through the birth canal; and a post-birth stage during which the placenta, or afterbirth, is delivered and the umbilical cord is cut.

The onset of labor

Interacting hormones from the placenta and the fetus are the chemical triggers for labor to commence. As birth nears, fetal cells produce oxytocin, which causes the placenta to release prostaglandins. Both hormones help to stimulate the myometrium, the muscular wall of the uterus (see pages 257 and 270), bringing on the muscular contractions of labor.

Stage one, initial (latent) phase: contractions begin

In the first stage of labor, muscular contractions begin and the cervix—the entrance to the uterus—dilates (opens).

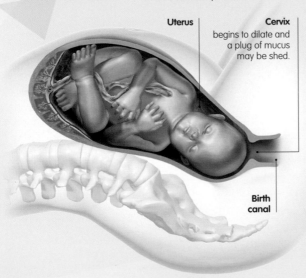

Uterus

Cervix
begins to dilate and a plug of mucus may be shed.

Birth canal

Stage one, active phase: contractions continue

The contractions of the uterus continue, often over several hours, and the dilating cervix is closely stretched—or "effaced"—over the infant's head.

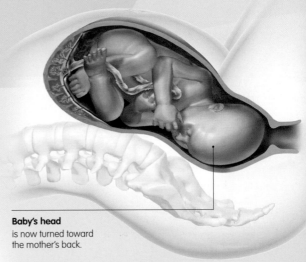

Baby's head
is now turned toward the mother's back.

Other hormonal triggers

Other hormones also play a part in labor. It is thought that the placenta releases CRH (corticotropin-releasing hormone), which appears to stimulate the fetus's adrenal glands to make and release the androgen DHEA (dehydroepiandrosterone). In the placenta, DHEA transforms in estrogen, which in turn contributes to uterine contractions.

Stage two: expulsion (delivery of the baby)

Intense, more frequent contractions propel the infant out of the uterus and through the birth canal.

Stage three: placental delivery

Milder contractions push out the placenta and other materials, collectively known as the afterbirth.

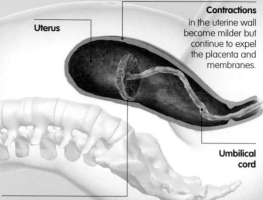

Uterus

Contractions
in the uterine wall become milder but continue to expel the placenta and membranes.

Umbilical cord

The afterbirth
consists of the placenta and other fetal membranes. It is delivered some minutes after the birth of the baby.

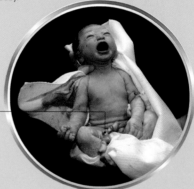

Umbilical cord
is cut, severing the vessels that have provided the baby with oxygen from the mother's bloodstream.

Contractions
push the baby out through the birth canal.

The length of labor

On average, labor takes about 18 hours from the first muscular contraction of the uterus to the delivery of the infant—but some births occur in just a few hours, while others may take a day or longer as the stages (shown here) slowly advance.

Breastfeeding

A female's breasts, or mammary glands, consist mainly of fatty tissue together with large glands that manufacture and release breast milk—to nourish a suckling newborn. Although the modern formula of artificial milk increasingly mimics breast milk, natural breastfeeding is still the best option for a baby.

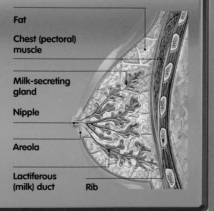

Fat

Chest (pectoral) muscle

Milk-secreting gland

Nipple

Areola

Lactiferous (milk) duct

Rib

First breaths

When an infant is finally separated from its mother, the placenta can no longer remove carbon dioxide from its blood. This change—along with other factors—stimulates centers in the infant's brain that regulate breathing. So, as its respiratory system begins to function, the baby takes its first breaths of air. The initial cries of the infant also serve to inflate its lungs, which helps to kick-start inhalation and exhalation.

GROWTH AND AGING

The human body changes dramatically as a child grows from infancy through to adolescence. Physical growth begins to slow around four years old, when most children have a command of verbal language and are developing good hand-eye coordination. By the age of 12, youngsters tend to be proportioned much like an adult, although they are not yet at their full height. The onset of puberty then reshapes their bodies with the secondary sexual characteristics.

Physical and mental changes

During infancy and early childhood, steady growth lengthens the body while the head becomes less prominent. By three years old, the head and torso are growing at a slower rate, while the limbs noticeably lengthen. Up until about the age of three, major changes are also taking place in the nervous system. Countless new neural connections form, based on gene-guided developmental processes, as well as on the child's interactions with the people around them and their exposure to stimuli in the larger world.

The evolving brain

After its early childhood growth spurt, the brain is relatively stable until shortly before puberty, when its neural wiring undergoes more major changes. Large numbers of synapses form between brain neurons and certain regions. Over the next few years, some of these connections are strengthened as nerve cell axons become sheathed in myelin—a process called myelination—while others wither. Much of this growth occurs in the prefrontal cortex, the area responsible for abstract thinking, judgment, and impulse control. Scientists now recognize that this process of growth and change in brain connections goes on throughout adult life.

Oligodendrocytes
such as this one can produce enough myelin to sheathe up to 50 neuron axons.

STUDY THE NEURAL CIRCUITRY OF THE BRAIN IN MORE DETAIL ON *PAGES 90–91*.

The aging process

Structural changes in proteins contribute to the effects of aging. In later life, collagen molecules become more rigid and less resilient. This affects the structure and functioning of the skin, blood vessels, and most internal organs. As our metabolism slows down, fatty deposits accumulate. Bone-forming osteoblasts become less efficient, so bone mass declines, and muscle mass decreases as skeletal muscle fibers waste away.

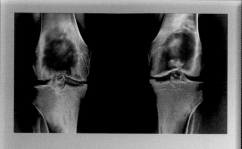

OSTEOARTHRITIS

About 90 percent of people over the age of 40, and virtually all people over 50, have some degree of osteoarthritis in their joints. This X-ray shows the narrowing of the spaces between the adjoining bones, due to the arthritic erosion of cartilage in the knee joints. The ratio of fat to muscle in the limbs also increases with age, further contributing to a decline in strength and mobility.

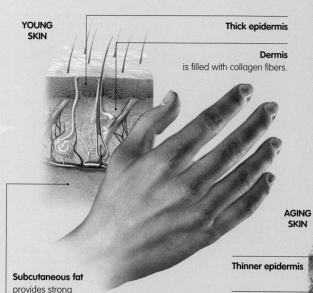

YOUNG SKIN

Thick epidermis

Dermis
is filled with collagen fibers.

Subcutaneous fat
provides strong support.

AGING SKIN

Thinner epidermis

Dermis
contains fewer collagen fibers.

Wrinkles and creases
appear due to changes in skin proteins over time—particularly the loss of elastin fibers.

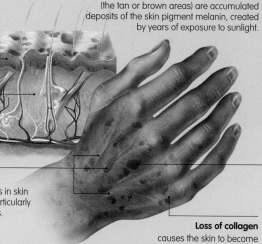

Liver spots
(the tan or brown areas) are accumulated deposits of the skin pigment melanin, created by years of exposure to sunlight.

Loss of collagen
causes the skin to become less supple and plump.

Active living

Physical activity, including regular weight-bearing exercise, can help to slow the physical effects of aging. Experts recommend maintaining a healthy lifestyle that includes a balanced diet, regular moderate exercise, positive social interactions, and stimulating mental activities. This is a positive recipe for happy, graceful aging.

GLOSSARY

Acetylcholine
A major neurotransmitter conveying signals between neurons in the central nervous system, and also between motor neurons and muscle gland cells.

Action potential
A nerve impulse.

Aldosterone
A steroid hormone from the adrenal cortex that acts (in the kidneys) to help regulate our blood pressure.

Allantois
One of the extra-embryonic membranes that develops in early pregnancy. It gives rise to the embryo's first blood cells and its bladder.

Allergy
An immune response against a substance that is normally harmless to the body.

Amino acids
Molecules that are the building blocks of proteins.

Androgen
A male sex hormone. Testosterone is the main human androgen.

Anemias
Blood disorders in which red blood cells do not supply sufficient oxygen to the body's tissues.

Antibiotic
A substance that kills or inhibits the growth of micro-organisms.

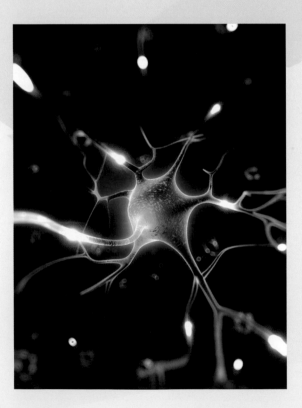

Antibody
Any of the defensive proteins produced by lymphocytes. An antibody binds to a specific antigen and flags it for destruction by other immune system cells.

Antigen
Any substance that stimulates a response by the immune system.

Antioxidant
A substance that can neutralize free radicals (uncharged molecules) before they cause damage to DNA or some other cell part.

Apoptosis
Genetically programmed cell death—a mechanism that helps to shape body parts during development, and which also destroys abnormal body cells.

Apoxia
A lack of oxygen.

Astrocytes
Branched glial cells in the brain that help to nourish brain neurons. They also perform other important support functions.

Autonomic nerves
Nerves associated with the autonomic nervous system, which regulates involuntary (or automatic) body functions.

Autosome
A chromosome that does not carry genes for sexual traits.

B cell
A type of lymphocyte (white blood cell) that arises in bone marrow, and which can make antibodies that act against foreign cells or substances during an immune response.

Benign
Not malignant, virulent, or infectious. A benign tumor is a non-cancerous tumor.

Bilirubin
An orange-yellow pigment that is formed in the liver by the breakdown of the protein hemoglobin. It is excreted in both bile and urine.

Brain lateralization
The assignment of certain brain activities, such as our functions of language and communication, mainly to one of the two cerebral hemispheres.

Carcinogen
A substance or agent that may have the potential to cause cancer in body tissues.

Cell
The small living unit of an organism. Individually, a cell's parts are not alive.

Cell-mediated immunity
Immunity conferred by the various kinds of activated T cells, which fight against infected or abnormal body cells that have been transplanted, and which also release chemicals that regulate immune responses.

Cerebrospinal fluid
A clear fluid that surrounds and cushions the tissues of the brain and spinal cord.

Chemoreceptor
A sensory cell that responds to chemical stimuli.

Chorion
One of several membranes that develop around an early embryo, and which becomes a major part of the placenta.

Chromosome
A DNA molecule and its associated proteins.

Cirrhosis
A chronic disease of the liver that is characterized by the degeneration of cells, inflammation, and a fibrous thickening of the organ's tissue. Cirrhosis is often the result of alcoholism or hepatitis (particularly hepatitis C).

Coeliac disease
A relatively common digestive condition in which the small intestine is hypersensitive to gluten (a mixture of two proteins that are present in cereals such as wheat), leading to difficulty in digesting some foods.

Complement system
A set of proteins that help to target and destroy pathogens (antigens) during our immune responses.

Congenital
Something present at birth, such as a condition or physical defect.

COPD
The acronym for chronic obstructive pulmonary disease, a collective term which includes the following conditions: chronic bronchitis, emphysema, and chronic obstructive airways disease.

Corpus callosum
A band of several hundred million neuron axons that connects the brain's right and left cerebral hemispheres.

Corpus luteum
A structure that develops after ovulation and secretes hormones (progesterone and estrogen) that prepare the uterus lining for a possible pregnancy.

Corticosteroid
A steroid hormone, secreted by the adrenal glands, that reduces inflammation in tissues.

Crohn's disease
A chronic, inflammatory disease of the intestine, affecting (in particular) the ileum and the colon, which is characterized by ulcers and fistulae.

Cytokine
Cytokines are a broad group of small proteins. They are a signaling substance that function in some of the body's immune responses.

Cytoplasm
The semifluid portion of a cell that contains all organelles except for the nucleus.

Cytoskeleton
A network of protein filaments that gives internal support and structure to a cell, and which plays a part in cell movement and division.

Diastole
A period during the cardiac cycle when the heart chambers relax and fill with blood.

Disease vector
An agent (such as a bug) that transfers a disease-causing pathogen from contaminated organisms or material to new hosts.

Dislocation
The displacement of a bone from a joint. Dislocation usually results in the tearing of joint ligaments, tendons—or both.

DNA
Deoxyribonucleic acid, a chemical that contains the genetic code for the development and functioning of a living organism. DNA contains sub-units called nucleotides.

DNA fingerprint
The unique sequence of nucleotides in a person's DNA. With the exception of identical twins, no two individuals have the same DNA sequences.

DNA repair
Natural processes in cells in which enzymes repair defects in strands of DNA.

Dominant gene
A version of a gene that makes another, "recessive" version of the same gene.

Dynamic equilibrium
The balance state that monitors the position of the head in response to movements such as rotation, acceleration, and deceleration.

Ectoderm
The outer-most tissue layer that forms in an early human embryo. Its cells give rise to the skin and nerve tissue.

Electrocardiogram (ECG or EKG)
A recording of the heart's electrical activity that can be detected through electrodes placed on the skin.

Endocytosis
An umbrella term for various energy-using processes through which cells absorb particles or molecules (such as proteins)—normally too large to pass through the cell's membrane—by engulfing them.

Endoderm
The inner-most tissue layer in an early human embryo. It gives rise to many of the young body's developing internal organs.

Endoplasmic reticulum
A system of internal cell membranes that are involved in the synthesis, modification, and transport of proteins and other molecules.

Endorphin
A chemical produced by the brain that acts as a natural painkiller.

Enkephalins
These are a type of endorphin.

Enzyme
A protein that speeds up, or catalyzes, chemical reactions in the body.

Erythropoietin
A hormone released by kidney cells that stimulates the production of red blood cells.

Exocrine gland
A gland that releases a product, such as sweat or tears, into ducts that deliver the substance to the surface of the skin, into a body cavity, or into a hollow organ.

Extracellular fluid
All body fluids—such as blood plasma—that are not contained inside cells.

Fistula
An abnormal or surgically created passage between a hollow or tubular organ and the surface of the body—or in between two hollow or tubular organs.

Fluoride
An inorganic anion (negatively charged ion) of the chemical element fluorine (F). It can aid dental health by strengthening tooth enamel, rendering it more resistant to decay.

Follicle
Inside a female ovary, a follicle is a structure where an oocyte (early egg cell) develops, along with associated cells that have other reproductive functions.

Foramen magnum
The largest opening in the skull, where the spinal cord connects with the brain stem.

FSH
The follicle-stimulating hormone that plays a key role in reproduction. Made in the pituitary gland, FSH stimulates the production of egg cells in females and sperm cells in males.

Gastrin
A hormone that stimulates the release of gastric juice, an acidic fluid that promotes the digestion of food. Gastrin is secreted into the bloodstream by the stomach wall in response to the presence of food.

Gene
A segment of DNA that contains instructions for building a particular protein. Genes are the basic units of heredity—the transmission of traits from one generation to the next.

Gene mutation
A change in the nucleotide sequence in a gene—for example, when a nucleotide is deleted.

Gene sequence
The order of the nucleotides that make up a person's genes.

Gene therapy
A technological procedure in which one or more normal genes are transferred into cells in order to correct a genetic defect.

Genetic code
The chemical correspondence between sequences of nucleotides in genes and amino acids in proteins. Each amino acid is encoded by a sequence of three nucleotides.

Genome
All the DNA in a full set of chromosomes.

Germ cells
The cells in reproductive organs that are specialized to give rise to eggs (in female ovaries) and sperm (in male testes).

Gestation
The full period of pregnancy, which lasts about 280 days.

GH
Growth hormone, also known as HGH (human growth hormone) and STH (somatotropin).

Ghrelin
An enzyme, made in the stomach lining, which stimulates appetite.

Glucagon
A hormone, formed in the pancreas, that promotes the breakdown of glycogen into glucose (in the liver).

Glycogen
The chemical form in which the body stores glucose. Glycogen is stored mostly in liver and muscle cells.

Gray matter
The nerve tissue in the cerebral cortex and spinal cord. Gray matter has nerve cell bodies, while white matter does not.

Growth factor
A signaling molecule that can cause cells to divide, leading to the growth of tissues and organs.

Gustation
Our sense of taste.

Hair cell
A type of mechanoreceptor that can trigger nerve impulses when it is bent or tilted.

Helper T cell
A type of T lymphocyte that facilitates our immune system reactions by activating and directing other cells in the body's immune responses.

Hemoglobin
The iron-containing protein in red blood cells that binds with and transports oxygen.

Hemostasis
The vital process of stopping blood loss, mainly through blood clotting.

Hepatic portal system
A set of blood vessels in the liver that receive nutrient-rich blood from the digestive tract via the hepatic portal vein.

Histamine
A chemical released by mast cells that promotes inflammation, as in the case of allergic reactions.

Homeostasis
A state of internal balance in the body that is achieved largely by mechanisms that adjust the chemical composition of blood and tissue fluid.

Hormone
A communication molecule, produced by an endocrine gland, that travels through the blood to target specific cells and tissues.

Hypodermis
A layer of connective tissue, located just below the skin.

Immune response
The body's physiological response to foreign materials (generally known as antigens).

Immunization
A procedure, such as vaccination, that provokes a mild immune response and confers immunity to a particular disease.

Immunodeficiency
An abnormal decrease in or total lack of immune responses.

Inheritance
The transmission of genetic traits, or characteristics, from parents to their offspring.

Innate immunity
General immune responses including inflammation and the activation of complement proteins.

Innervation
The supply of nerves to an organ or other body part.

Insulin
A hormone produced in the pancreas by regions of hormone-producing cells called the islets of Langerhans. It regulates the level of glucose in the blood.

Intercostal muscles
Sets of muscles between the ribs. The external intercostals contract to lift the ribs (to aid inhalation), while the internal intercostals pull the ribs back down (to aid exhalation) during breathing.

Interferons
A family of proteins that help to regulate immune responses to viruses and some kinds of cancer cells.

Internal environment
The internal fluid environment that surrounds body cells. It consists of blood and tissue fluid, but does not include the fluid inside cells.

Interneuron
Interneurons are neurons in the brain that communicate only with other neurons.

Intervertebral disk
A cartilaginous disk between spinal vertebrae.

Jaundice
A condition characterized by the yellowing of the skin and/or the whites of the eyes. It arises from an excess of the pigment bilirubin, which may be caused by a blockage in the bile duct, liver disease, or the excessive breakdown of red blood cells.

Karyotype
A complete collection of the chromosomes in a somatic (body) cell. It usually shows all 23 pairs of human chromosomes.

Keratin
A protein found in cells of the epidermis, and in hair and nails.

Killer T cell (cytotoxic T cell)
A type of lymphocyte that directly destroys cells infected with particular viruses or bacteria.

Lactation
The production and secretion of milk from a woman's mammary glands (breasts).

Leptin
A hormone created by fat cells. It regulates the amount of fat stored in the body—by adjusting both the sensation of hunger and the expenditure of energy.

Leukocyte
The general term for a white blood cell.

LH
The luteinizing hormone. Released from the anterior pituitary, LH triggers ovulation in females and testosterone production in males.

Lipid
A greasy or oily compound, used in cells for energy or to build parts such as cell membranes.

Lithotripsy
A treatment that uses waves of ultrasound to break down a kidney stone (or other internal stone) into smaller particles, which may then be passed out of the body in urine.

Lymph
The tissue fluid carried in the vessels of the lymphatic system.

Lymphocyte
A type of white blood cell, such as a T cell or B cell, that participates in our immune responses.

Lymph vascular system
The vessels of the lymphatic system, which collect and transport lymph.

Lysozyme
An antibacterial enzyme found in tears, saliva, and sweat.

Mast cell
A type of white blood cell in tissues. Mast cells release inflammatory chemicals such as histamine.

Mechanoreceptor
A sensory receptor that responds to mechanical pressure.

Meiosis
The type of cell division that produces gametes (sperm and eggs). Only cells in the testes and ovaries divide by meiosis.

Memory cells
A subset of T and B cells that remain in the body after an immune response, and that subsequently can mount a stronger, more rapid response to the same antigen.

Meninges
Membranes that cover the brain and spinal cord.

Menopause
The gradual cessation of menstruation in mature females. Menopause normally occurs when a woman is in her late forties or early fifties.

Menstrual cycle
The cyclic shedding of blood and endometrial tissue from the uterus of a non-pregnant female.

Metabolism
A collective term for all the chemical processes and reactions in body cells, through which they obtain and use energy.

Metastasis
The development of secondary malignant growths in a different part of the body, separate from the primary site of cancer.

Microvillus
One of the hairlike projections emanating from the surface of some epithelial cells—as in the lining of the small intestine, for example. Microvilli are specially adapted to absorb substances.

Mitochondrion
A cell organelle in which the cellular fuel ATP is formed.

Mitosis
The type of cell division by which our body tissues grow and body cells replicate.

Monoclonal antibodies
Antibodies produced in a laboratory. They are created by cells descended from a single "parent" cell.

Motor neuron
A neuron that carries motor impulses from the central nervous system to the muscles and glands of the body.

Motor unit
In muscle tissue, this is a neuron and all of the skeletal muscle fibers it controls.

Mucous membrane
A thin, moist membrane containing mucus-secreting glands. Mucous membranes line the body cavities that open to the outside.

Muscle fiber
A single muscle cell, composed of bundled myofibrils.

Muscle tissue
Tissue that can contract (shorten) when it is stimulated by nerve impulses. The three types of muscle tissue are cardiac, skeletal, and smooth muscle.

Mutation
A change in the chemical make-up of a gene. Mutations may occur spontaneously or due to the effects of a virus, ionizing radiation, a chemical, or some other factor.

Myelin sheath
A fatty, insulating wrapping around the axons of many motor and sensory nerves. It is formed by the outer membranes of Schwann cells.

Natural killer (NK) cells
Lymphocytes that mount a general attack against a foreign material or substance in the body.

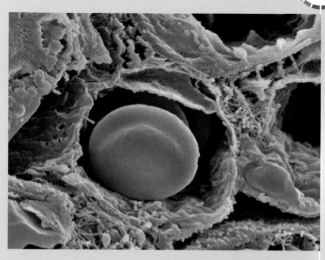

Negative feedback
A mechanism of homeostasis in which a change in some biological condition triggers a response that counteracts the altered condition.

Nerve impulse
A brief reversal of electrical voltage across the cell membrane of a neuron. Nerve impulses pass information between nerve cells and other parts of the body. An impulse is also known as an action potential.

Nerve tract
A cablelike bundle of neuron axons (the threadlike parts of nerve cells) in the central nervous system.

Nervous tissue
The category of body tissue that includes neurons and associated support cells.

Neuroendocrine System
A control center in the brain— the parts of the hypothalamus and pituitary gland that interact to control many physiological functions of the body.

Neuroglia
Cells that provide physical and metabolic support to neurons. More than half of all our nervous tissue consists of neuroglia.

Neuromuscular junction
The junction where a motor neuron forms a synapse (crossing point) with a skeletal muscle fiber.

Neuron
A nerve cell.

Neurotransmitter
Any of the signaling chemicals released by nerve cells.

Nucleic acid
A long, chainlike molecule composed of nucleotides. DNA and RNA are both types of nucleic acids.

Nucleus
The cell organelle that contains most of the cell's genetic material, in the form of DNA organized in chromosomes.

Nutrient
A substance not naturally made in the body, but which is required for the proper functioning of the body's cells, tissues, and organs.

Olfaction
Our sense of smell.

Oncogene
A gene that causes cancer. Oncogenes generally develop from previously normal genes that have undergone a mutation of some kind.

Oocyte
A developing egg cell.

Organelle
In cells, an organelle is a sac or compartment, enclosed by a membrane, that has a particular function.

Osmoreceptor
A sensory receptor that detects changes in the volume of water in a particular body fluid.

Ovarian cycle
The cycle in an ovary, lasting (on average) 28 days, during which a follicle develops and an egg is ovulated.

Oxytocin
A hormone from the hypothalamus that stimulates uterine contractions during labor, as well as the release of milk from a female's mammary glands, or breasts.

Parasite
An infectious organism that obtains nourishment from the tissues of its host.

Parasympathetic nerves
Nerves involved in physiological processes that maintain normal body functions such as digestion and excretion. These nerves are part of the autonomic divisions of the peripheral nervous system.

Pathogen
A disease-causing organism.

Pericardium
The membrane that encloses the heart. It consists of an outer, fibrous layer and an inner, double-layer of serous (serum-producing) tissue.

pH scale
A scale that is used to measure the relative acidity of blood and other body fluids. It ranges from 0 (most acid) to 14 (most alkaline, or basic). A pH of 7 is "neutral."

Pheromone
A substance released from an exocrine gland that serves as a social communication signal between members of the same animal species.

Plasma
The fluid part of blood.

Plasma cell
A type of B cell that produces our antibodies.

Pleura
One of a pair of serous (serum-producing) membranes that line the thorax and enclose the lungs.

Polygenetic trait
A trait, or characteristic, that results from the influence of several different genes.

Positive feedback
A homeostatic mechanism that intensifies a change from an original condition. The intensifying labor contractions, experienced during childbirth, are an example of this process.

Prion
An infectious particle that consists only of protein.

Proprioreceptor
A sensory receptor involved in monitoring the position of body parts. Proprioreceptors are associated with our joints, tendons, and ligaments.

Prostaglandin
Prostaglandins are a group of chemical compounds that influence many body functions, such as blood pressure and smooth muscle contractions.

Protein
Proteins are chemical compounds that have a specific biological function. They exist in many different molecular forms and are essential structural components in all living organisms. Required for cell growth and repair.

Receptor
A protein in or on a cell that is activated by a specific stimulus. Sensory receptors are examples.

Recessive gene
A version of a gene that can be masked by a different, "dominant" version of the same gene. A trait governed by a recessive gene is usually seen only when a person inherits the gene from both of his or her parents.

Releasing hormone
A hypothalamus hormone that signals the anterior pituitary to release one of its hormones.

RNA
Ribonucleic acid. In human cells, genetic instructions in DNA are converted into RNA, which then directly guides the cell's response to those instructions.

Secondary sexual characteristic
A trait such as beard growth,

genital, or breast development that is associated with mature maleness or femaleness, but which is not directly involved in sexual reproduction.

Sensory adaptation
In a sensory system, a process in which the firing of nerve impulses, generated by receptors, slows or stops—even though the stimulus remains constant.

Sensory area
A region of the cerebral cortex that processes sensory information and produces a conscious sensory perception.

Sensory neuron
A neuron in the peripheral nervous system that carries impulses generated by the sensory receptors.

Sensory receptor
A sensory cell or structure that can detect a particular type of stimulus, such as light, pressure, or a chemical.

Septicemia
The poisoning of the blood, caused in particular by bacteria or their toxins.

Serum
An amber-colored, protein-rich liquid that separates out when blood coagulates.

Sex chromosome
An X or Y chromosome, which carries genes that determine an embryo's gender.

Solute
A minor component in a solution. Solutes are dissolved into a liquid solvent.

Somatic senses
The "body" senses of touch, pressure, temperature, and pain.

Somatosensory cortex
The brain region that processes signals coming from the skin, muscles, and joints.

Spasm
An abrupt, involuntary contraction of one or more muscles.

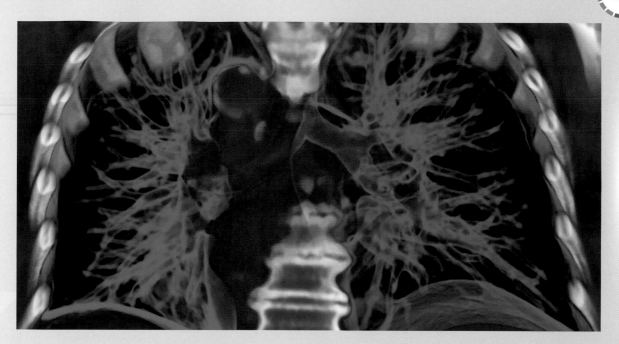

Special senses
The senses of smell, taste, vision, and hearing. Our "general" senses are those where the sensory receptors are more widespread, associated with the skin, muscles, joints, and viscera (the internal organs of the main body cavities).

Sphincter
A ring of muscle that can contract and relax to control the passage of substances through an opening in the body—or an opening that connects two different parts of an organ system.

Static equilibrium
The balancing sense that monitors the position of the head in relation to the ground and the effects of gravity.

Stem cell
An unspecialized cell that can divide repeatedly and give rise to descendants, which then develop into specialized cells.

Stimulus
A form of energy, such as light or pressure, that activates a sensory receptor in the body.

Suppressor gene
A gene with activity that inhibits other, generally cancer-causing genes (which are known as oncogenes).

Sympathetic nerves
As part of the autonomic nervous system, these nerves operate to spur physiological processes—such as changes in heart rate in response to stress or excitement.

Synapse
The gap between nerve cells, across which nerve impulses are transmitted (through the release of neurotransmitters).

Systemic circuit
The cardiovascular circuit running between the heart and the body tissues.

Systole
In the cardiac cycle, this is the period in which the heart chambers contract and pump blood out of the heart.

Tastant
A chemical that is detected by the taste buds.

T cell
A type of lymphocyte (white blood cell) that becomes specialized in the thymus and functions in specific immune responses.

Triglyceride
The most common form of fat in the blood. Triglycerides are the major form of stored fat in the body and are a vital source of energy for the body's metabolism.

Tumor
An abnormal mass of cells that may be either benign or malignant (cancerous).

Ulcerative colititis
A long-term condition in which the colon and rectum have become inflamed.

Urea
A waste product of protein metabolism that is excreted in urine by the kidneys.

Vasoconstriction
A reduction in the lumen (space) inside a blood vessel when the muscle in the vessel wall contracts.

Vasodilation
An increase in the lumen (space) inside a blood vessel when the muscle of the vessel wall relaxes.

Villus
One of the tiny, finger-shaped projections of the lining of the wall of the intestines. Villi can absorb substances such as nutrients.

White matter
Nerve tissue that has many myelinated (myelin-coated) axons. But unlike gray matter, it does not contain nerve cell bodies.

X chromosome
A sex chromosome with genes that cause an embryo to develop into a female, if the embryo receives one X chromosome from each parent.

Y chromosome
A sex chromosome with genes that cause an embryo to develop into a male.

Zygote
The first cell of a new individual, produced when a sperm cell fertilizes an egg cell.

INDEX

ACKNOWLEDGEMENTS

Picture credits
The publisher would like to thank the following people for permission to reproduce their images
(t = top, b = bottom, c = centre, l = left, r = right):

8cl Alain Pol, ISM/Science Photo Library (SPL); 8bl Du Cane Medical Imaging Ltd/SPL; 8br (x 4 images) Wellcome Department of Cognitive Neurology/SPL; 8r Simon Fraser/SPL; 9tl Nancy Kedersha/SPL; 9cl Bernard Benoit/SPL; 9bl Dr. Arnold Rivera/SPL; 9tr Steve Gschmeissner/SPL; 9cr Biophoto Associates/SPL; 9br RVI Medical Physics, Newcastle/Simon FraserSPL; 12–13 Dr. Gopal Murti/SPL; 16bl D. Phillips/SPL; 16bc David M. Phillips/SPL; 17br Juergen Bergen/SPL; 18bl CNRI/SPL; 18br SPL; 19tr Rr. Gopal Murti/SPL; 20bl Dr. Gopal Murti/SPL; 21tr CNRI/SPL; 23t Alfred Pasieka/SPL; 23b James King-Holmes/SPL; 24tl Steve Gschmeissner/SPL; 24tr Eric Grave/SPL; 24bl Nancy Kedersha/SPL; 24br Steve Gschmeissner/SPL; 25tr Steve Gschmeissner/SPL; 25br Steve Gschmeissner; 26tl Susumu Nishinaga/SPL; 26tr Steve Gschmeissner/SPL; 26br Dr. Gilbert Faure/SPL; 29tr Cavallini James/BSIP/SPL; 31tr Edelmann/SPL; 33tr Professor Michel Brauner, ISM/SPL; 34–35 Professors P.M. Motta, K.R. Porter and P.M. Andrews/SPL; 36cl Biophoto Associates/SPL; 38cl Steve Gschmeissner/SPL; 39tr Biophoto Associates/SPL; 39br Hannah Gal/SPL; 40tr Manfred Kage/SPL; 40br CNRI/SPL; 42c Professors P.M. Motta, K.R. Porter and P.M. Awndrews/SPL; 44tl D. Phillips/SPL; 44tr Dr. P. Marazzi/SPL; 44bl Dr. P. Marazzi/SPL; 44br Sinclair Stammers/SPL; 45tr J.C. Revy, ISM/SPL; 46–47 SciePro/SPL; 50br Biophoto Associates/SPL; 52tr Vincent Starr Photography/SPL; 53tr Steve Gschmeissner/SPL; 53br Damien Lovegrove/SPL; 54tr Sebastian Kaulitzki/SPL; 54bl Orkan, ISM/SPL; 56bl D. Roberts/SPL; 58–59c Science Picture Co./SPL; 59tr Philippe Psaila/SPL; 59br Philippe Psaila/SPL; 63tr Simon Fraser, Royal Victoria Infirmary/SPL; 63tr Medical Images, Universal Images Group/SPL; 64–65c SciePro/SPL; 65cr Dr. P. Marazzi/SPL; 66–67 SPL; 69br Severin Schweiger/SPL; 70bl SciePro/SPL; 70–71c SciePro/SPL; 71tl SciePro/SPL; 71tr SciePro/SPL; 71r SciePro/SPL; 71cr SciePro/SPL; 72b Scientifica, Visuals Unlimited/SPL; 73tr BSIP, Cavallini James/SPL; 79br Science Picture Co./SPL; 81tr SPL; 81br Alfred Pasieka/SPL; 83br Volker Steger/SPL; 84–85 C.J. Guerin, phD, MRC Toxicology Unit/SPL; 86b SciePro/SPL; 88cl Sebastian Kaulitzki/SPL; 91tr Silvia Riccardi/SPL; 91br Thomas Deerinck, NCMIR/SPL; 95tr Otis Historical Archives, National Museum of Health and Medicine/SPL; 96cl Zephyr/SPL; 98cl Pascal Goetgheluck/SPL; 98–99tc Science Picture Co./SPL; 99tr Dr. Keith Wheeler/SPL; 99br Hannah Gal/SPL; 102cl Science Picture Co./SPL; 103br SPL; 105tr BSIP, Chassenet/SPL; 106cl Deep Light Productions/SPL; 106br Evan Oto/SPL; 107br Professor Michel Zanca, ISM/SPL; 108bl Living Art Enterprises, LLC/SPL; 108cr Zephyr/SPL; 109cl Zephyr/SPL; 109bl CNRI/SPL; 109bcr CNRI/SPL; 112bl Hank Morgan/SPL; 112bcl Hank Morgan/SPL; 112br Allan Hobson/SPL; 113br Massimo Brega/Look At Sciences/SPL; 114cl Peter Bowater/SPL; 116br Russell Kightley/SPL; 117br Lea Paterson/SPL; 118cl Sebastian Kaulitzki/SPL; 118cr Biophoto Associates/SPL; 119tl Corbin O'Grady Studio/SPL; 120c Marc Phares/SPL; 122–123 Steve Gschmeissner/SPL; 127br Vincent Starr Photography/Cultura/SPL; 128bl Mauro Fermariello/SPL; 129bc Bluestone/SPL; 130br Laguna Design/SPL; 131tl Steve Gschmeissner/SPL; 132bl SPL; 132br SPL; 133bl SPL; 133br SPL; 134cl Annabella Bluesky/SPL; 135tr Chassenet/BSIP/SPL; 135cl Sue Ford/SPL; 137cr Professor Tony Wright, Institute of Laryngology and Otology/SPL; 139br Susumu Nishinaga/SPL; 141tr Frans Lanting, Mint Images/SPL; 141cl Science Picture Co./SPL; 141cr Science Picture Co./SPL; 141bl Science Picture Co./SPL; 141br Science Picture Co./SPL; 142cl Omikron/SPL; 143bl Anatomical Travelogue/SPL; 143tr Chassenet/BSIP/SPL; 143cr Charles D. Winters/SPL; 144cl Tony Camacho/SPL; 144cr Steve Gschmeissner/SPL; 145c Eye of Science/SPL; 146bl SPL; 147br Adrianko/Cultura/SPL; 148tr Alfred Pasieka/SPL; 148bl Science Picture Co./SPL; 149cl Spencer Sutton/SPL; 149cr Adam Gault/SPL; 150–151 Steve Gschmeissner/SPL; 154cl Alfred Pasieka/SPL; 154cr SciePro/SPL; 155cl Alfred Pasieka/SPL; 155tr SPL; 155cr Steve Gschmeissner; 156bc Kate Jacobs/SPL; 158cl SciePro/SPL; 158tl Steve Gschmeissner/SPL; 159bc Dr. M.A. Ansary/SPL; 160bl Alfred Pasieka/SPL; 161br Herve Conge, ISM/SPL; 163br Alfred Pasieka/SPL; 164bl Monty Rakusen/Cultura/SPL; 165tr Professor P. Motta/Department of Anatomy/University "La Sapienza", Rome/SPL; 165br Sidney Moulds/SPL; 166cl Ria Novosti/SPL; 166br Roman Andrade 3Dciencia/SPL; 167t Roger Harris/SPL; 167cr Laguna Design/SPL; 168cl Zephyr/SPL; 168cr Steve Gschmeissner/SPL; 169tr Ian Hooton/SPL; 169cr Ian Hooton/SPL; 170bl Omikron/SPL; 170cr CNRI/SPL; 171tl David R. Frazier/SPL; 172cl Gustoimages/SPL; 173t Western Opthalmic Hospital/SPL; 173cl Houin/BSIP/SPL; 173bl SciePro/SPL; 174–175 SPL; 178cl Bob L. Shepherd/SPL; 179br Manfred Kage/SPL; 182cr SPL; 183tl Asklepios Medical Atlas/SPL; 183cl David Leah/SPL; 183br Sovereign/ISM/SPL; 184bl Steve Gschmeissner/SPL; 185tr Zephyr/SPL; 187cl Steve Gschmeissner/SPL; 187c NIBSC/SPL; 187cr Professors P.M. Motta and S. Correr/SPL; 188bl Zephyr/SPL; 188cr Alfred Pasieka/SPL; 189tr Steve Gschmeissner/SPL; 190cl BSIP, B. Boissonnet/SPL; 191tr Eye of Science/SPL; 192–193 Science Picture Co./SPL; 194cr Science Picture Co./SPL; 196bl Sebastian Kaulitzki/SPL; 197tr Biophoto Associates/SPL; 197br Michael Hanson, Mint Images/SPL; 199cl Pixologicstudio/SPL; 200cl Amélie Benoist/BSIP/SPL; 201cr Ian Hooton/SPL; 203tl Dr. Tony Brain/SPL; 203cl Eye of Science/SPL; 203cr Moredun Animal Health Ltd./SPL; 204–205 SPL; 208cr SPL; 209tr MCS/SPL; 210bl Dr. Mark J. Winter/SPL; 211tr Francis Leroy, Biocosmos/SPL; 211br Claus Lunau/SPL; 212blt NIAID/National Institutes of Health/SPL; 212blb Eye of Science/SPL; 212blr CNRI/SPL; 213tr Power and Syred/SPL; 213cl Science Picture Co./SPL; 213cr SPL; 214cl Science Picture Co./SPL; 216cl Ian Hooton/SPL; 217t Science Picture Co./SPL; 217cl J.C. Revy, ISM/SPL; 218cl Steve Gschmeissner/SPL; 219tl Steve Percival/SPL; 219cr Dr. Kari Lounatmaa/SPL; 220cl David Scharf/SPL; 220cr Clouds Hill Imaging Ltd./SPL; 221cr CNRI/SPL; 221br Steve Gschmeissner/SPL; 222cr NIBSC/SPL; 223tl Life In View/SPL; 224–225 Steve Gschmeissner/SPL; 228bl Laguna Design/SPL; 229cl Herve Conge, ISM/SPL; 229cr Dr. P. Marazzi/SPL; 231tl Susumu Nishinaga/SPL; 231c Laguna Design/SPL; 231cr; Laguna Design/SPL; 232cl David M. Martin, MD/SPL; 233br Science Picture Co./SPL; 234bl Microscape/SPL; 235br Scott Camazine/SPL; 237cl Science Picture Co./SPL; 237br SPL; 239tr SciePro/SPL; 239br Dr. P. Marazzi/SPL; 241bl Ian Boddy/SPL; 242–243 Manfred Kage/SPL; 246c Manfred Kage/SPL; 250cr GCA/SPL; 250bl Jon Stokes /SPL; 250br Michel Brauner/ISM/SPL; 251cr Professor P.M. Motta et al/SPL; 251br

Chassenet/BSIP/SPL; 252cl Du Cane Medical Imaging Ltd./SPL; 252c CNRI/SPL; 252cr David McCarthy/SPL; 253tr Antonia Reeve/SPL; 253cr AJ Photo/Hop Americain (American Hospital of Paris)/SPL; 254–255 Eye of Science/SPL; 257tl Steve Gschmeissner/SPL; 257cl Steve Gschmeissner/SPL; 258cr Animate4.com/SPL; 259bl Steve Gschmeissner/SPL; 261cl Professor P. Motta/Department of Anatomy/University/SPL; 262cl Eye of Science/SPL; 262cr CNRI/SPL; 264bl Zephyr/SPL; 265cr Thierry Berrod, Mona Lisa Production/SPL; 265br Zephyr/SPL; 266cl Edelmann/SPL; 267tr Steve GSchmeissner/SPL; 268bc Lea Paterson/SPL; 268cbr Professors P.M. Motta and S. Makabe/SPL; 269tr Edelmann/SPL; 271tr Neil Bromhall/SPL; 271br Scott Camazine/SPL; 273cr Keith/Custom Medical Stock Photo/SPL; 274cr Janie Airey/SPL; 274br Steve Gschmeissner; 275tr Alain Pol, ISM/SPL; 275bl Zero Creatives/Cultura/SPL; 276bl Sebastian Kaulitzki/SPL; 279 tr Steve Gschmeissner/SPL; 280bl Neil Bromhall/SPL; 281t Du Cane Medical Imaging Ltd./SPL. All other images Shutterstock.

Illustration credits

The publisher would like to thank the following people for permission to reproduce their artworks:

All body illustrations are by Argosy Publishing, www.visiblebody.com, with the exception of some additional artworks from the following illustrators:

Andrew Davies/Creative communication: 153bc, 161tr; Peter Bull Art Studio: 52b, 63tcl, 63bcl, 72tr, 103t, 104r, 105l, 153b, 176br, 223br; Peter Bull Art Studio/Argosy Publishing: 266br, 267bl, 267br, 268l, 268cl, 268c, 268cr, 269cl, 269br, 270c, 270cr, 271cl, 271cr. Science Photo Library (SPL): 46–47 SciePro/SPL; 58–59c Science Picture Co./SPL; 64–65c SciePro/SPL; 70–71 (all artworks) SciePro/SPL; 86b SciePro/SPL; 98–99tc Science Picture Co./SPL; 102cl Science Picture Co./SPL; 108cr Zephyr/SPL; 109cl Zephyr/SPL; 141cl Science Picture Co./SPL; 141cr Science Picture Co./SPL; 141bl Science Picture Co./SPL; 141br Science Picture Co./SPL; 148bl Science Picture Co./SPL; 183tl Asklepios Medical Atlas/SPL; 196bl Sebastian Kaulitzki/SPL; 199cl Pixologicstudio/SPL; 211br Claus Lunau/SPL; 214cl Science Picture Co./SPL; 233br Science Picture Co./SPL; 237cl Science Picture Co./SPL; 239tr SciePro/SPL; 276bl Sebastian Kaulitzki/SPL.

From other Weldon Owen titles/properties: *Insiders: Human Body*: 16cr (Argosy), br (Argosy), 17tr (Argosy), 27cl (Argosy), 27tr (Argosy), 130tl (Argosy). *A Day In The Life Of Your Body*: 19tl (Argosy), 19bl (Argosy), 19cr (Argosy), 42bl (Argosy).